THE

INTERNATIONAL

DESIGN

YEARBOOK

THE INTERNATIONAL DESIGN YEARBOOK

2

EDITOR

EMILIO AMBASZ

GENERAL EDITOR
DEYAN SUDJIC

ASSISTANT EDITOR
HILARY MORE

ABBEVILLE PRESS · PUBLISHERS · NEW YORK

The Publisher and editors would like to thank the
designers and manufacturers for submitting
work for inclusion in this book, Peter Popham for
his help on the collection of Japanese material,
and the following sources for use of photographs:
plates 67, 427 and 478, Hiroyuki Hirai; 107,
Augusto Eira; 168—171, 263 and 264, kindly
lent by the National Museum of Art, Kyoto; and
186, Peter Williams Studio.

Designer: Peter Bridgewater

Library of Congress Catalog number 0883-7155
ISBN 0-89659-663-X

Typeset by Composing Operations Ltd, England
Printed in Hong Kong by Mandarin Offset
International Ltd

First Edition

CONTENTS

PREFACE

This is the second volume of the *International Design Yearbook*. It brings together a selection of the best, the most characteristic, the most distinctive and the most memorable domestic designs of 1986 from around the world. Taken together they provide a survey that pinpoints the new directions currently being followed by designers.

This year the selection has been made by Emilio Ambasz. Through his choices, the talents of a younger generation can be seen emerging in the five main fields of domestic design: furniture, lighting, tableware, textiles and metal and electrical products. Entries are arranged into these five areas and, within these, into further broad groupings — for example, where common themes or sources of inspiration can be detected. Within the category of furniture in particular, the reader will find groupings ranging from the strictly functional and rational in approach to form on the one hand — pieces generally made from metal with a straightforward graphic outline — to poetic pieces and art or craft objects at the other extreme, where utility is seen as irrelevant or takes a low priority.

While the book attempts to cover all the kinds of domestic design, work is selected for inclusion only where it is considered of a high enough standard — given the objectives of the designer — or where it is felt to be important for its representative nature. Entries in the book are accompanied by brief captions. Critical commentaries are interspersed within sections where it is felt appropriate to link groups of objects or remark on special work. In addition, each category of design has its own introduction, recording new developments within the field. Details of designers and suppliers, together with a list of further reading, are provided at the end of the book.

This is a particularly stimulating and rewarding moment for looking at design. The orthodoxies of stylistic schools have, for the moment, been overturned, and more experimentation is possible than has been attempted for decades. Interestingly, in Britain, France and certain other countries design is being deliberately promoted as part of government policy, attracting substantial investment and propaganda efforts. The design landscape is changing rapidly. While Italian manufacturers still dominate the prestige end of the high-design furniture market, their domination is no longer as unquestioned and automatic as it once was. Companies such as Cassina and Zanotta, and Arteluce and Artemide in lighting, do continue to flourish, thanks to their enormous reputation and their long histories of impressive design collections. They still set the pace, drawing on designers from around the world, and can still be relied on to produce annual ranges of new work that will set a standard for others to match. But in terms of creativity, their leadership seems less secure than was once the case. Outside the hothouse of Milan, new creative centres are emerging; in particular, the cities of Paris and Barcelona have once more begun to make themselves felt. They are becoming alternative places in which reputations can be made, and in which there are adequate outlets and manufacturers to produce substantial enough quantities of new work to justify the recognition of the existence there not merely of influential individuals but of influential 'schools' of design. These however are still in their infancy. Manufacturers still possess only modest resources in both money and equipment. Thus their designs do not have the highly engineered and elaborately finished quality of the famous Italian firms; instead they go for pieces with a raw directness, making strong attention-grabbing statements rather than subtle observations.

In Paris, President Mitterrand's government has set a premium on design, going to great lengths to create showcases for the talents of new designers in order to attract the attention of industry and of overseas markets. The President's own apartments in the Elysée Palace are graced by pieces made by an assortment of younger designers, and new ranges of furniture for public buildings have also been selected by competition. Apart from the celebrated Philippe Starck, many others in Paris are attracting attention, including Martin Szekeley, Jean-Michel Wilmotte and Ronald Sportes. New companies such as Tribu now have the confidence to bring in the talents of non-French designers such as Paolo Deganello and Gaetano Pesce.

In Barcelona, the creative upsurge accompanying the re-emergence of the Catalan national identity has found expression partly through design: a society bent on modernization is putting a high priority on design as a medium for demonstrating its changing circumstances. Barcelona's best-known names are Oscar Tusquets — one of the generation which is forming the new establishment in the city — and Javier Mariscal, a one-time member of the Memphis group who belongs to the younger generation.

The new work in Paris and Barcelona is in striking contrast to the technicolour whimsy of the avant-garde elsewhere in recent years. This new design, strongly graphic, sparse in its materials and shapes, seems like a bread-and-water antidote after the excess of cream cakes that made up the design diet in the early 1980s.

In London the wit and surrealism of Ron Arad and others seem to echo these new themes. And England is also the centre of the new tradition of artist-craftsmen designers. Some, such as Jaak Floris van den Broecke, the new Head of Furniture Design at the Royal College of Art, make their own work as a second-best alternative to mass production. Others take the opposite standpoint, and treat their pieces as art one-offs — an attitude increasingly prevalent in the United States, typified by the Art et Industrie group of designers, artists and makers.

Revivalism still flourishes, with ever more obscure classics of the 20th century unearthed and put into production, often for the first time. A steady stream of Eileen Gray pieces continues to flow each year, and 1986/87 sees the addition of Eliel Saarinen to the pantheon of reissued designers, beside Marcel Breuer and Arne Jacobsen.

Product design has become, more than ever, a fascinating and significant area. Reflecting this, the Yearbook has further strengthened its coverage of the subject, including a broad cross-section of consumer and electrical goods, from clocks to TV sets. It shows the transformation that is overtaking these once mundane objects, which are no longer regarded as simply utilitarian but are now expected to display all kinds of levels of meaning and expression.

In so many areas of product design it is Japan which is assuming leadership. Instead of merely copying, Japan is now an innovator, producing a torrent of new goods. The major Japanese manufacturers constantly revise their catalogues, offering new ranges, new colour treatments and new styling. In fact in 1986/87 Japan is a force to be reckoned with in all areas of domestic design, from textiles to table-ware and from lighting to furniture. The Yearbook has benefited from the contribution of a Tokyo-based correspondent who has written an essay appraising these new developments.

Worldwide, product design has always lagged some distance behind furniture design in breaking with the orthodoxies of the recent past. There now seems to be evidence however that an alternative to the rationalist modernist aesthetic of product design is firmly establishing itself, typified equally by Ron Arad's concrete hi-fi equipment and by the toy-like tiny pastel TV sets made by Sharp.

1986 has been a year of significant changes in the world of design, and this book will provide a lasting record of them.

Deyan Sudjic

THE 1986 DESIGN ZOO

My task in the compilation of the Yearbook was that of making the final selection, and of casting a larger look over the whole shifting universe of contradictory, redundant, eccentric and sometimes just plain lovable design creatures to emerge in 1986. I have not been in charge of gathering the animals which compose this zoological catalogue. That task, as well as that of commenting critically on them, was the responsibility of Deyan Sudjic.

Since I cannot vouch that we have one example of each kind of design represented in our zoo, to avoid establishing rigorous taxonomies I tried rather to look them over to classify families and mutational tendencies. As I meditated on this matter however it became quite evident that the offspring of one year of world design provided too thin a sample for analysis. The body of the material is still very much alive, and does not yet allow for dissection. As in the case of living animals, one can only approach the individual creations with care and seek to touch them with great caution. I have tried, therefore, to comment on the animals populating the 1986 design zoo by identifying some tendencies and changes without attempting a conclusive analysis. I hope the reader will forgive me the views expressed here which do not provide a definitive theoretical structure.

I should like to begin by identifying two design animals which can be said to represent stylistic families. They reach a size, in many cases, no larger than a chair. The first, belonging to one of the most curious families to have evolved, runs the American prairies; the second, a distantly related type, is quite often seen populating the northern European continent. Fifty years ago there was little evidence of either of these schools, whether in the Grand American Design Desert or in the northern European woods. These two recent trends share a common origin in the early 1970s.

The exhibition 'Italy: The New Domestic Landscape', presented in 1972 at the Museum of Modern Art, New York, had a deep and pervasive impact, not least in promoting these strands of evolution. For the first time the American public was invited to conceive of design not only as a product of the creative intelligence, but also as an exercise of the critical imagination. The exhibition aimed at helping visitors to realize that design in general, and Italian design in particular, did not simply mean creating objects to satisfy functional and emotional needs: it illustrated that the processes and products of design could be used to make a critical commentary on our society. The exhibition was something of a shock to American designers. Here they found themselves facing another breed of designer, unafraid of curves and capable of taking an unabashed delight in the sensual attributes of the materials he or she used. For many American and northern European designers — sternly trained in the Bauhausian tradition of deductive analysis, strict functionalism and rigorous pragmatism — the flair and panache of the Italians were almost offensive. The fabric of their professional repressions was unceremoniously torn open by the creations of their Italian counterparts — to the extent that, it seemed, some of them were aggrieved enough to want to file a writ of complaint against Italian Design: a) for having created beautiful objects in complete disregard of all prevailing rules, b) for having shamelessly seduced the public with these products, and, what was even worse, c) for having seduced the designers themselves.

Over a decade later, we find that Italian design thus spawned many gifted offspring. Like their Italian colleagues, American and northern European designers have grown fonder of, and very dexterous with, colours, curves, patterns and textures. Once the unbending seekers of eternal truths following in the footsteps of their Bauhausian ancestors, these designers have now learned how to make peace with the ephemeral. Design, once perceived as yet another means of achieving redemption through sensory deprivation, has now begun to open its tightly closed fist to embrace fashion and caress ornament. So a breed of designer has appeared who frankly takes joy in the exercise of his stylistic gifts. Perhaps in 1992 we shall be able to see whether the new designers' debt to Italian design goes beyond, and deeper than, mere resemblance.

In the meantime, as we look back from today's Italian productions, we realize that the 1972 show marked the highpoint of Italian design as a free-wheeling creative process. Since then a considerable part of Italian activity has concentrated upon improving the quality of established models. Particular attention is paid, for example, to considering how different materials can be gracefully juxtaposed and deftly combined; how component elements can be well built and better joined; how the quality of colours, patterns and textures can be subtly enhanced. Since 1972 many products of Italian design have travelled from the museum to the market place. Once these objects were the fancied harbingers of social changes to come: today, we realize that they have become an integral part of society. If they have not helped to fulfil early Utopian promises, these products have nevertheless greatly enhanced the quality of our daily existence; if they have fallen short of being pathmarks in our long voyage to a better tomorrow, they have served us nobly as pleasant companions in our daily travails. The Italian products of the last decade have given pleasure, performed faithfully, and — why not say it — have also tickled our fancy and flattered our pride. We have bought them gleefully and paraded them with delight. They have, in some small but true way, helped us through the day and soothed us through the night. Handsome and wholesome, these products have served us well. If they have sometimes failed to move our hearts they have however always touched our minds and altered our senses. What greater badge of honourable service can be bestowed upon an object and the culture which created it?

Another sub-group has emerged from these powerful Italian origins. It is called 'Memphis', and is an animal whose forebears were already fully fledged in concept, if not in actuality, in the 1970s. Memphis's beginnings at that time were immediately identified with Milan, and, more specifically, as the offspring of Ettore Sottsass. In the 1970s, Ettore, in his role of the Holy Ghost as Guru, created, with his loyal disciples, a number of controversial objects of great originality and with a strong ideological flavour. They were greatly celebrated by a few, who saw in them a criticism of the consumer society concealed as admiration to the point of idolatry. A small number of specimens created by Memphis were shown at the exhibition 'Italy: The New Domestic Landscape', mentioned above. Yet somehow, for about a decade thereafter, the products of Memphis seemed to disappear — only to reappear, along with Ettore Sottsass, some five years ago. In a new guise he tried his magic once more, and controversy was reborn — albeit without the political edge, since he now believed that salvation was possible only with a stylistic spearhead.

When I first saw the Memphis exhibition in 1980, I felt compelled to suspend critical judgment. I liked what I saw, in the same spontaneous way one may find oneself charmed by a hyperactive, red-haired freckled kid with a disarmingly prankish smile. I saw Ettore, always the Pied Piper, not leading the children away but rather joining them in play. I could not help being touched. The myths of both Faust and the Phoenix were here in the form of a ritual of design rebirth. When children begin to perceive the world, they interact with it through fables and toys. They assign to the latter magical properties and powerful attributes; thus a chair lying on its back can become a locomotive or a platform in outer space. I perceived in Memphis's creations many layers of meaning, from the obvious enquiries into the future of ornament to deeper questions about the psychological and liturgical roles which objects such as furniture may play. The analytical observer could find all of this and more in Memphis's output. To me, Memphis's fascination resided in the fact that the designer, having realized that he had little chance of physically affecting the broader urban environment, had chosen to take refuge in the interior of the house — the last domain of individual freedom. There, in domestic security, the designer dreamt of himself as a gracious host while Debussy played in the background, or as a subversive agent manufacturing magic talismans endowed with the power to redeem the dreariness of everyday routine.

Memphis reintroduced the totem and the altarpiece into the home. Some Memphis objects have, for me, the same lovable characteristics as a household pet. One can hold them in one's arms, one can play with them, one can cover them up at night, and they, in turn, reassure us that they will never leave us; they will never know need or grief; their 'misdeeds' will always be forgivable and easy to rectify by actions as simple as the passing of a wet rag over a plastic laminated surface; they will be forever youthful, eternally vibrant. To the sensual gratification which ornamented surfaces and complex patterns give us, the Memphis designers added a dimension of wistfulness for a state of innocence before design.

Until the middle of 1985 the Memphis group's achievement was seen more as an act of the will than as a product of continuous experience; but then we assumed that this was because it was so young (or rather, we should say, 'they' were so young, because in the process of rebirth, the Phoenix once more destroyed himself and Ettore declared Memphis dead — for him, Memphis had become a catch-all name, a grab-bag where many banal items cohabited with a few moralist pieces — and still Memphis is with us: it has undergone several incarnations). Yet already in 1980 it was possible to foresee that Memphis's contribution to the progress of design was going to be greater than that of many acts of will, more forceful stylistically than its arcane and metaphysical and aesthetic postulates might have suggested on first examination. First Milan, then Barcelona, Los Angeles and Tokyo, started to buzz with the murmurs of traditional designers, telling each other *sotto voce*, 'Perhaps we ought to recognize that colour, texture, pattern and ornament are legitimate; perhaps we ought to recognize that forms other than the rectangular are from now on acceptable, if we look at what the youngsters are doing; perhaps we should bow to the fact that formal redundancy and symbolism have received the avant-garde's *imprimatur* and are being purchased as fast as they can be packaged; perhaps we ought to acknowledge that emotional needs demand satisfaction as peremptorily as pragmatic ones. . .'.

Now that the older generation has seen the way forward, a younger generation is beginning to play with the possibilities: everything can be merry and colourful, even though the progenitor of the trend has deserted them. As we look at our menagerie, it may seem that many design animals are left orphaned. But if we look more closely, we can see that some orphans are beginning to fend for themselves. Perhaps their father has 'left' them not because they abandoned his stance but because he recognized that his young family might produce strong and vital designs of their own in the years to come. And perhaps next year's *International Design Yearbook* will show whether this is really happening.

Emilio Ambasz

JAPANESE DESIGN: BACK TO THE NATIVE BASICS

Scouring the department stores of Ginza or the electrical stores of Akihabara for a key to the personality of Japan's contemporary design, one can apply only the word 'pragmatic', apparently, to everything. These people will do anything, it seems, to move the goods. Not even the smallest minnow of a trend gets through their net. 1950s curves and pastels, high-tech dials and controls, sub-Bauhaus boxes, even the odd item which might slip into a survey of good design — all these and many more are present in riotous profusion.

When the products are observed coolly as the work of a single nation, it is the lack of inherent, commonly shared characteristics which is the most striking fact about them. Here, one would say, is the work of a nation with very little history or tradition of its own, and a correspondingly vast appetite for the forms and traditions of countries whose history is richer.

In fact the story of the origins of government-sponsored good design in Japan reflects just such a condition of cultural poverty and hunger. The prototype of the Japan Industrial Design Promotion Organization, roughly equivalent to Britain's Design Centre, was set up as a division of the Ministry of International Trade and Industry in 1958 — because, as an MITI pamphlet explains, 'of a pressing need felt by the MITI to establish some mechanism within its organization to deal with the increasing number of claims from abroad against the illegal use of design on the part of . . . Japanese enterprises'.

Masahiro Mori's classic soy sauce pot, 1958, was awarded a JIDPRO G-Mark and is still on the market. It is designed to harmonize with Japanese dishes and utensils

These claims were to be 'dealt with' by prevailing on Japanese companies to design their products themselves, and by honouring those who did so satisfactorily. Each year the JIDPRO selected well-designed goods and bestowed on them what they termed the 'G-Mark', as an indication of 'good design based on true originality', and as an encouragement to other Japanese enterprises 'to realize the importance of original design development'.

Partly as a result of JIDPRO's initiative, Japan gradually outgrew its phase of flagrant imitation — though inevitably the more developed West remained the basic source of inspiration. During the 1950s, industrial designers who had cut their teeth in the immediate post-war years on commissions for the American military came to maturity, designing refrigerators and other domestic appliances for the Japanese market, which was beginning its slow climb to affluence.

Tendo Mokko's dining table and chair set, 1961, was an attempt to re-style Japanese traditional dining furniture in the light of Western design standards without obliging the nation to get up off the floor

National's Japanese-style stereogram 'Asuka', 1964, a late product of the age of nationalistic design, was intended to fit discreetly into a tatami-matted room

In the same decade Sony developed its first transistor radio and began selling it worldwide. This marked the earliest modern manifestation of what has long been one of the strongest distinguishing features of Japanese design: the penchant for miniaturization. The culture that produced bonsai and netsuke (the carved ornament worn at the girdle) had now discovered a contemporary way to express the urge. The theme has been persistent ever since, recent manifestations including Sanyo's range of diminutive travelling irons and hairdryers and the thousand-and-one varieties of Walkman.

During the 1960s and 1970s, as the Japanese economy drew level with and then overtook those of much of the West, industrial designers grew in confidence and originality and felt it even less necessary to follow the West's lead blindly. The improving quality and low price of all sorts of Japanese-made commodities, from hi-fis to motorcycles, forced the overseas competition back into the outer darkness; in such cases, design originality was forced on the Japanese, for there were no models left.

As Japanese firms grew in strength, a striking difference from Western firms in equivalent fields became apparent. The great companies of Europe — Braun, Olivetti, Jaguar, Citroën and so on — achieved their reputations on the basis of design integrity. No matter how much their products changed, they always possessed some identifiable character that was unmistakable.

No such phenomenon exists in Japan. Not even the most renowned firms have what might be described as a 'look'. Sony is often written about abroad in the same sort of terms used to describe the European greats, as if it were inviolably unique in some important way, but the reality is different. In Japan the pioneering firm takes the risk (as Sony did, famously, with the *Walkman*), and, if it is lucky enough to have a hit, reaps the advantage for a brief period while competitors wait on the sidelines. After that, however, the Japanese market is a vicious free-for-all: any new product or feature which is seen to be paying off is bound to be seized by a rival and closely imitated.

As a result a tremendous premium is put on rapid, even manic, innovation, whether based on technological innovation (rare), on stylistic fiddling around, or on permutating the existing variables one more time. This last ploy was particularly favoured from the late 1970s on, engendering a multiplicity of new combinations of less-than-brand-new technologies: radio with cassette player, radio with portable TV, radio with camera, radio with clock and so on *ad nauseam*.

To avoid commercial disaster, all firms in the same mass-market field are obliged to cover all angles. If Sony invent it, National, Toshiba, Hitachi, Mitsubishi, Sharp and the rest must cover it as soon as the market is confirmed. Once a firm does well with a large-scale ghetto-blaster, the others cannot pass up the challenge on the grounds that the exercise is demeaning. Sharp may make a splash with pastel-

Sony's classic transistor radio, 1958, is 10.6 by 6.3 by 25 cm (4¼ by 2½ by 9¾ in), and still looks good today

Olympus's 'Pearlcorder', 1976, another landmark in the trend towards miniaturization, is 14 by 6.6 by 2.25 cm (5½ by 2½ by ¾ in)

National's portable TV, 1982, is 18.7 by 17.6 by 31.7 cm (7⅜ by 6⅞ by 12½ in)

Sanyo's travelling iron, 1982, is 3.6 by 15.5 by 7.7 cm (1⅜ by 6 by 3 in), and weighs just 0.4 kg (¾ lb)

coloured radio-cassettes for girls in their teens; others cannot neglect to strive to appeal to the same people.

The ruthless determination with which Japanese firms woo every section of the market, without any notions of territoriality, explains their power to terrify as competitors of the West. Those Western companies which did not sink without trace, mostly made a dash for the upper end of the market where name and snob value sell. Philips remain in the middle ground, increasingly resembling a somewhat anonymous Japanese firm. The one recent operation which makes a clear, bold response, on equal terms, to the Japanese challenge, is the Swatch series of watches (plates 463–465), with their low prices, high quality, and rapid turnover of designs aimed at many different sections of the market. When Citizen came up with a remarkably similar range at almost the same time that Swatch made its Japanese début, it was no surprise.

****

The proliferation of styles, colours and combinations, often with no significant technological advance to justify changes, reached a peak at the end of the 1970s and then ran into a reaction. It was all too gratuitous, and products with intrinsic design merit were rare. There was a yearning for simplicity and minimalism; for clean, uncluttered design, which was realized in Sony's *Profeel* of the early 1980s – a TV apparently without a tuner, as sleekly elegant when looked at from the back or side as from the front.

This urge to minimalism still has life today. An interesting new twist is given by the National 'floor TV'. Clearly inspired by the *Profeel*, with its slick, flat, screwed-down screen and grilled, contoured back, the novelty of this set is that it is intended exclusively for use on the floor. The screen is tilted ten degrees upwards.

Japan's traditional lifestyle was entirely floor-bound; National's recognition of the floor space neatly symbolizes the most interesting trend to gather strength through the first half of the 1980s, one which connects at many points with the attraction of minimalism – a new awareness of Japanese tradition, and a desire to revive and reinterpret its lineaments. This is particularly significant because of the passive but vital role that traditional Japanese design has played in the formation of what we mean by the word 'modern'.

When the West rediscovered the everyday objects of Japan in the middle of the last century, after a gap (caused by the Tokugawa Shogun's policy of almost total isolation) of more than two hundred years, people were immensely impressed. Their first appearance came at London's Great Exhibition of 1851; ironically, because these alien but oddly compelling forms went on to play a major part in the revolution of taste of the following seventy years – a revolution against the age of madly profligate ornamentation which the Crystal Palace was seen to have embodied.

Traditional Japanese design was noteworthy most of all for its elegant simplicity. The pots, spoons and bamboo whisks of the tea ceremony, the handsome chests of drawers and intricately arranged built-in cabinets found in aristocratic residences, the sensitivity to texture demonstrated by the straw tatami flooring, the handmade paper, the traditional fencing – all these proved enormously attractive, and the lack of fussiness was part of the appeal. Ornamentation was encountered in the architecture, most famously in the Tokugawa mausoleum at Nikko, but the prevailing aristocratic taste of Japan favoured forms of striking plainness which were nevertheless much more than baldly functional.

There was nothing either accidental or merely utilitarian about traditional Japanese design. It was the product of a long and highly sophisticated tradition, focused on the tea ceremony, which saw the attainment of beauty – in plastic form, in motion and gesture, in

Sony's integrated amplifier, 1965, established the dominant hi-fi aesthetic for years to come: the cool, uncompromisingly professional look, making the living-room a substitute for the recording studio. Before this, the controls of audio equipment were either hidden or made to look as simple as possible: afterwards, the stress was on difficulty and complexity

texture, in taste — as an expression of religious feeling.

During the centuries that European art, fine and decorative, was undergoing spasm after spasm of change, Japanese aristocratic taste was directed steadily inward: on the attainment in, say, a bowl or vase, in a splash of ink or in an interval of time, of a melancholy kind of stillness and quietness. When the two traditions, Western and Japanese, were brought deliberately into contact with each other some 130 years ago, great shock was felt on both sides. But after the shock had subsided, the responses of East and West were very different.

In the West, Japanese plainness began slowly to infiltrate into Western sensibilities. The process was accelerated by such events as the publication of Edward Morse's classic *Japanese Homes and their Surroundings* in 1886 and the Chicago World's Fair of 1893, where Frank Lloyd Wright absorbed the Japanese influence that was soon to find expression in his 'Prairie' houses. The qualities that by the 1920s were to be identified with modern architecture and the Bauhaus owed a huge debt to Japan. Honesty to materials, the beauty of asymmetrical design, modularity, the rejection of ornament — all these quintessentially modern tendencies derived in part from traditional Japanese practice.

The times permitted Japan no such slow accommodation, however. Acutely aware of the West's technological and military superiority, the Japanese began importing the products and standards of the West, everything from hairstyles to steam engines, as fast as they were able. Traditional Japanese things, meanwhile, were accorded their own limited sphere, and maintained it pretty well inviolate from the onset of modernization in the 1860s to the defeat by the Allies in 1945. When they relaxed — at home after work, or at festivals — the Japanese of this period invariably slipped back into their kimono and geta, and sat cross-legged on tatami. After an initial period of confusion in the early years of modernization, the two worlds of *wa-fu* (Japanese style) and *yo-fu* (Western style) were kept rigidly apart.

As a result of this separation, Japan's traditional style has until recently had remarkably little influence on that country's modern designers. The traditional Japanese interior may have been an important source of inspiration for the West, but inspiration was the limit of it: until recently, the Japanese played no more active a part in the development of Western interior design than, say, the Easter Islanders played in the development of modern sculpture.

This situation has now changed radically, because the first generation to be born after the war has come into its creative prime. If it is true, as Andrea Branzi says in *Architecture in Love*, that 'the history of modern architecture corresponds to the history of the modern chair', it is easy to understand why Japan's active participation in modern design has been so long in coming about; for the generation now entering its forties is the first in the nation's history to have been brought up on, under and around chairs.

The American occupation that followed Japan's defeat in World War II did not kill off the nation's traditional culture, but it did, more than any event before or since, transform the quality of everyday Japanese life. Western clothes became more and more the norm, even after hours, while most post-war homes came equipped with only a single traditional room.

The post-war generation thus grew up with little or no sense of inferiority to, or distance from, the culture of the West, at least in its material manifestations. The view of things now was from chair-height, and it was of a world of cars and motorbikes and expressways, of TV and hi-fi, and of the utilitarian Western standards of design that were a part of that world. This was normality; and for the most sophisticated of this generation, especially for those who later travelled abroad to study, it had neither the strangeness nor the romance it had possessed for their fathers.

Japan Victor Company's portable radio with TV, 1975

Sony's black-and-white TV with FM/AM radio and cassette recorder, 'Jackal', 1976, which took the tendency to complexity to fetishistic lengths with its multiplicity of dials, levers, gauges and knobs

Towards the end of the 1970s, sated with the richly eclectic diet of the past years, some members of this generation began to pine for what had been discarded, to cast around for ways to affirm not just a modern but a specifically Japanese identity. Leading figures in architecture, interior design and fashion all felt this trend, a trend which is reflected in much of the Japanese work featured in the present book.

Fascination with the native tradition has been a recurring feature of Japanese design this century, reviving whenever fear of the erosion of national identity reaches a certain level. In the 1930s it was manifested by a boom in the popularity of rattan furniture, and went easily with the nationalism of that decade. The early 1960s saw the next big wave, with Katsuo Matsumura's sitting platforms for use in place of sofas in carpeted, Western-style rooms, and with the popularity of Isamu Noguchi's paper and bamboo lampshades.

But the revival during the past six years has been the most internationally significant. Many more Japanese designers now have experience of studying and working abroad. They are on the same wavelength as their foreign counterparts, and closely in touch with new developments worldwide; but they also carry enough weight to influence the West in return.

The architect Arata Isozaki is one of these. His sidetable and bench employ rough-hewn stone in a way that recalls the use of rocks in Japanese gardens. Isozaki emphasizes that chance played an important part in these designs, the arrangement of colours, for example, having been selected by throws of a dice. The accidental is a vital element in many traditional Japanese arts such as ink painting and ikebana. Hiroshi Morishima is another such designer. He spent from 1967 to 1973 studying and working in the United States, one result of which was an upsurge of his interest in the materials and forms of Japanese tradition. In his work he reinterprets that tradition, using handmade paper for lamps, roller blinds and screens. The tactile qualities of the paper are fully exploited and yet his materials fit comfortably into the context of modern, Western-style rooms (plate 371). Masayuki Kurokawa, an architect like his even better-known brother Kisho, is also prolific and versatile. The smooth, rounded contours of his stainless-steel boxes, pen trays and condiment sets demand to be caressed, and subtly employ the contrast between the coldness of the material and the sensuality of the form. Starkly simple, their effect is the opposite of puritanical.

In the field of products, National's design for the floor TV has already been mentioned as evidence that Japanese style in the typical modern Japanese house is no longer confined to a particular room reserved for formal occasions: more and more people, hankering for the green smell of tatami and the cosy, grounded feeling the Japanese enjoy when they sit on it, have been bringing Japanese features into the rooms they use every day — paper shoji windows, exposed columns and beams and areas of tatami, and now possibly National's TV.

But of all the design areas, perhaps textiles have provided the greatest scope for bringing modern technology and a traditional sensibility together to produce radically new designs. Junichi Arai is unquestionably the leader in this field. Now famous as the principal supplier of fabric to Issey Miyake, Arai was born into a traditional weaving and dyeing environment. With his superb sense of colour and texture, he yokes the high-craft standards of Japan's traditional artisans to the design capabilities offered by the computer. For the first time ever, Japanese designers such as Arai enjoy sufficient international respect for their work to affect that of their peers in the West.

Peter Popham

Sony's elegant 'Trinitron Colour Monitor', 1980. In the reaction from complexity, all the controls were concealed from view, and all surfaces back and front were as sleek and sheer as they could be made

Toshiba's 'Black 10', 1982, continues the minimalistic theme

ACKNOWLEDGMENT All photographs are courtesy of the Japan Industrial Design Promotion Organization.

Michael Graves. Photograph © Larry Shlim 1981

DESIGN AS A CONSUMER DURABLE

In the last few years a small number of designers of domestic products have become stars. This is one of the more noteworthy transformations to have taken place in the design world during the 1980s. For a number of manufacturers, the value of employing such illustrious designers lies not so much in the quality of their work, but in the cachet that attaching their names to products can bring. There is a story to illustrate the phenomenon at its most extreme. A pencil manufacturer attempted to engage Gae Aulenti to 'design' a lead pencil for him. 'But how can I improve on existing pencil design?', she reportedly objected. Yet there are now several firms, ranging from Swid Powell in New York to Alessi in Italy, who are building their success on the portfolio of 'names' whom they have recruited. In the case of the latter company at least, this is a success equally solidly based on the quality of the designs and workmanship themselves.

The importance of the designer name can be explained partly by the increasing celebrity fixation of a media-oriented world. Warhol's notorious prophecy of a climate in which everyone would be famous for fifteen minutes has almost come true in the sphere of design. Indeed in some ways, design has moved more and more into the orbit of the high-speed fashion business, a commodity to be consumed greedily by the media-jaded, on a par with jeans, music, soap opera and royalty. As a result, designers may achieve brief periods of fame and fortune, but all too soon find themselves discarded, sucked dry of ideas and individuality, their work exhausted of meaning and content.

Such well-known figures as Michael Graves have already faced this process. After elevation almost overnight from the comparative obscurity of academic life in Princeton, respected by his peers but largely unknown outside the world of architecture, and consequently starved of sufficient outlets for his talents, Graves has become a public figure. Now he is in demand for 'high-profile' projects – fashion shops for Diane von Fürstenberg, furniture for Sunnar and Memphis –, lends his name to shopping-bags, and has in 1986 produced a kettle for Alessi (plate 475) which has reportedly attracted the interest of Nancy Reagan herself. But his prolific output has brought a backlash: his portrait has appeared in *Women's Wear Daily* overprinted with a damning red cross. The peril of becoming fashionable is the prospect of becoming as quickly unfashionable, and the process can be regarded by others as trivializing a designer's serious work.

The glamour of celebrity is not the only motivation for manufacturers to use and endorse the designer star system. They increasingly recognize that the *identity* which their products project is of critical importance to their commercial success. Sometimes it is a matter of reassuring the anxious, diffident consumer that his purchase will reflect well on his taste and judgment. For the insecure as well as for the fashion-conscious, this is best done by a process of association. 'If X has put his or her name to designing Y, then I can be secure, confident that I have made a socially acceptable choice,' runs the reasoning. To get the message across, the designer's signature needs to be readily visible. The prominent display of acceptable addresses provides similarly attractive associations: once it was the ostentatious advertisement, on packaging or product, of branches in Paris, Milan and New York that counted; now it is the addition of a street name – Via Montenapoleone, Fifth Avenue, Bond Street.

What works for the reassurance of individuals holds good, too, for the confidence of companies. Names can provide manufacturers with a ready entry into world markets, and the same names appear

Tea set for Alessi by Michael Graves, 1984

working for countries all over the world. A Taiwanese electronics company, for example, may not be known in Europe, but if it employs Mario Bellini to style its products, then it can be sure that his name at least will open doors. Equally, the first step for a traditionally minded furniture company hoping to extend its appeal might be to engage the services of an individual such as the universally respected Vico Magistretti to establish its new credentials.

A further reason for the star trend is the increasing standardization of products. In many areas of the market for consumer goods, the basic performance of the leading brands is indistinguishable. Hi-fi equipment, motor cars and so on, within a given price category, have roughly similar levels of performance whoever makes them. In these circumstances, all that remains to supply the vital added ingredient of product differentiation is design. Given the high costs of prototyping and development, the choice of a bankable designer as consultant helps to ease the minds of marketing departments.

There are some designers however who, like the Frenchman Philippe Starck, revel in the star phenomenon for the opportunities that it brings. Starck, who began his career as a designer working for Pierre Cardin, is only too well aware of the workings and the fickleness of the system. Nevertheless he asserts he finds it fascinating: 'It guarantees you work, and I need that guarantee: I'm a creative junkie, and I have to design every day.' Starck is the man who scored a notable success at last year's Milan Furniture Fair with his designs for Driade; he was also called in by Renault to design a special version of their Espace model, half-way between a car and a van; by Teraillon, to create a new set of scales; by Thompson, to undertake TV sets; by the Japanese for new watches; by Du Pont for cigarette lighters; and he has even designed a soda-pop bottle. And when the mass-market French mail order company of 3 Suisses went looking for a 'name' to come up with a furniture collection which would sell alongside their usual folding pine and chintz, it seemed natural to turn once more to Starck.

What is it then that makes the Starck signature so valuable to so many? Setting to one side for a moment his highly individual talent, Starck has been fortunate in his timing. His severe, sharply graphic designs came to prominence at just the right moment to provide an antidote to the continuing, excessively rich diet of Memphis imitators. Then he received two much-publicized commissions: the first from President Mitterrand for his personal apartments at the Elysée Palace, the second the fashionable Café Costes in the Les Halles area of Paris. Hence he is courted by half a dozen leading furniture manufacturers, and his designs are made by, among others, Driade, Baleri and Disform.

But while Starck seems content to ride the crest of the wave, turning the eccentric workings of stardom to his apparent advantage, there are others who have attempted the same course, and found it not without problems. Ettore Sottsass jr began the Memphis group fully conscious of the possibilities for exploiting the media's weakness for celebrities and sensationalism. These erstwhile arch-manipulators of public interest have however now been consumed themselves by the response which their designs have prompted; the Memphis name has been endlessly pirated, borrowed by T-shirt shops in London, and used by apartment blocks in New York. Even Sottsass has begun to express disenchantment with the Memphis movement. Introducing the 1986 Memphis collection, Barbara Radice, Sottsass's right-hand associate and Memphis's spokeswoman, described its character in bleak terms: 'It recalls the foggy, metropolitan moods of *Blade Runner* and of *The Terminator*, where the reckless post-nuclear hero moves against the blackened, wasted background of a presumed day after.'

In fact however, Memphis's current work is not a true celebration of *Mad Max* design — this was a field explored a few years ago by

Ettore Sottsass jr, Memphis's genius

(below) 'President M' table by Philippe Starck, 1985, designed for use in the Elysée Palace

(bottom) Philippe Starck

(top) Typewriter for Olivetti by Mario Bellini, 1983

(above) Black 201 TV set for Brionvega by Marco Zanuso and Richard Sapper, 1969. The Museum of Modern Art, New York (gift of Brionvega)

Gaetano Pesce, with his charred plastic tables for Cassina. In reality, the 1986 Memphis style is more in the nature of an abdication. 'Memphis are getting rid of the Memphis style,' says Radice; 'These pieces of furniture are neither optimistic nor playfully childish nor ironic, but obscure and overbearing.' In short, however one describes the work, Memphis have changed tack, conscious of having been neutralized by the very mechanisms which the group itself had exploited with such skill. Radice highlights the problem when she talks of 'the increasing quantity and spread of information which has destabilized, and is in the process of breaking, the sense of continuity and steadiness left to culture. Ideas, theories and programmes lose credibility from day to day. Fashions and fads are born and burnt out in closer and closer cycles.'

The notoriety of the Memphis group has nonetheless ensured a ready flow of work of many kinds for its members — though they design now as individuals as much as together. People such as George Sowden, Nathalie du Pasquier, Michele De Lucchi and Matteo Thun have themselves become stars.

Designers such as Vico Magistretti are longer established, belonging to the first generation to have devoted their entire careers to the creation of furniture. The classic period of modernism from Breuer to Eames saw the production of many important and long-lived designs. But without exception these were the creations of architects, who concentrated only briefly on furniture and then moved on to other concerns. From the 1960s onwards, Magistretti, Achille Castiglioni, Richard Sapper and one or two others have committed themselves almost exclusively to furniture, lighting and product design.

Both Magistretti and Castiglioni have been able to remain one step ahead of censure in *Women's Wear Daily*; in Magistretti's case this was thanks to the continuing freshness and undemanding charm of his ideas, in Castiglioni's to his inventiveness. Magistretti's *Villabianca* chair (named after his favourite London restaurant), designed for Cassina's 1985–86 collection along with the *Edison* table, is typical of his style (plates 38–42), though hardly vintage Magistretti at his best. He has also produced new lights for Venini. Castiglioni's output for 1985–86 is equally prolific: lights for Flos (plates, 224, 225), tableware (inevitably) for Alessi (plate 299), and pieces such as a coat-stand for Zanotta (plate 494).

Names such as theirs have become synonymous with modern design. Magistretti's beech chair for Cassina in the early 1960s, his moulded plastic *Selene* chair for Artemide of 1969, the *Maralunga* sofa for Cassina of 1973, and the *Atollo* lamp for O Luce of 1977 have each in their different ways become classics. Achille and Pier Giacomo Castiglioni's *Toio* light of 1962 for Flos, with its witty and highly inventive assembly of found elements into a low-voltage uplighter, Castiglioni's tractor-seat chair and many other pieces have also achieved classic status. Manufacturers still seek these designers out today, in the hope of finding themselves equally important new pieces for their catalogues, and basking in the reflected prestige that such designs bring to the rest of their ranges.

Rapidly acquiring similar status are Mario Bellini and Richard Sapper. These two have both been more involved in the field of consumer electronics than Magistretti and the Castiglioni brothers. Bellini has long worked with Olivetti, designing typewriters and calculators, as well as acting as a consultant for Japanese hi-fi firms and for Lancia Cars. His furniture includes the leather *Cab* chair for Cassina. Sapper began his career collaborating on electrical products, in particular radios and TV sets for Brionvega (with Marco Zanuso). He achieved his first resounding success with the *Tizio* light, produced from 1972 for Artemide. The *Tizio* is a masterly synthesis of formal values and new technology, being one of the earliest lights to make

(top) Portable radio for Brionvega by Marco Zanuso and Richard Sapper, 1968. The Museum of Modern Art, New York (purchase)

(above) 'Tizio' light for Artemide by Richard Sapper, 1972

*Detail of a table by Norman Foster, 1986.
Photograph Richard Davies*

Norman Foster

use of a quartz halogen source, with a low-voltage transformer that allows the metal arms of the light to be used to conduct electricity. Its status as a cult object was confirmed in 1985 when Artemide began to make a white version. Since the *Tizio*, Sapper has designed a limited amount of furniture, the *Tantalo* clock, a kettle and a coffee-maker for Alessi. Both Bellini and Sapper have shown themselves especially capable of designing consumer products which rise above the mundanely functional, and which offer tactile pleasures besides.

The star system undoubtedly regulates more and more the careers of its members. Now, they take on tasks ever further removed from their original specialisms. Giorgio Giugiaro for example, who began his career as a car designer producing such renowned models as the Volkswagen *Golf*, has since then turned his hand to designing everything from wrist watches to pasta shells. Ferdinand Alexander Porsche, no longer involved with the family car firm, has also taken the process to an extreme, diversifying into wrist watches, suitcases, sunglasses, smokers' pipes, and more recently chairs and lights.

The trend is particularly true of architects, who constitute a disproportionate number of the designer stars. Renzo Piano, a new recruit, designed the Beaubourg arts centre in Paris with Richard Rogers; he has since undertaken an experimental car for Fiat, and most recently a table for Fontana. Even such previously aloof figures as Norman Foster and James Stirling are now being assiduously courted by manufacturers eager to add their names to the growing repertoire of famous-name furniture.

Architects have long provided much of the intellectual underpinning for design. In an increasingly questioning period, their ideas are now finding a direct expression in areas of design outside architecture. Their growing involvement in fields such as the ceramics and glassware commissioned by Swid Powell — the firm has called on everyone from Hans Hollein to Architectonica — may well reflect an increasingly desperate search for content in design.

Deyan Sudjic

Swid Powell: a few designer stars, including Richard Meier (far left), Andrée Putman (third from left), Arata Isozaki (fourth from left), Stanley Tigerman (sixth from left) and Robert Stern (fourth from right)

F U R N I T U R E

Italy remains the pre-eminent home of contemporary furniture design: most of the major companies committed to producing high-quality new design are based there. But it is no longer quite the dominant cultural force that it once was. Much of the most interesting new work is coming from countries, or perhaps more accurately from cities, which are just beginning to find a voice of their own. Paris, Barcelona, New York and London do not yet begin to measure up to Milan. But there is a distinct air of change, and it is coming from those cities. For one thing, much of the new work has a simple directness, and can be made without the huge factories of the big Italian companies and the massive investments in tooling and craftsmanship which they require. Designers in Paris and Barcelona are prepared to work within the constraints of low-investment technology. Simple metal-bending machinery is all that is needed in some cases. Yet the work of the group of designers from the Via stable in Paris, or of Ron Arad's One-Off in London, does not look gauche when set against the high finish of the established manufacturers.

Looking back, perhaps the Memphis eruption can be interpreted as a kind of *fin-de-siècle* outpouring of emotion, mushrooming everywhere for a brief moment then disappearing again equally quickly, leaving only the more provincial manifestations behind. It is a path, incidentally, which corresponds exactly to the somewhat longer trajectory of Art Nouveau. The Memphis group itself now says that it has changed its style. The new pieces may have individual force, but they no longer exhibit the single coherent flavour that Memphis works once had.

As Memphis's adherents percolate through the Italian mainstream, some older designers, such as Magistretti, mark time. Others, such as Bellini, have their attention focused outside the field of domestic furniture, for the time being at least. This pause, if that is what it is, has left Italy's more enterprising manufacturers looking around for a means of filling the void. Inspiration has come mainly from those new voices outside Italy that are beginning to make themselves heard. France has produced Philippe Starck, whose work, wrong-headed though it may sometimes be, seems most to have caught the mood of the moment for a new purposeful approach. And it is he whom Driade have recruited. Zanotta have belatedly discovered Oscar Tusquets, an architect from Barcelona, a city which has begun to enjoy a creative rebirth in the years since democracy was restored to Spain. This process has accelerated, thanks to Spain's recent accession to the Common Market.

How much of the promise of all this diversity will mature has yet to be seen. Markets for its results still need to be found, and many of the manufacturers involved are still working on shoe-string budgets. But for the moment, the prospects seem encouraging.

1 PAULO NAVA
Sofa, *Gli Abiti*
Foam-covered steel structure, with canvas padding and
Dacron covering. The outer covering is treated like a
piece of clothing, designed to change with the seasons, by
Gianfranco Ferre.
Two-seater sofa: H 78 cm (30¾ in). W 168/210 cm
(66/83 in). D 84/130 cm (33/51⅛ in)
Manufacturer: B & B Italia, Italy

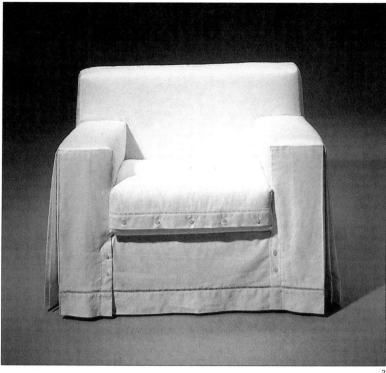

2

3

● Gianfranco Ferre is one of the most interesting of Italy's fashion designers. Originally trained as an architect, he has managed to avoid the pitfalls of too literal a transfer of the disciplines of this background to the field of clothes design. He has collaborated with Paolo Nava, an architect who turned to furniture, on B & B Italia's new armchair seating. In the process they have carried through an idea which has intrigued several designers for some time, treating their furniture coverings as clothing. Ferre has produced a series of covers for Nava's armchairs which can be replaced at will, with different styles and colours appropriate to each season.

2–4 PAOLO NAVA
Armchairs and sofas, *Gli Abiti*
Foam-covered steel structure, with canvas padding and Dacron covering. The outer coverings are treated like a wardrobe of clothes in different colours and textures, designed to change with the seasons, by Gianfranco Ferre.
Armchair: H 78 cm (30¾ in).
W 108/150 cm (42½/59 in).
D 84/130 cm (33/51⅛ in)
Two-seater sofa: H 78 cm (30¾ in).
W 168/210 cm (66/83 in).
D 84/130 cm (33/51⅛ in)
Three-seater sofa: H 78 cm (30¾ in).
W 228/270 cm (90/106½ in).
D 84/130 cm (33/51⅛ in)
Manufacturer: B & B Italia, Italy

6,7 BRUNO ROTA
Sofas and armchairs, *Wein-Wein Collection*
Black leather upholstered set; armchairs, a two-seater and a three-seater sofa.
Armchair: 80 cm (31½ in). W 104 cm (41 in). D 90 cm (35½ in)
Two-seater sofa: 81 cm (32 in). W 170 cm (67 in). D 91 cm (36 in)
Three-seater sofa: 82 cm (32¼ in). W 229 cm (90⅛ in). D 92 cm (36¼ in)
Manufacturer: Franz Wittmann, Austria

4

5 TITINA AMMANNATI AND GIANPIER VITELLI
Chair, *Kilkis*
The metal frame is embedded in
permanently shaped foam, raised from
the floor by epoxy-painted flexible steel
bars and nylon gliders. The position of the
back can be altered. Covers can be fabric
or leather, plain or quilted
H 81–95 cm (32–37½ in)
Manufacturer: Brunati, Italy

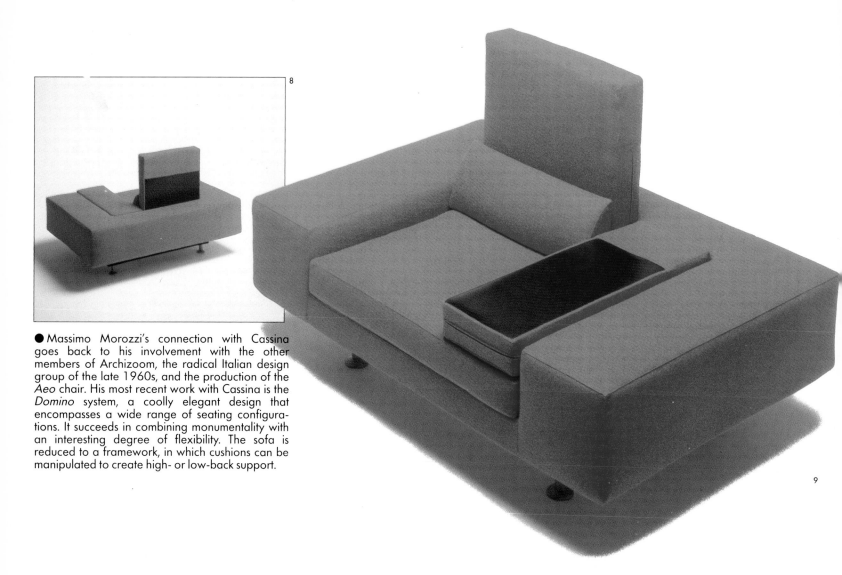

8

9

● Massimo Morozzi's connection with Cassina goes back to his involvement with the other members of Archizoom, the radical Italian design group of the late 1960s, and the production of the *Aeo* chair. His most recent work with Cassina is the *Domino* system, a coolly elegant design that encompasses a wide range of seating configurations. It succeeds in combining monumentality with an interesting degree of flexibility. The sofa is reduced to a framework, in which cushions can be manipulated to create high- or low-back support.

11

10, 11 JEAN-PIERRE CAILLÈRES
Table, *Basculator*
With a metal base and glass top this table can be positioned at three different levels: low/intermediate/high.
H 45/58/74 cm (17½/23/29 in).
W 75 cm (29½ in). L 140 cm (55 in)
Manufacturer: Papyrus, France

10

8, 9 MASSIMO MOROZZI
Sofa, *Domino*
Small, medium or large sofa with wooden
frame and foam padding, built up from
adjustable components. There is a full-
length seat cushion and small back
support cushion. The removable and
independent high-back cushions have a
steel frame and thick leather insert.
Upholstered in fabric or leather in a
variety of colours.
H 94 cm (37 in). W 150/210/300 cm
(59/83/118 in). D 100 cm (39½ in)
Manufacturer: Cassina, Italy

12, 13 YRJO KUKKAPURO
Chairs, *Project A-500*
Light-weight general-purpose chairs in
birch plywood and epoxy-painted steel.
The upholstery covers come in a variety of
fabrics.
H 42 cm (16½ in). L 52 cm (20½ in).
W 42 cm (16½ in)
Manufacturer: Avarte, Finland

12

13

14

15

14 ISAO HOSOE
Tables, *Haru*
Small adjustable tables that can be
arranged to form surfaces for different
uses. The tops are printed and varnished
in a variety of colours.
H 40 cm (16 in). D of top 50 cm (20 in)
Manufacturer: Arflex, Italy

16

15 ISAO HOSOE
Seating, *Haru Collection*
Range of furniture: ottoman, high-back
and low-back armchairs, two-size sofa
with low or high backs, stuffed with foam
and fitted with removable covers.
H 92 cm (36 in). L 113/171/220 cm
(44½/67½/87 in). W 92 cm (36 in)
Manufacturer: Arflex, Italy

16 ANTTI NURMESNIEMI
Chair, *Tuoli*
Versatile adjustable chair: the
independent back moves and the angle it
forms with the seat can be altered to
change the sitting position. With a frame
of polished chromed steel; the foam
padding is covered with fabric or leather
upholstery.
H 78 cm (31 in). W 65 cm (25½ in).
L 154 cm (60½ in)
Manufacturer: Cassina, Italy

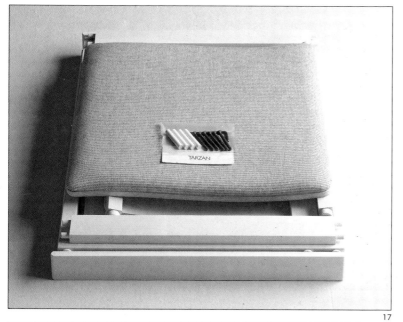

17

18

17, 18 SIMO HEIKKILÄ
Chair, *TZ2 Tarzan*
Folding chair in birchwood with a cotton
and wool cover.
H 86 cm (34 in). L 56 cm (22 in). W 59 cm
(23 in)
Manufacturer: Tarzan Furniture Factory,
Finland

20 BRUNO ROTA
Table, *Pantos*
Square and rectangular tables with glass
tops. All with varnished tubular metal
bases.
H 70 cm (27½ in)
Square: 130 cm (51¼ in) square
Rectangular: L 200/260 cm
(78¾/102⅜ in). W 100/130 cm
(39⅜/51¼ in)
Manufacturer: B & B Italia, Italy

19

● Mario Bellini is a designer of a
younger generation than, for
example, Vico Magistretti (see pages
36–37), and one whose work is
altogether more sensual in its
exploitation of the tactile sense than
Magistretti's. Yet he too keeps to the
conventions built up around the
restrained Italian look of the early
1970s.

19 MARIO BELLINI
Sofa, *Excelsior*
Two-seater, with metal structure embedded
in polyurethane foam, cushions in
polyurethane and Dacron and covers in
leather or fabric. The seat cushions and
head rest adjust to various sitting positions.
H 82 cm (32¼ in). L 163 cm (64 in).
W 89 cm (35 in)
Manufacturer: B & B Italia, Italy

20

21

● Lella and Massimo Vignelli are two Italian
designers who now work mainly in America. Their
new chairs for Knoll have the strong graphic quality
and colour sense that typify all their work.

21 LELLA AND MASSIMO VIGNELLI AND DAVID LAW
Chairs, *Handkerchief*
Lightweight stackable chairs, with steel wire frame
supporting a fibreglass and polyester seat and back.
H 73.5 cm (29 in). W 58.5 cm (23 in). D 57.5 cm (22½ in)
Manufacturer: Knoll International, USA

22

23

22, 23 GIANFRANCO FRATTINI
Table, *Capri*
Square or rectangular table of black
lacquered beechwood. The cantilevered
structure carries interchangeable tops,
available in wood, glass, leather or sheet
steel, all in various colours.
H 74 cm (29 in). L 136/231 cm
(53½/91 in). W 96 cm (38 in)
Manufacturer: Cassina, Italy

24 WALTER GERTH
Desk/chair, *Crea*
Cabinet with medium-density fibreboard
panels and adjustable chrome-plated
support. Both desk and chair are mounted
on an integral base.
H 84–129 cm (33–51 in). W 75 cm
(29½ in). D 52 cm (20½ in)
Manufacturer: Strässle Söhne,
Switzerland

24

25 KAZUO KAWASAKI
Couch and chair, *Ton Ton*
Two seating units: an upper unit with a rounded back and seat, and a modular seating unit. Frame in polyurethane-covered steel tubing with a rigid wooden base.
Upper unit: H 46 cm (18 in). L 80 cm (31½ in). W 80 cm (31½ in)
Under unit: H 46 cm (18 in). L 80 cm (31½ in). W 80 cm (31½ in)
Manufacturer: Maruichi Selling, Japan

25

26 ENZO MARI
Chair, *Tonietta*
Frame in natural-finished aluminium alloy or fire-lacquered black or white. Seat and back covered in cow-hide in a variety of colours.
H 83.5 cm (33 in). W 39 cm (15½ in). D 47 cm (18 in)
Manufacturer: Zanotta, Italy

27 ENZO MARI
Table, *Trevi*
Three-legged table in natural-finished steel.
H 70 cm (27½ in). D 53 cm (21 in)
Manufacturer: Zanotta, Italy

26

27

28 GIANFRANCO FRATTINI
Chair, *Caprile*
Black lacquered beechwood frame with
leather back and seat in a variety of
colours.
H 80 cm (31½ in). W 48 cm (19 in).
D 51 cm (20 in)
Manufacturer: Cassina, Italy

29 MICHELE DE LUCCHI
Armchair, *Motel*
Painted tubular steel frame with
upholstered seat in black fabric.
H 70 cm (27½ in). W 77 cm (30 in).
D 62 cm (24½ in)
Manufacturer: Bieffeplast, Italy

28

29

30, 31 ULRICH BOEHME AND WULF SCHNEIDER
Chair, *S320* and sofa, *S340*
Beech and steel-rod frame. The chair has
a moulded plywood seat which can be
plain or upholstered.
H 46 cm (18 in). W 61 cm (24 in). L 57 cm
(22½ in)
Manufacturer: Gebrüder Thonet, West
Germany

30

31

32

33

32 RENZO PIANO
Table, *Teso*
Almost entirely in glass; the legs are fixed
to the top with a steel tension bar that
passes through the leg to create a rigid
joint with the table top.
H 72 cm (28½ in). L 240 cm (95 in).
W 80 cm (31½ in)
Manufacturer: Fontana, Italy

33 OSCAR TUSQUETS
Trolley, *Teulada*
Black fire-lacquered steel trolley for TV
and video which has an adjustable width.
H 65 cm (25½ in). W 59–83 cm
(23–33 in)
Manufacturer: Zanotta, Italy

34, 35 STEFAN WEWERKA
Units, *Cella*
Furniture treated as interior architecture,
in natural and lacquered woods, consisting
of five units: bookshelves and shelves;
chest of drawers; couch; floor container;
high seat with desk. Also shown,
Wewerka's kitchen tree, a minimal kitchen.
Sofa with bookshelf: H 223 cm (88 in).
L 200 cm (79 in). W 109 cm (43 in)
Chest of drawers: H 123 cm (48½ in).
L 65 cm (25½ in). W 40 cm (16 in)
Couch: H 11 cm (4¼ in). L 223 cm (88 in).
W 172 cm (67½ in)
High seat with desk, overall: H 132 cm
(52 in). L 120 cm (47 in). W 63–89 cm
(25–35 in)
Office combination/floor container:
H 216 cm (84½ in). L 185 cm (72¾ in).
W 120 cm (47¼ in)
Kitchen tree: H 196 cm (77 in). D 120 cm
(47 in)
Manufacturer: Tecta Möbel, West
Germany

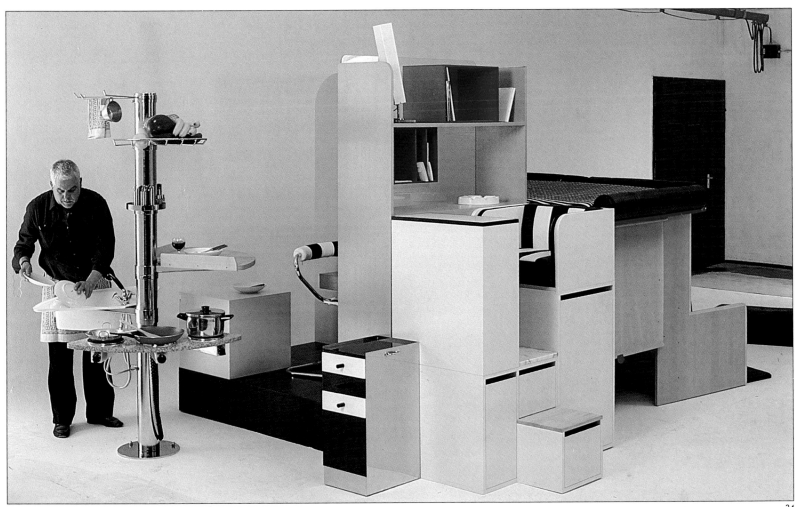

34

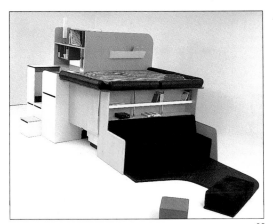

35

36

37

● Wewerka, an artist as well as a designer, has produced for Tecta a number of pieces which come closer to architecture than to furniture in the scope of what they offer. His kitchen tree includes storage capacity with sink and hot-plate, and his bed/storage box is equally versatile; not only can you sleep in it but it forms a room divider, a wardrobe and even has a desk flap.

36, 37 KAIROS
Table, *Servese*
In rigid polyurethane with cast-iron base on two wheels. The lacquered top with drawer is adjustable in length.
H 55–70 cm (21½–27½ in). D 50 cm (19⅝ in)
Manufacturer: B & B Italia, Italy

● Despite the often frantic experiments of some furniture designers with form, colour and imagery in the last decade, a vigorous, less flamboyant tradition still exists. As a significant proportion of the total output of the world's furniture industry, it might be called the mainstream of contemporary furniture design, and embraces such figures as Mario Bellini (see page 28) and Vico Magistretti. It would not be unfair to call Magistretti a functionalist. The vocabulary of his designs takes as its starting-point straightforward ideas of usability. Magistretti accepts the status quo: to him design is there to make life more pleasant, not to provoke or to upset. And as a functionalist Magistretti remains firm in his grasp of shapes, materials, colours and textures that build upon the idea of 'good design' as it was developed through the 1960s and 1970s. The result is restrained and simple, rather than extravagant and complex.

38

39

40

41

38, 40, 41 VICO MAGISTRETTI
Armchairs, *Villabianca*
Stackable chairs with stained beechwood
frames and seats and backs in polyester
resin, named after Magistretti's favourite
restaurant in London. Fabric (plate 38) or
leather (plate 41) removable covers with
incorporated padding.
H 78 cm (31 in). W 53 cm (21 in). D 53 cm
(21 in)
Manufacturer: Cassina, Italy

38, 39, 42 VICO MAGISTRETTI
Tables, *Edison*
Rectangular and circular tables. Glossy
enamel steel base in a variety of
colours with natural birch finish or glass top.
H 72.5/74 cm (28½/29 in)
Square: 140 cm (55 in) square
Rectangular: L 140 cm (55 in). W 225 cm
(89 in)
Circular: D 150 cm (59 in)
Manufacturer: Cassina, Italy

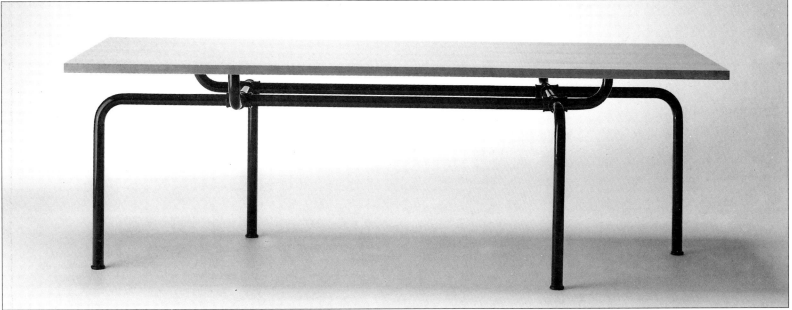

42

43

43, 44 OSCAR TUSQUETS
Table, *Varius*
Wooden frame with bronze feet and glass
top.
H 70 cm (27½ in). L 200 cm (79 in).
W 110 cm (43 in)
Manufacturer: Casas, Spain

● Outside the Italian sphere, the sober Scandinavians — whether the younger teams such as Pelikan Design from Copenhagen, or the older established names such as the Finn Antti Nurmesniemi (page 27) — are generally more successful than those who brashly attempt to ape the Italians. Their unpretentious, straightforward if sensitive detailing and shapes have the strength of purpose and integrity lacked by the more heavy-handed attempts at originality of some of their compatriots.

45

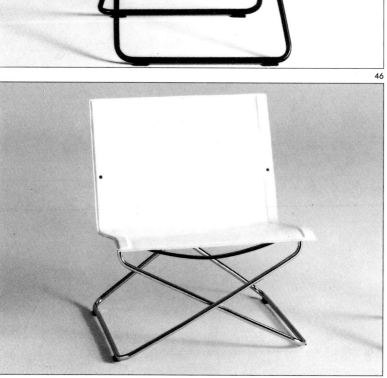

46

47

45–47 PELIKAN DESIGN
Chairs
Available with or without arms. Frame in either black lacquered metal or polished chrome, covering in black rubber or leather in a variety of colours.
H 77/84 cm (30⅜/33 in). W 50/70 cm (19½/27½ in). D 60/80 cm (23½/31½ in)
Manufacturer: Cappellini, Italy

48 OLE SCHJOLL
Armchair, *Arch Chair*
In laminated plywood.
H 71.5 cm (28in). D 68cm (26¾in). W 60 cm (23½in)
Manufacturer: Altaform, Denmark

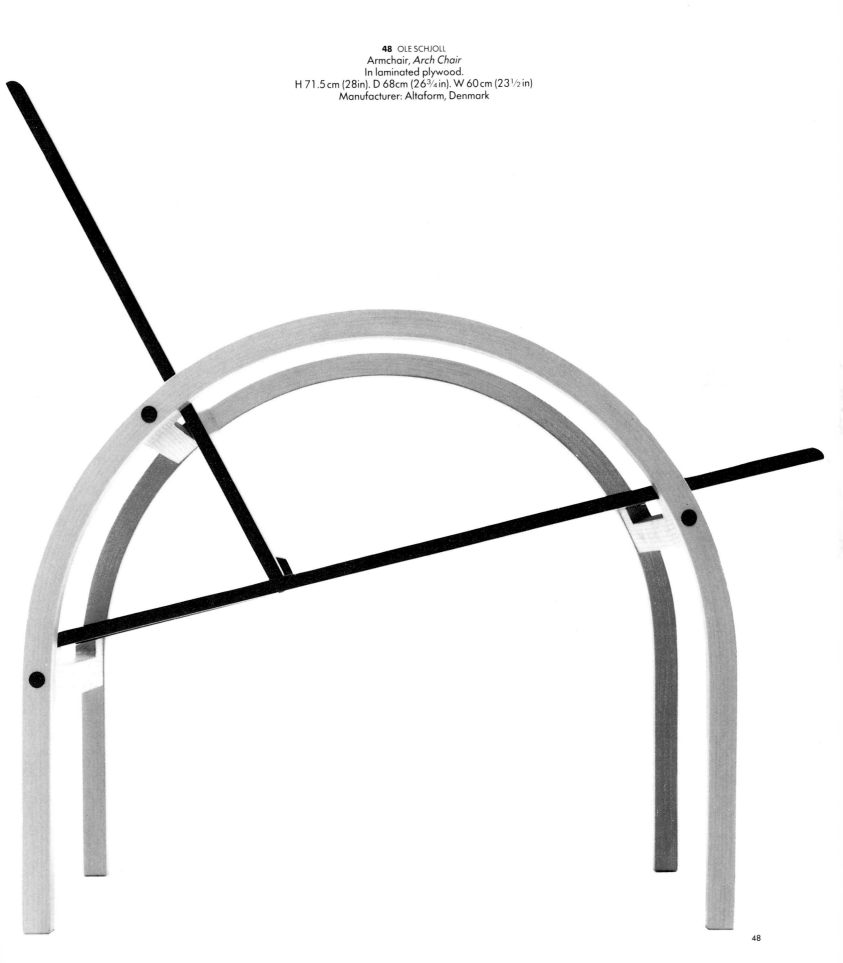

49, 50 GIOTTO STOPPINO
Sideboard, *Playbox*
In lacquered wood, equipped with
internal wiring to contain bar, fridge, TV
and hi-fi equipment. The small door has a
circular window, the larger slides open on
runners.
H 156 cm (61½ in). L 52 cm (20½ in).
W 156 cm (61½ in)
Manufacturer: Acerbis International, Italy

49

50

51 JOCHEN FLACKE
Cabinet, *Life-Service*
In lacquered medium-density fibreboard,
this series of units with drawers slots
together to form one large unit.
H 99 cm (44 in). L 52–104 cm (20–41 in).
W 52 cm (20 in)
Manufacturer: Rosenthal, West Germany

51

52 GASPARE CAIROLI
Chairs, *Terna*
Folding and stackable chairs in metal and
synthetic resin. The back rest is in fabric,
leather or rubber. Available in many
colours.
H 80 cm (31½ in). W 40 cm (15½ in).
D 48 cm (19 in)
Manufacturer: Seccose, Italy

53 GASPARE CAIROLI
Table, *Bingo*
Folding table with synthetic resin top and
painted metal structure. Available in many
colours.
H 80 cm (31½ in). L 48 cm (19 in).
W 48 cm (19 in)
Manufacturer: Seccose, Italy

52

53

● Designed as a student project in her final year at London's Royal College of Art, Mary Little's armchair is now in limited batch production — so far only for distribution in France. Its combination of strong formal values with an intelligent analysis of its practical function shows considerable maturity.

54

55

54, 55 MARY LITTLE
Armchair
Arms and seat in wood on a steel tube frame. The back is rubber and the feet turned nylon with a polyester finish.
H 75 cm (29½ in). W 90 cm (35½ in).
D 70 cm (27½ in)
Manufacturer: Mary Little, UK

56 PAOLO PIVA
Chair, *Arcosa*
Black leather-covered steel with steel arms and leather back.
H 86 cm (33⅞ in). W 58 cm (22⅞ in).
D 51 cm (20⅛ in)
Manufacturer: B & B Italia, Italy

56

57

57 BRUNO POZZI
Table, *Battista*
White laminated top on aluminium legs.
H 74 cm (29 in). D of top 80 cm (31½ in)
Manufacturer: Ciatti, Italy

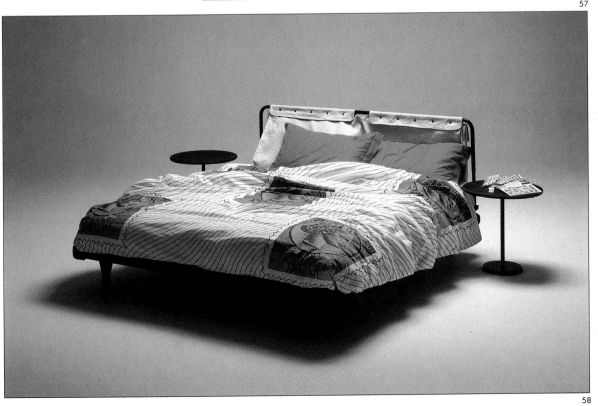

58

58 GIUGIARO DESIGN
Bed
Steel-frame wheeled bed.
L 195 cm (77 in). W 85/140/170 cm
(33½/55/67 in)
Manufacturer: Axil, Italy

59

60

● Matteo Thun's sideboard is one of his range of designs for Bieffeplast which capitalize on that company's commitment to technological innovation in manufacturing processes. It is fabricated using sheet steel, processed through a computer-controlled folding press of the type used in the manufacture of refrigerators and washing machines, and ornamented with a pattern of punched holes.

59 JOUKO JARVISALO
Chair, *Mondi Light*
Steel frame, chromed or powder-coated. The back rest is form-pressed plywood and the upholstery leather or fabric.
H 78.5 cm (31 in). L 59 cm (23 in).
W 54 cm (21 in)
Manufacturer: Inno Tuote, Finland

60 JOUKO JARVISALO
Chair, *Mondi Soft*
Steel frame with form-pressed plywood back rest, upholstered in fabric or leather.
H 75 cm (29½ in). L 75 cm (29½ in).
W 62.5 cm (24½ in)
Manufacturer: Inno Tuote, Finland

61 MATTEO THUN
Storage unit, *Madia*
In the *Container System* range. In enamelled folded steel, the top in printed laminate and glass and the doors perforated. Available in black and white or red and black.
H 209 cm (82¼ in). W 100 cm (39¼ in).
D 65 cm (25½ in)
Manufacturer: Bieffeplast, Italy

62, 63 BORGE LINDAU AND BO LINDEKRANTZ
Chair, *Planka*
In enamelled plywood with leather, sheet-metal or fabric seat. The swivelling base plate is enamelled steel and the seat frame and neck frames are chrome-plated.
H 110 cm (43 in). W 42 cm (16½ in).
D 68 cm (27 in)
Manufacturer: Lammhults, Sweden

62

63

64 PETER MALY
Armchair, *Zyklus*
In chromed steel tubing, with the upper part in coloured lacquer. The cover material and the leather are available in various combinations and colours.
H 72 cm (28¼ in). W 75 cm (29½ in).
L 85 cm (33½ in)
Manufacturer: COR-Sitzkomfort, West Germany

65 JOCHEN HOFFMANN
Sofa, *Trio*
Versatile sofa which can be used as a two-seater with two leg rests, a three-seater with one leg rest or a four-seater. The head rests are also adjustable. The beech frame is supported by lacquered-finished metal. The upholstery comes in a variety of different fabrics.
Manufacturer: Firma Franz Fertig, West Germany

64

65

66 GEMMA BERNAL AND RAMON ISERN
Bedhead, *Liron*
Bedhead on metal support to which the
bedside table is attached – a movable
tray, lamp and lacquered ash vertical
surface. Available in single or double size.
Single: H 580 cm (228⅓ in). W 1554 cm
(611¾ in).
Double: H 640 cm (252 in). W 2884 cm
(1135½ in)
Manufacturer: Disform, Spain

67 MASAYUKI KUROKAWA
Armchair
In aluminium alloy and plastic.
H 67.5 cm (26½ in). L 48.5 cm (19 in).
W 60 cm (23½ in)
Manufacturer: Nippon Light Metal, Japan

66

67

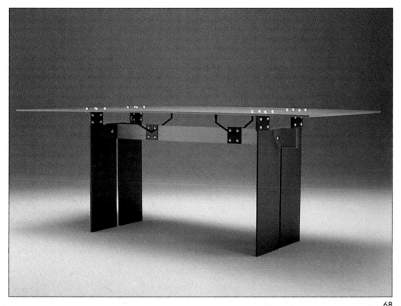

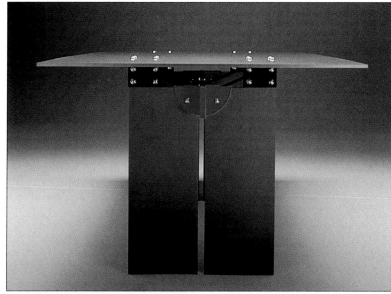

68

69

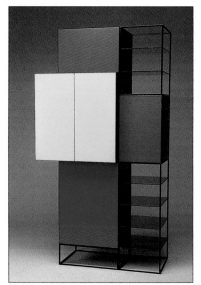

70

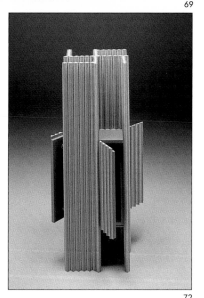

72

68, 69 SETSUO KITAOKA
Table
Dining-table in steel.
H 75 cm (29½ in). L 200 cm (78¾ in).
W 100 cm (39⅜ in)
Prototype

70 ARNOLD MERCKX
Sideboard, *Harmony*
Range of units made up of square and
rectangular pieces, dividers and elements
with glass doors and shelves.
H 90 cm (35½ in). Top W 200 cm (79 in).
Unit W 120 cm (47¼ in). D 48 cm (19 in)
Manufacturer: Pastoe, The Netherlands

71, 72 SETSUO KITAOKA
Screen, *Byobu*
Folding screen in colorcore.
Each panel 24 cm (9½ in) by 24 cm
(9½ in) by 14 cm (5½ in)
Prototype

71

73 ANGELO MANGIAROTTI
Table, *La Badoera*
Legs in stone and top in walnut with either
a transparent finish, matt black lacquered
ash or transparent ash.
H 74 cm (29 in). L 240 cm (95 in). W 84 cm
(33 in)
Manufacturer: Poltronova, Italy

73

74 JEAN-PIERRE CAILLÈRES
Chair, *Chaise Longue*
In black and blue timber.
L 180 cm (71 in). W 65 cm (25½ in)
Manufacturer: Papyrus, France

74

75

76

77

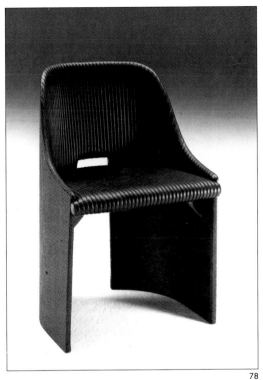

78

79

75 PIOTR SIERAKOWSKI
Mirage Table
Base in aluminium finished in black or grey Nextel; the top is pencil-edged glass.
H 72.5 cm (28½ in). W 91.5 cm (36 in) L 193/213.5 cm (76/84 in)
Manufacturer: Koch + Lowry, USA

76 GERARD TAYLOR
Desk
The desk top is made in three panels — leather-covered work surface/briar veneer/dark grey — and supported on a black steel frame. The circular table to the left houses a cupboard.
H 74.5 cm (29¼ in). L 220 cm (87 in). W 93 cm (36½ in).
W of wings 75 cm (29½ in)
Prototype
Manufacturer: Gordon Russell, UK

77 DANBER
Table, *Chamisso*
Timber, with glass top, and black and white legs.
Manufacturer: Danber, Italy

78 AFRA AND TOBIA SCARPA
Chair
Chair with or without arms in curved plywood. The back and seat have quilted padding in either fabric or leather.
H 75 cm (26½ in). W 52 cm (20 in). D 53 cm (21 in)
Manufacturer: Maxalto, Italy

79 MARCELLO MORANDINI
Unit, *Corner*
Black plywood corner unit veneered with ash.
H 218 cm (86 in). L 107 cm (42 in). W 28 cm (11 in)
Manufacturer: Rosenthal, West Germany

80 PETER VAN DER HAM
Sofa, *Sandwich*
A wooden shell with a horizontal spring,
upholstered with pre-formed foam
covered in fabric.
H 72 cm (28½ in). W 190 cm (75 in).
D 82 cm (32½ in)
Manufacturer: Artifort, The Netherlands

80

81 MARIO MARENCO
Table, *Mimi*
Round-cornered top with base in stone.
The table is pivoted to permit rotation and
sideways movement.
H 28 cm (11 in). Top: 100 cm (39½ in)
square
Manufacturer: B & B Italia, Italy

81

82

83

82–84 LELLA AND MASSIMO VIGNELLI AND DAVID LAW
Table, *Serenissimo*
The legs are four large-diameter metal columns treated to evoke Venetian stuccowork. They are interconnected by a natural-finish metal framework. The top is treated plate glass, giving a semi-opalescent effect.
H 70–72 cm (27½–28½ in). L 160 cm (63 in). W 145 cm (57 in)
Manufacturer: Acerbis International, Italy

84

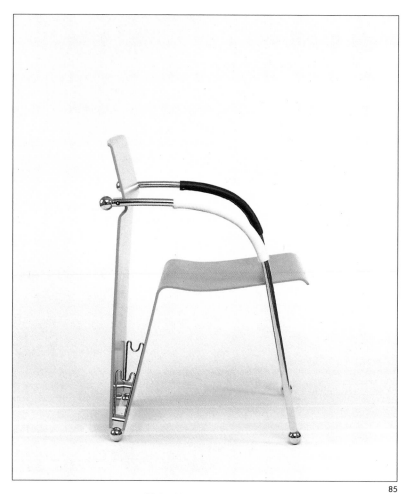

85

85, 86, 89 HANS-PETER RAINER
Armchair, *Metropolis*
Stacking, shaped lacquered plywood chair with leather
sleeves and detachable upholstery.
Manufacturer: Thonet, Austria

87 PENTTI HAKALA
Chair
High-backed armless chair in wood and
steel tubing.
H 110 cm (43½ in). W 50 cm (19½ in)
Prototype
Manufacturer: Lily River, Finland

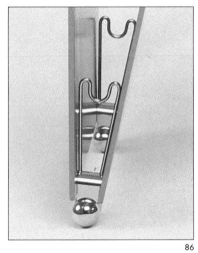

88 ERNST BERANEK
Chair, *Fit Forms*
Stackable solid beech chair with seat and
back in punched shaped plywood.
Lacquered in a range of colours.
H 106 cm (42 in). W 43 cm (17 in). D 56 cm
(22 in)
Manufacturer: Thonet, Austria

89 HANS-PETER RAINER
Table, *Metropolis*
Chrome knock-down table with wood,
melamine, glass or cast marble top.
Available in six sizes.
Manufacturer: Thonet, Austria

86

87

88

89

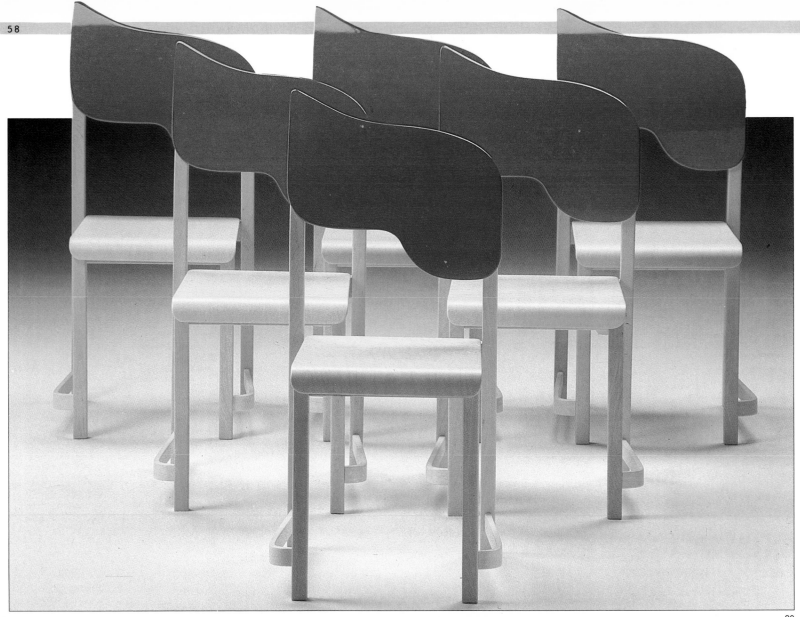

90

● When furniture designers turn their hands to wit, they need to exercise the lightest of touches: the occasions when you actually want a table or a set of chairs to make you laugh are few and far between. Rita Taskinen's *Flag* chairs, and the *State* table – presumably it can be cut to the shape of the country of your choice – thankfully make perfect design sense even without the joke.

90, 91 RITA TASKINEN
Table, *State* and chairs, *Flag*
Table in medium-density fibreboard and lacquered tubular steel. Chairs in solid birch and lacquered bent plywood.
Table: H 72 cm (28 in). W 130 cm (51 in). L 150 cm (59 in)
Chair: H 86 cm (34 in). W 42 cm (16½ in). D 51 cm (20 in)
Manufacturer: Proforma, Finland

91

92, 93 SERGIO ASTI
Table, *Ontario*
An occasional table on wheels with a
bottom shelf of lacquered wood and
shaped top shelf of crystal plate,
supported on marble elements.
H 35 cm (13½ in). Square 140 cm (55 in)
Manufacturer: Morphos, Acerbis, Italy

93

92

94

94 GIOVANNI OFFREDI WITH SAPORITI ITALIA
Armchair, *Daun*
Cushioned adjustable armchair is
connected to the back with hinges and
balanced in different positions on two
rods. The movement is hidden by a plate
at the base, leaving joints and releasing
lever exposed.
H 100 cm (39 in). W 80 cm (32 in). L 83 cm
(33 in)
Manufacturer: Saporiti Italia, Italy

95

96

97

98

99

95 FRANCO RAGGI
Cupboard and table, *Carton*
Beech frame cupboard lacquered in matt
black. The transparent-finished top is
decorated with opening lateral supports
and silver-plated handle. Matt black
lacquered beech frame table with top
decorated internally and matt black
lacquered exterior. Extension supports in
matt lacquer.
Cupboard: H 90 cm (35½ in). W 120 cm
(47 in). D 60 cm (23½ in)
Table: H 90 cm (35½ in). W 114/241 cm
(45/95 in). D 72 cm (28½ in)
Manufacturer: Poltronova, Italy

● Jaak Floris van den Broecke, now
Professor of Furniture Design at the
Royal College of Art in London, takes
a different tack from those designers
labelled as craftsmen with whom he
is generally grouped. For him, making
furniture by hand is of less significance than the design of what he
makes. In this sense he regards his
works as prototypes for machine-
made production.

100

96–99 JAAK FLORIS VAN DEN BROECKE
Seat, *S.E.T.T.L.E.*
Upholstered seat on a metal frame.
H 130 cm (51 in). W 200 cm (79 in).
L 200 cm (79 in)
Prototype
Manufacturer: Furniture Designers, UK

100 JURGEN LANGE
Cupboard, *Headline*
Grey- and pink-lacquered wood cupboard
with glass doors, with pink-lacquered
metal column supporting pivoting shelf.
H 213 cm (84 in). 1,000 cm (393½ in)
square
Manufacturer: Behr Möbelfabrik, West
Germany

101 WALTER GERTH
Chairs, *Spass*
A series of seven chairs with a family
resemblance, in green-dyed plywood
with red-lacquered tubular steel legs.
H 79 cm (31 in). W 45 cm (17½ in).
D 62 cm (24½ in)
Manufacturer: Strässle Söhne,
Switzerland

101

102

103

104

102–104 PAOLO DEGANELLO
Tables, *Artifici*
The bases are made of quartz and marble aggregate, the four struts are in natural cherrywood, and the top is composed of two sheets of crystal with an insert of non-slip plasticized fabric.
H 37.5 cm (15 in). L 63.5–120 cm (25–47 in)
Manufacturer: Cassina, Italy

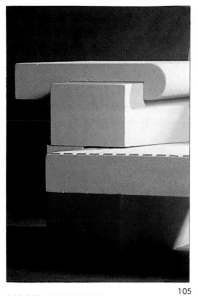

105

105, 106 MARIO BELLINI
Benches
Carved stone benches in red sandstone and white marble, designed for manufacture by Indian artisans and shown at the Cooper-Hewitt Museum 'Golden Eye' exhibition.
Prototypes

106

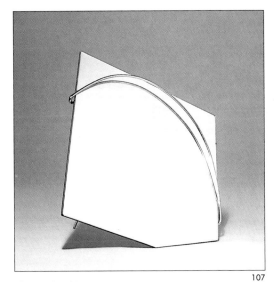

107 ALVARO SIZA
Mirror, *Esquisse*
Mirrored glass decorated with chrome steel rods.
20 cm (8 in) square, with corner missing. 4 mm ($\frac{1}{8}$ in)
thick, supported on 2 mm ($\frac{1}{16}$ in) wire
Manufacturer: Alvaro Siza, Portugal

108 PAOLO DEGANELLO
Dressing-table, *Grande Spichio*
With shelves and hanging mirror.
H 240 cm (94$\frac{1}{2}$ in). W open 115 cm (45$\frac{1}{4}$ in).
W closed 60 cm (23$\frac{1}{2}$ in)
Manufacturer: Tribu, France

109 MARTIN SZEKELY
Shelves, *Bibliotheque Pi*
In lacquered wood.
H 167 cm (65$\frac{3}{4}$ in). W 80 cm (31$\frac{1}{2}$ in)
Manufacturer: Tribu, France

107

108

109

110 MASAKI MORITA
Table, *Floraqua*
Circular table with domed base supported
on four tubular legs.
H 75 cm (29½ in). D 135 cm (53 in)
Manufacturer: Tribu, France

111 SIMON DESANTA
Chair, *Flying Carpet*
Single-seater cantilever chair with a base
of cast aluminium and sprung tubular steel
frame. Cushion covers come plain or
patterned.
H 100 cm (39½ in). W 105 cm (41½ in).
D 105 cm (41½ in)
Manufacturer: Rosenthal, West Germany

110

111

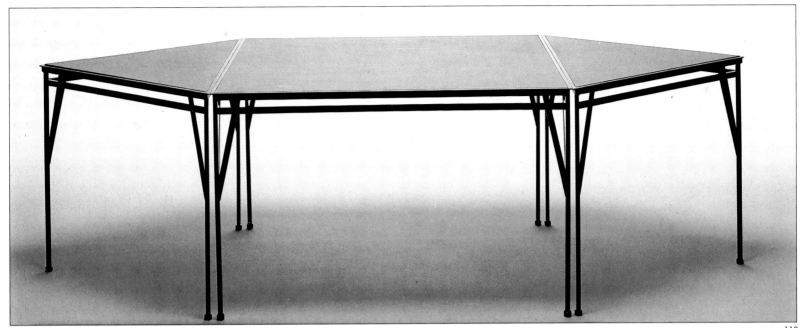

112

112 ABDENENGO
Table, *Tux*
Three-section table with stone top and
black-painted steel structure.
H 73 cm (28¾ in). Top 76 cm (30 in) square
Manufacturer: Bieffeplast, Italy

114

113, 114 MAURIZIO PEREGALLI
Armchair
Tubular steel with perforated steel seat.
Available in a variety of finishes.
H 77 cm (30½ in). L 53 cm (21 in)
Manufacturer: Zeus, Italy

113

115

116

118

● The fame of Mario Botta's sternly geometric houses in his native Ticino has spread around the world, and he is now attempting a series of much larger, but equally sober, rationalistic public buildings. His interest in furniture is a more recent development. It displays a similar preoccupation with simple geometric forms, here made from tensely stressed metal, sometimes to more successful effect than at other times.

115, 118 MARIO BOTTA
Chair, *Quinta*
Painted perforated plate metal, with metal tube frame.
H 92 cm (36 in). L 45 cm (18 in)
Manufacturer: Alias, Italy

116, 117 MARIO BOTTA
Armchair, *Sesta*
Perforated and stretched-steel painted
frame with seat and cushions in leather or
fabric.
H 95 cm (37¹⁄₂ in). W 100 cm (39¹⁄₂ in).
D 100 cm (39¹⁄₂ in)
Manufacturer: Alias, Italy

119 MARIO BOTTA
Sofa, *Sesta*
Two-seater sofa with perforated
stretched-steel frame. Seat and cushions
in leather or fabric.
H 95 cm (37¹⁄₂ in). L 155 cm (61 in)
Manufacturer: Alias, Italy

119

● The idea of producing an object that is both a piece of furniture and a light lies behind Sebastian Conran's dressing-table. The mirror is illuminated, echoing Eileen Gray's classic mirror, while the storage drawer below folds out in use, supported by its wheeled leg.

● Ron Arad's company One-Off is perhaps the most interesting of Britain's burgeoning small designer/maker furniture businesses. Arad's pieces explore decay, destruction and also the creative recycling of found objects and cannibalized bits of machinery. In the past year he has begun a closer collaboration with the Milan-based Zeus organization. Here the table scarred with etched and ground glass is from One-Off, but the chairs are Zeus's.

120 SEBASTIAN CONRAN
Dressing-table, *Vanity Femme*
White metal dressing-table with drawers and circular mirror attachment.
H 1800 cm (708½ in). D 500 cm (197 in)
Manufacturer: Sebastian Conran/Authentics, UK

121 RON ARAD
Table
Etched glass-topped table with folded, welded sheet metal supports. The chairs are by Maurizio Peregalli (see plates 113, 114).
H 75 cm (29½ in). L 153 cm (60 in).
W 153 cm (60 in)
Manufacturer: One-Off, UK

122 MINALE, TATTERSFIELD AND PARTNERS
Chair, *Parmesan*
Steel with tubular framework and perforated steel seat with hammer finish.
H 77 cm (30½ in). W 46 cm (18 in).
D 43 cm (17 in)
Manufacturer: Cubic Metre Furniture, UK

120

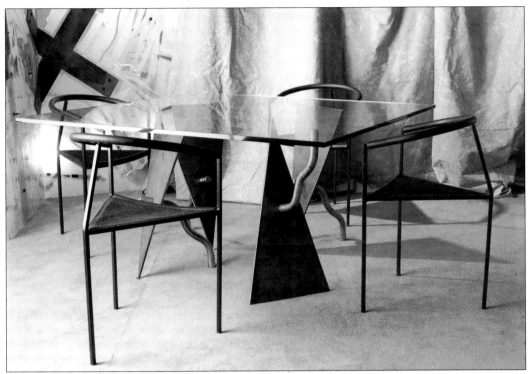

121

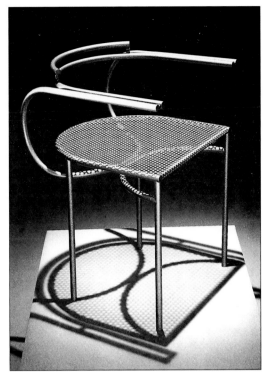

122

● Rodney Kinsman's work in Britain for OMK, the furniture company of which he is managing director, and in Italy for Bieffeplast, with whom he has long been associated, has become a rare example of British sophisticated furniture design. Disappointingly, while it is regarded as 'mainstream modern' in Italy or America, far too many British retailers see it as avant-garde. Through the 1960s and 1970s, Kinsman's design was distinguished by its toughness, and its industrial-looking detail. In the last two years he has begun to work in a more attenuated, softer manner. The *Tokyo* chair is poised and elegant, with its graphic outline sharp and clear.

123 RODNEY KINSMAN
Chairs and stool, *Tokyo*
Chairs with steel tube frame and upholstered fabric seat.
Chair H 71 cm (28 in). W 43 cm (17 in).
D 40 cm (15¾ in)
Stool H 88 cm (34½ in). W 43 cm (17 in).
D 37 cm (14½ in)
Manufacturer: OMK Design, UK

123

124

125

126

124, 125 PHILIPPE STARCK
Chair, *Mrs Frick*
Black-painted steel folding chair.
H 85 cm (33½ in). Top H 48 cm (19 in).
D 38 cm (15 in)
Manufacturer: 3 Suisses, France

126, 128 PHILIPPE STARCK
Table, *Tippy Jackson*
Three-legged bent-steel folding table with
turned sheet-steel top, varnished in dark
metal grey.
H 71 cm (28 in). D 120 cm (47¼ in)
Manufacturer: Aleph, Italy

● Philippe Starck's rise to international prominence has been exceptionally rapid, fuelled partly by the publicity that his interiors have attracted. Starck, who likes to work at break-neck speed, is so prolific that he has produced a steady stream of designs, keeping him continually in the headlines.

His sparse, spare, geometric style has a freshness that reflects his working method: a series of rapid sketches in which he finalizes his ideas, ready to hand over to his assistants working with manufacturers. 'I don't let them change *anything*,' he says. His resulting designs, somewhat arbitrarily named after characters from the science fiction novels of Philip Dick, have both the advantages and disadvantages of this fluency.

127

There are certainly plenty of them to choose from, produced by a puzzlingly large number of manufacturers. Two of his best-known works are the *President M* table (manufactured by Baleri) for the private apartments of the Mitterrands at the Elysée Palace, followed by a range of folding tables for Aleph/ Driade, another Italian manufacturer.

'I try to design in a French way,' says Starck. 'I don't want to make copies of Italian designs ... I try to give my work a French feeling of balance.' To this end, Starck's work takes playful risks with gravity. The chairs and tables tend to rely on three legs rather than the customary four, and have a single-minded devotion to hinges.

128

129

130

127 PHILIPPE STARCK
Chair, *Pratfall*
Varnished black steel tubing frame with bent plywood back lacquered in semi-opaque black. Seat is covered in black leather.
H 86 cm (34 in). W 61.5 cm (24 in). D 78 cm (31 in)
Manufacturer: Aleph, Italy

129, 130 PHILIPPE STARCK
Table, *Titos Apostos*
Three-legged, folding table of steel tubing, with turned sheet-steel plates and top. Varnished in metal, gold and silver.
H 71 cm (28 in). D 85 cm (33½ in)
Manufacturer: Aleph, Italy

131

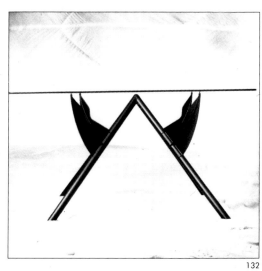

132

132 PHILIPPE STARCK
Table, *President M*
Clear glass top mounted on opaque black-varnished steel tubing legs.
H 75 cm (29½ in). Top 136 cm (53½ in) square
Manufacturer: Baleri Italia, Italy

134 PHILIPPE STARCK
Armchair, *Richard III*
In moulded rigid plastic, varnished in metallic silver.
Leather-covered seat pad.
H 91 cm (35¾ in). W 92 cm (36 in). D 82 cm (32¼ in)
Manufacturer: Baleri Italia, Italy

133

131, 133 PHILIPPE STARCK
Table, *Nina Freed*
Folding table with epoxy-coated metal base, available with a choice of tops: wood or glass, and rectangular, square or round, with a black or silver base.
H 72 cm (28¼ in). D 128 cm (50¼ in)
Manufacturer: Disform, Spain

134

135

137

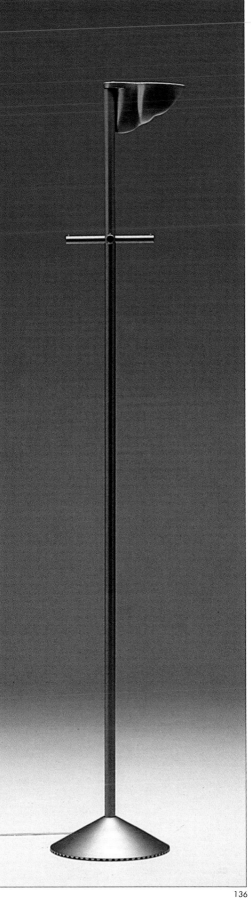

136

135 PHILIPPE STARCK
Cabinet, *Le Bureau du Théâtre du Monde*
Free-standing cabinet designed to house a hi-fi system or
drinks tray with an assortment of records and tapes, with a
folding top and front storage compartments. Epoxy-
coated sheet metal body in black, gold or silver.
H 114 cm (44¾ in). W 69 cm (27¼ in)
Manufacturer: 3 Suisses, France

136 PHILIPPE STARCK
Uplighter, *Roi Egon Groat*
Floor-standing uplighter,which can also be used as a
coatstand. Lacquered steel body in silver or gold. 500 W.
halogen lamp.
H 189 cm (74½ in)
Manufacturer: 3 Suisses, France

137 PHILIPPE STARCK
Wardrobe, *Fred Zafsky*
Two-door wardrobe available in mirrored or epoxy-
coated steel versions with external shelves.
H 164 cm (64½ in). W 102 cm (40¼ in). D 53 cm (20¾ in)
Manufacturer: 3 Suisses, France

138

139

140

138 PHILIPPE STARCK
Chair, *Von Vogelsang*
Steel tubing frame with bent perforated
metal seat. All varnished in light metal
grey.
H 71.5 cm (28 in). W 54 cm (21 in).
D 51 cm (20 in)
Manufacturer: Aleph, Italy

139 PHILIPPE STARCK
Table/seat, *Mickville*
Three-legged folding structure in steel
tubing with turned sheet-steel top.
Varnished in metal azure and semi-
opaque black.
Total H 80.5 cm
(32 in). H of surface
48 cm (19 in).
D 38 cm (15 in)
Manufacturer:
Aleph, Italy

140 ALESSANDRO MENDINI
Armchair, *San Leonardo
Collection*
Leather club armchair,
designed in
traditional form.
H 100 cm (39½ in). W 102 cm (40 in).
D 85 cm (33½ in)
Manufacturer: Matteo Grassi, Italy

● Italy has a tradition of well-known architects and designers who edit magazines – *Casabella*, for example, was for many years edited by Ernesto Rogers, and Gio Ponti edited *Domus*. As a result, each publication tends to have a very clear-cut stance. For Alessandro Mendini, the pattern has been different. True, he was initially a designer with Nizzoli Associates; but it was his work as an editor, first at *Casabella*, then *Modo* and until 1985 *Domus*, that first attracted attention. That platform allowed him to move back towards design once more, initially with the didactic, polemical and overwrought 'art' furniture that he devised for Studio Alchymia. Now his *Leonardo Collection* – vaguely Art Deco, upholstered pieces for Matteo Grassi – has moved beyond irony into a curious kind of anonymity, swallowed up perhaps by the system of which he has long been a critic.

● De Pas, D'Urbino and Lomazzi's sofa for Zanotta is a self-conscious and knowing adaptation of the vocabulary that Le Corbusier created for the *Grand Confort* armchair of the 1920s. The original rectilinear form has been subverted by the introduction of a wilful rippling curve.

141, 142 JONATHAN DE PAS, DONATO D'URBINO AND PAOLO LOMAZZI
Sofa, *Onda*
With an exposed frame of stainless steel, upholstered in polyurethane/Dacron. The covering is removable and can be of leather or fabric.
H 72 cm (28½ in). W 195 cm (76½ in). D 78 cm (31 in)
Manufacturer: Zanotta, Italy

141

142

143

● Like Alessandro Mendini, Paolo Deganello approaches design from a radical perspective. Deganello is a former member of the now dissolved Studio Archizoom. Its members saw design and architecture as a medium for commentary on the nature of the society which produced them. Deganello came to terms with the constraints of working for the big commercial manufacturers some time ago, and his one-time radicalism is now restricted to a fondness for surrealistically mixing materials, and in his trademark flag motif — shown here in these otherwise restrained bookshelves.

144

143, 144 PAOLO DEGANELLO
Bookcase, *Inprimis*
Metal-structure bookcase with medium-density fibreboard shelves coloured with aniline. Bases are in quartz and polyester in two different colours.
H 213 cm (84 in). W 30 cm (12 in).
L 121–152 cm (48–60 in)
Manufacturer: McLandia, Italy

145 SERGIO ASTI
Bed, *Okura*
Double bed with metal de-mountable structure, in dark red or grey paint finish. The upper parts of the support tubes are chrome-plated metal. Two adjustable metal arms hold small tables at each side.
H 66 cm (26 in). L 228 cm (90 in).
Maximum W 285 cm (112¼ in)
Manufacturer: Misura Emme, Italy

145

146 JEAN-PIERRE CAILLÈRES
Bureau
In timber, with a black or blue lacquered finish.
H 88 cm (34¾ in). L 154 cm (60½ in).
W 90 cm (35½ in)
Manufacturer: Papyrus, France

147 CHRISTIAN THEILL
Chair, *Frac*
Gloss-lacquered beech frame in a variety of colours. The seat and back are covered in leather, also available in a variety of colours.
H 87 cm (34¼ in). W 42 cm (16½ in).
D 39 cm (15½ in)
Manufacturer: Poltronova, Italy

146

147

148

149

148 SERGIO ASTI
Display stands, *Araldo*
Stands in matt-surface, two-tone lacquered
wood. They have five semi-circular shelves
in a pyramid arrangement, diameter
93 cm (36½ in) at the bottom and 61 cm
(24 in) at the top.
H 166 cm (65½ in). W 93 cm (36½ in).
D 93 cm (36½ in)
Manufacturer: Acerbis International, Italy

149 SERGIO ASTI
Bookcase, *Periplo*
Free-standing bookcase in matt-surface,
two-toned lacquered wood on castors.
Four shelves held by three uprights.
H 97.5 cm (38⅜ in). W 52 cm (20½ in).
D 54 cm (21½ in)
Manufacturer: Acerbis International, Italy

150 GEORGE SOWDEN
Armchair, *Zaragoza*
In painted wood with curved arms and
decorated seat and back.
H 86.5 cm (34 in). W 48 cm (18¾ in).
D 58 cm (22¾ in)
Manufacturer: George Sowden; made by
Pier-Luigi Ghianda, Italy

150

151

151 PETER SHIRE
Floor lamp, *Cahuenga*
Two-tier cylindrical light on chrome legs with blue feet,
containing three PL9 lamps.
H 100 cm (39⅜ in). D at widest point 50 cm (19¾ in)
Manufacturer: Memphis, Italy

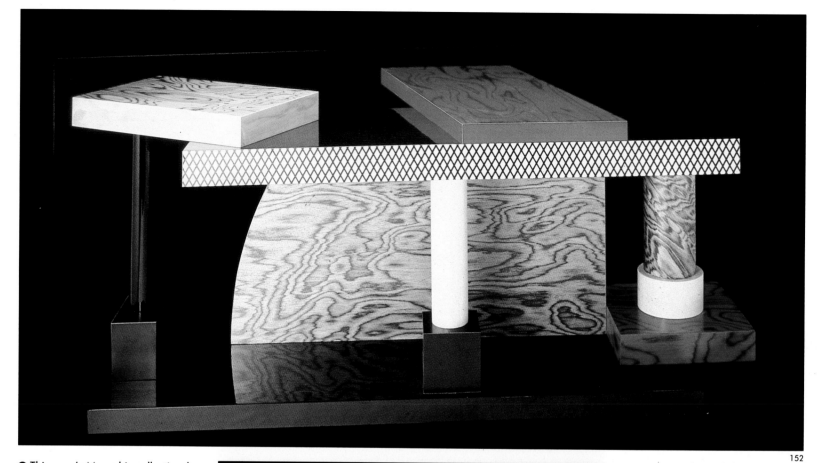

152

● This year's Memphis collection has been transported from the original Milan showroom, where the movement was launched in 1981, to a new and permanent home in the handsome surroundings of an eighteenth-century mansion, elegantly restored by Michele De Lucchi. It is dangerous to take Ettore Sottsass jr, the sad-eyed genius of the Memphis group, at face value when he starts talking in aphorisms. But one can reasonably read into what he says of the new collection a view of what has happened to Italian design in general. Describing the half-disassembled building blocks and sombre colours that characterize Memphis's new work — work which seems 'barbaric', to use his own adjective — Sottsass says that it 'is

more or less what could happen to a Roman villa inhabited by a Hun'.

There are several statements by members of the Memphis group which suggest that the Memphis style, with its childlike charm, is over. Be that as it may, the group is now talking about turning itself into a more businesslike organization, producing, if not huge numbers of products, then at least great enough quantities to put them within reach of a group larger than the wealthy collectors who were its original supporters. To this end, Ernesto Gismondi, owner of the successful lighting company Artemide, has taken a stake in the company and has to some extent reorganized its structure.

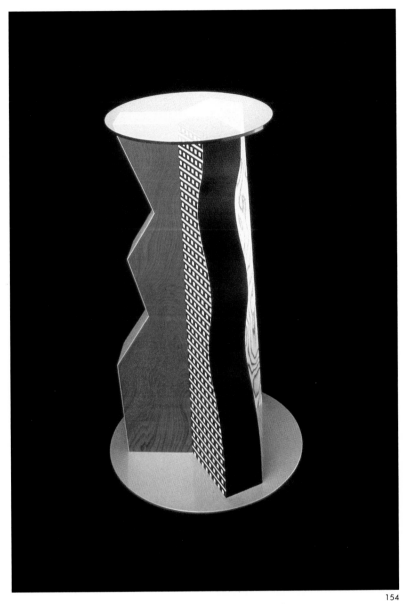

154

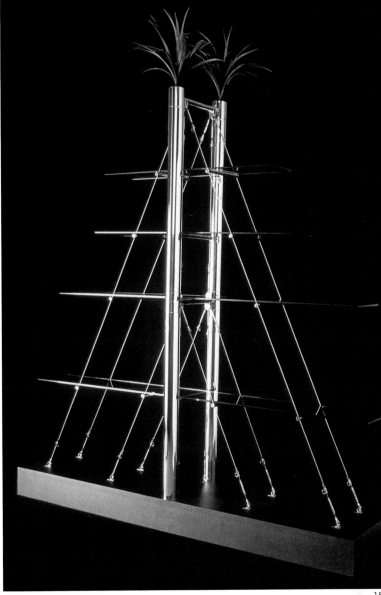

155

154 ETTORE SOTTSASS JR
Table, *Ivory*
Side table in reconstituted veneer and plastic laminate, with a glass top and circular base.
H 100 cm (39½ in). D 48 cm (19 in)
Manufacturer: Memphis, Italy

155 ANDREA BRANZI
Bookcase, *Magnolia*
In metal and plastic laminate with glass shelves and plastic palms.
H 208 cm (82 in). W 200 cm (79 in).
D 50 cm (20 in)
Manufacturer: Memphis, Italy

152 ETTORE SOTTSASS JR
Console, *Tartar*
In reconstituted veneer and plastic laminate.
H 78 cm (31 in). W 195 cm (77 in).
D 85 cm (33½ in)
Manufacturer: Memphis, Italy

153 ETTORE SOTTSASS JR
Sideboard, *Freemont*
In reconstituted veneer, plastic laminate, aluminium and gilded wood.
H 183 cm (72 in). W 190 cm (75 in).
D 60 cm (24 in)
Manufacturer: Memphis, Italy

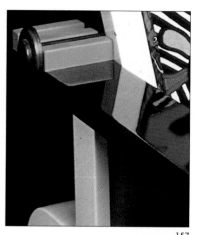

157

● George Sowden and Nathalie du Pasquier, respectively English and French but both living in Milan, work individually and together, as members of Memphis and independently. Sowden works on Olivetti's industrial design programme, particularly on computer keyboards, du Pasquier on textiles. Their chairs (plates 150, 158, 159, 164, 166 and 167) are a project on which they collaborated outside the Memphis umbrella, although the affinities with Memphis are clear.

156, 157 GEORGE SOWDEN
Armchair, *Mamounia*
Armchair in lacquered wood, plastic laminate and velvet. The fabric covering is designed by Nathalie du Pasquier (plates 382, 387).
H 120 cm (47¼ in). W 72 cm (28½ in).
D 80 cm (31½ in)
Manufacturer: Memphis, Italy

156

158 GEORGE SOWDEN
Armchair, *Alhambra*
In wood with curved arms and sides.
H 91.5 cm (36 in). W 48 cm (18¾ in). D 55 cm (21½ in)
Manufacturer: George Sowden; made by Pier-Luigi
Ghianda, Italy

158

159

159 GEORGE SOWDEN
Armchair, *Cadiz*
Painted wood with curved arms.
H 89 cm (35 in). W 40 cm (15¾ in). D 55.5 cm (21¾ in)
Manufacturer: George Sowden; made by Pier-Luigi
Ghianda, Italy

160 MICHELE DE LUCCHI
Room divider, *Scarlet*
In plastic laminate and metal.
H 243 cm (96 in). W 180 cm (71 in).
D 85 cm (33½ in)
Manufacturer: Memphis, Italy

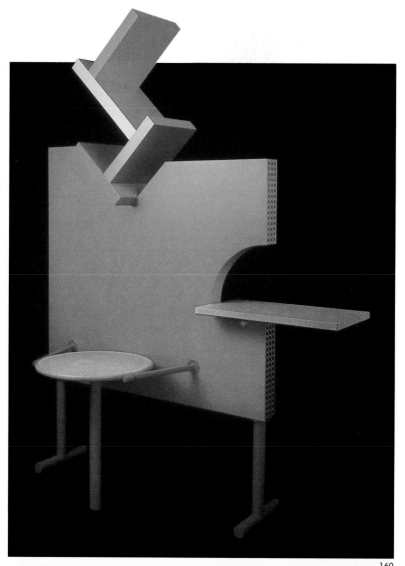

160

161 MICHELE DE LUCCHI
Mirror, *Dorian*
Circular mirror set in lacquered wood of
different shades.
H 33 cm (13 in)
Manufacturer: Memphis, Italy

161

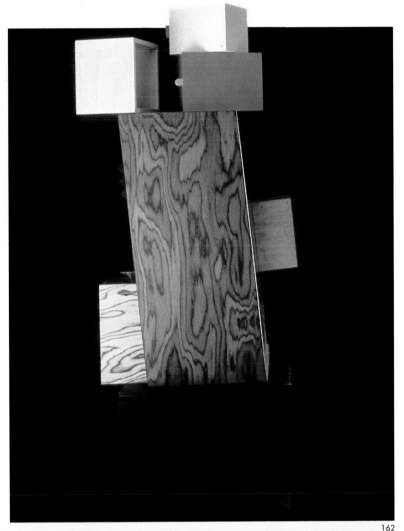

162

162 MARCO ZANINI
Cabinet, *Amazon*
In reconstituted veneer and lacquered wood.
H 205 cm (71 in). W 80 cm (31 ½ in).
D 51 cm (20 in)
Manufacturer: Memphis, Italy

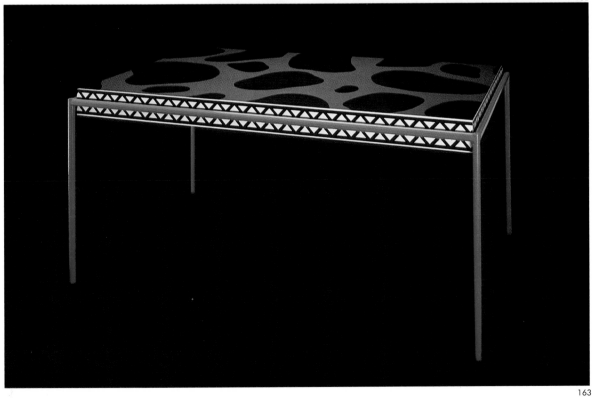

163 MICHELE DE LUCCHI
Table, *Burgundy*
In plastic laminate and painted metal.
H 72 cm (28 ½ in). W 155 cm (61 in).
D 105 cm (41 ½ in)
Manufacturer: Memphis, Italy

164

164 NATHALIE DU PASQUIER
Chair, *Esmeralda*
In wood and plastic laminate. The back and arms are
covered with patterned fabric.
H 93 cm (36½ in). W 60 cm (23½ in). D 50 cm (19½ in)
Manufacturer: Nathalie du Pasquier; made by Pier-Luigi
Ghianda, Italy

165 NATHALIE DU PASQUIER
Sideboard, *Emerald*
In wood and plastic laminate with a
curved mirror.
H 190 cm (75 in). W 100 cm (39½ in).
D 40 cm (16 in)
Manufacturer: Memphis, Italy

165

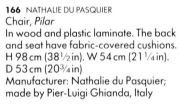

166 NATHALIE DU PASQUIER
Chair, *Pilar*
In wood and plastic laminate. The back
and seat have fabric-covered cushions.
H 98 cm (38½ in). W 54 cm (21¼ in).
D 53 cm (20¾ in)
Manufacturer: Nathalie du Pasquier;
made by Pier-Luigi Ghianda, Italy

167 NATHALIE DU PASQUIER
Chair, *Mercedes*
Lacquered wood with fabric-covered seat
cushion.
H 98 cm (38½ in). W 55 cm (21½ in).
D 50 cm (19½ in)
Manufacturer: Nathalie du Pasquier;
made by Pier-Luigi Ghianda, Italy

166

167

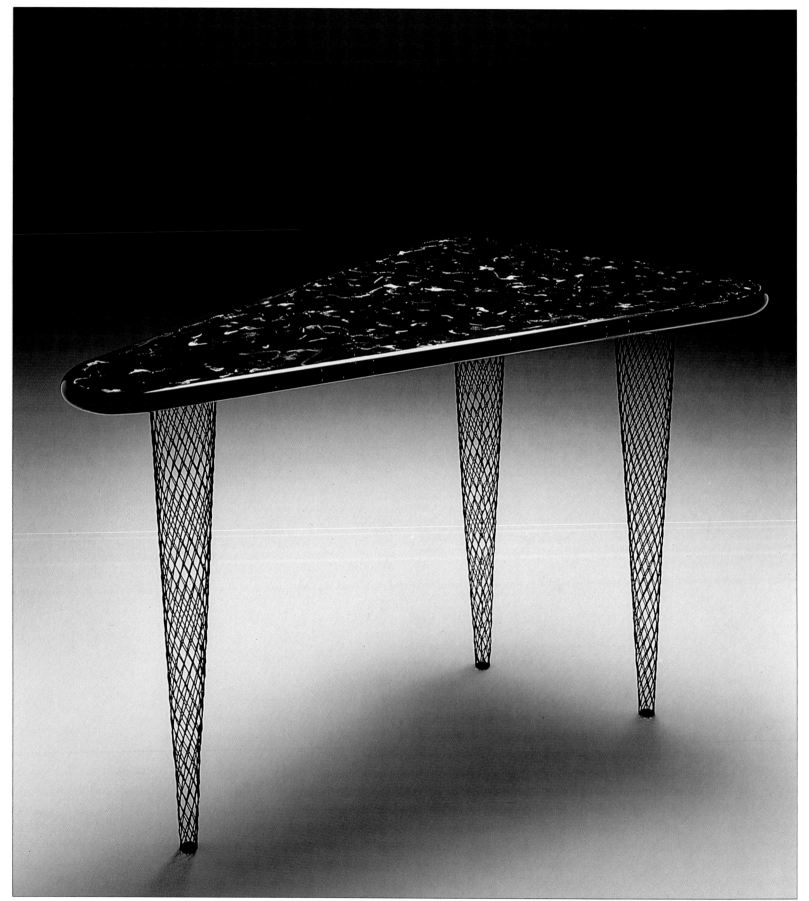

● Shiro Kuramata's work, as always, combines immaculate workmanship with a surreal elegance that sometimes veers away from furniture in its practical capacity towards the purely sculptural. His disturbing but memorable chair is virtually the ghost of a Thonet bentwood café chair. An actual chair was wrapped in steel, then incinerated. The metal, all that was left, was then plated. His tables play similar tricks, apparently floating on legs that seem too fragile to support them.

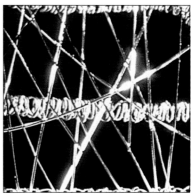

170

169, 170 SHIRO KURAMATA
Chair, *Homage to Hoffman, Begin the Bigin*
Chair frame in steel rod with enamel-plated finish.
H 83 cm (32½ in). L 54 cm (21½ in). W 45 cm (17½ in)
One-off
Manufacturer: Ishimaru, Japan

169

171 SHIRO KURAMATA
Table
Three-legged table with metal legs supporting a shaped glass top.
H 70 cm (27½ in)
One-off
Manufacturer: Ishimaru, Terada and Top Tone, Japan

168 SHIRO KURAMATA
Table
Three-legged table in plywood and metal.
H 70 cm (27½ in)
One-off
Manufacturer: Ishimaru, Terada and Top Tone, Japan

171

● Art et Industrie is an informal group of young American designer-artists based around a New York gallery. Many have a design or architectural background, although others are trained as sculptors or painters. Their work is perhaps more aptly regarded as an 'installation' than as furniture in the conventional, functional sense. But there is no reason to dismiss it on those grounds alone: after all Rietveld's *Red Blue* chair could be similarly described. Art et Industrie's adherents absorb ideas that spring from both design and art, and synthesize them in a sometimes unsettling hybrid, which may in turn provide fresh imagery for the disciplines from which they are drawn.

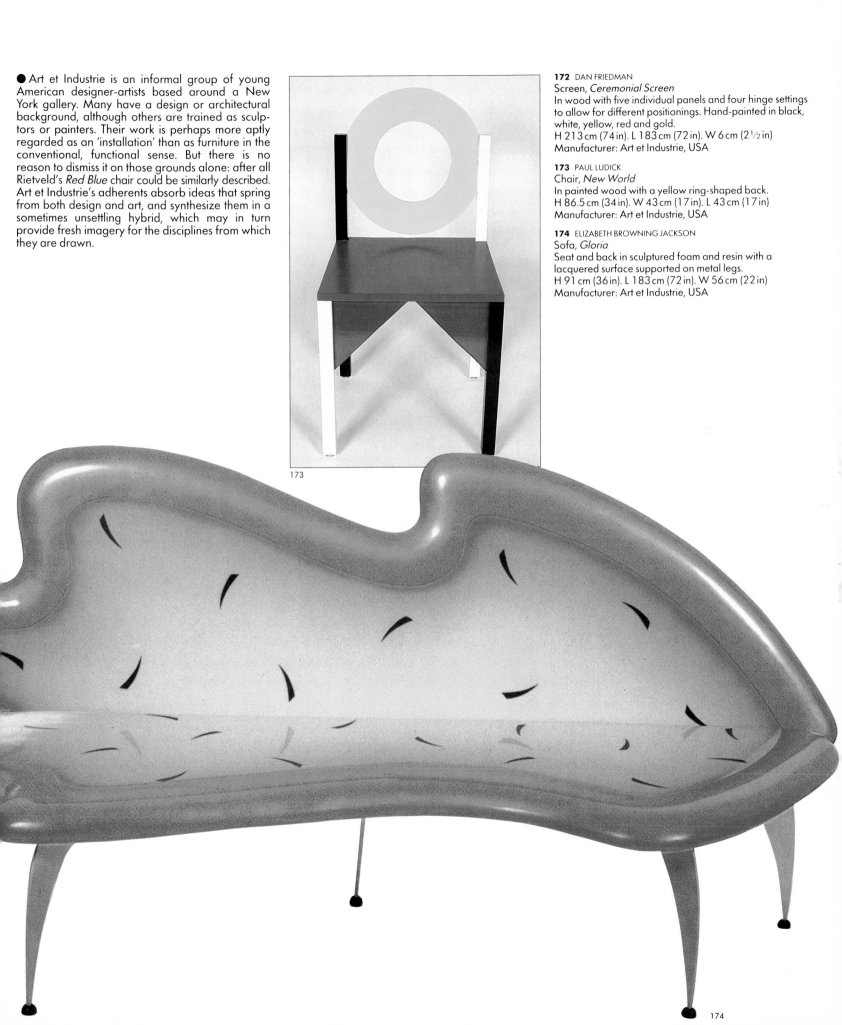

173

174

172 DAN FRIEDMAN
Screen, *Ceremonial Screen*
In wood with five individual panels and four hinge settings to allow for different positionings. Hand-painted in black, white, yellow, red and gold.
H 213 cm (74 in). L 183 cm (72 in). W 6 cm (2½ in)
Manufacturer: Art et Industrie, USA

173 PAUL LUDICK
Chair, *New World*
In painted wood with a yellow ring-shaped back.
H 86.5 cm (34 in). W 43 cm (17 in). L 43 cm (17 in)
Manufacturer: Art et Industrie, USA

174 ELIZABETH BROWNING JACKSON
Sofa, *Gloria*
Seat and back in sculptured foam and resin with a lacquered surface supported on metal legs.
H 91 cm (36 in). L 183 cm (72 in). W 56 cm (22 in)
Manufacturer: Art et Industrie, USA

175 PAUL LUDICK
Chair, *Apartheid*
One of an edition of twenty chairs, each
one of painted and patterned wood, in
this case with a chain-link back.
H 86 cm (34 in). L 43 cm (17 in). W 43 cm
(17 in)
Manufacturer: Art et Industrie, USA

176 JAMES HONG
Bookcase/room divider, *Clear Space*
In lacquered wood and aluminium with
glass sides and cast concrete base.
H 203 cm (80 in). L 193 cm (76 in).
W 56 cm (22 in)
Manufacturer: Art et Industrie, USA

175

176

177

177–180 THOMAS LEAR GRACE
Chair, *Lorry Chair*
Moulded plywood sides and solid maple
seat. Available in a variety of colours.
H 91 cm (36 in). L 68 cm (27 in). W 40 cm
(16 in)
Manufacturer: Dean Luse, USA

178

179

180

181 CHARLES VANDENHOVE
Table
In wood with patterned top.
H 72.5 cm (28½ in). D 130 cm (51 in)
Manufacturer: Desiron & Lizen, Belgium

182 CHARLES VANDENHOVE
Chair
Aluminium with moulded back and seat in
covered polyurethane foam.
H 120 cm (47 in). L 63 cm (24¾ in).
W 63 cm (24¾ in)
Manufacturer: Desiron & Lizen, Belgium

183 CHARLES VANDENHOVE
Armchairs
In various woods with leather back and
seat and brass arm supports.
H 84 cm (33 in). W 44 cm (17 in).
D 48.5 cm (19 in)
Manufacturer: Desiron & Lizen, Belgium

184 CHARLES VANDENHOVE
Cupboard
Semi-cylindrical two-door cupboard in
wood.
H 117 cm (46 in). D 95 cm (37½ in)
Manufacturer: Desiron & Lizen, Belgium

181

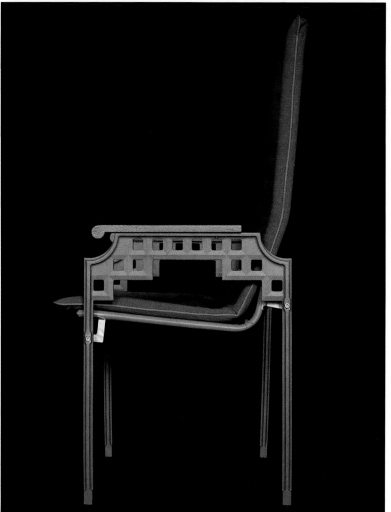

185 HIROSHI MORISHIMA
Screen, *Wagami Carta Byobu*
Screen in handmade Japanese paper.
H 150 cm (59 in). L 276 cm (109 in)
Manufacturer: Otaki Paper Land, Japan

182

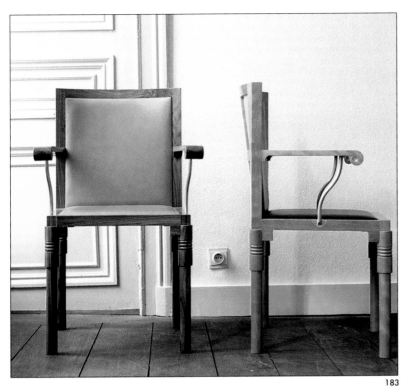

183

184

185

186

● The craft revival, originating in Britain and America, is a more complex movement, and a far less homogeneous one, than might at first sight appear. It can include pieces of furniture that are virtual abstractions, made from frankly industrial materials, such as Erik de Graaff's steel frame and medium-density fibreboard chairs. It can equally include painstakingly crafted pieces that use precious timbers; here the emphasis is on the making, and sometimes on the semi-mystical relationship that may or may not exist between patron and maker — a tendency represented principally by the English craftsman John Makepeace. One of his best-known students, David Linley, is represented here with a costly but attractive screen.

186 DAVID LINLEY AND MATTHEW RICE
Screen, *Venetian Screen*
Six-panelled wood veneer folding screen using stained and natural woods in marquetry design.
H 214 cm (84 in). W 366 cm (144 in)
Manufacturer: David Linley Furniture, UK

187 FRED BAIER AND CHRIS ROSE
Table, *Refectory Table*
Large oak refectory table.
H 71 cm (28 in). L 700 cm (276 in).
W 120 cm (48 in)
Prototype
Manufacturer: Professional Woodworkers
UK

187

188

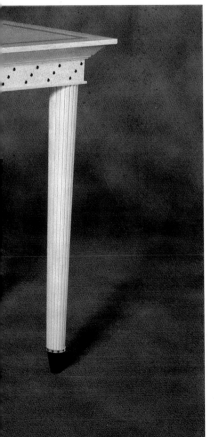

189

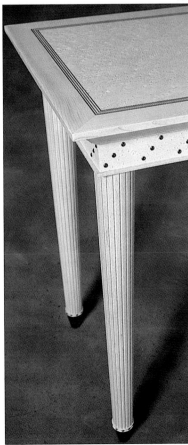

190

188 ERIK DE GRAAFF
Armchair, *High Armchair*
Metal frame, with seat-back and high
arms in medium-density fibreboard.
H 102 cm (40 in). L 66 cm (26 in).
W 68.5 cm (26 in)
Manufacturer: Degraaff Furniture, UK

189, 190 RICK WRIGLEY
Writing table
Maple desk held with black oxide screws.
H 75 cm (29½ in). W 89 cm (35 in).
D 51 cm (20 in)
Manufacturer: Rick Wrigley Furniture,
USA

192 KAZUKO FUJIE
Screen/seating unit, *Watari-dori (Migratory Bird)*
In plywood with a Japanese linden veneer, Sutein colouring and a clear polyurethane matt finish. Designed for and used in the lobby of the T2 studio in Tokyo.
H 115 cm (45 in). W 430 cm (180 in).
D 96 cm (38 in)
One-off

191

191, 193 KAZUKO FUJIE
Screen, *Coquille*
In plywood with a Japanese linden veneer and natural grain finish.
H 180 cm (71 in). W 400 cm (157 in).
D 150 cm (59 in)
One-off

192

193

194

● In India, handicraft is potentially a huge national resource. This is now — intriguingly — being harnessed by a group of entrepreneurs who have commissioned well-known Western designers to design pieces for hand production using India's traditional skills. These figures include Sir Hugh Casson, Mario Bellini (page 62) and Charles Moore.

194, 195 CHARLES MOORE
Desk
Wooden and brass desk displayed at the Cooper-Hewitt Museum 'Golden Eye' exhibition and designed for manufacture in India. The architectural interior contains painted wooden folk toys.
Prototype

195

● Reproduction is not quite the right word for the increasingly common practice of searching out obscure masters of the modern movement and putting into production designs from their earlier oeuvre. Eileen Gray's furniture was made in tiny numbers when she designed it. And by the late 1970s, when Zeev Aram had succeeded in manufacturing the first of her re-editioned pieces, she had died. In fact Aram often had to rely on contemporary photographs, because no surviving examples of the originals could be found. But these Gray pieces, and other works like them, are not reproductions: they make no attempt to simulate age. For these products of the machine, precision and finish are much more important than patina. Since that first Gray piece emerged, a steady stream of rediscovered works is put into production each year.

Eliel Saarinen, the Finnish architect who emigrated to America and established the Cranbrook Academy, is one of the more surprising choices of designer. With Belotti's *Homage to Chareau*, he has reinterpreted, fairly faithfully, a sofa from Pierre Chareau's famous *Maison de Verre*. Arne Jacobsen's *The Number Two*, made in 1985 by Fritz Hansen, is a variation on his famous *Ant* chair, designed in the 1950s.

197 ELIEL SAARINEN
Table and chair, *Blue Table and Chair*
Wooden chair with fanned back and upholstered seat. Table with straight legs and lower shelf with lacquered top.
Table: H 71 cm (28 in). L 76 cm (30 in) square. W 76 cm (30 in).
Chair: H 76 cm (30 in). W 63.5 cm (25 in). D 50 cm (19½ in)
Manufacturer: Adelta, Finland

196, 198 MARCEL BREUER
Chair, *Isokon Long Chair*
Formed in laminated beech with wool upholstery in a range of six colours. A re-issued classic design of the 1930s.
H 86 cm (34 in). L 142 cm (56 in).
W 61 cm (24 in)
Manufacturer: Windmill Furniture, UK

199 ARNE JACOBSEN
Chair, *The Number Two*
On chromed steel legs with a high-gloss shell, this was Jacobsen's favourite chair, *The Ant*, from 1952, but has not previously been in production.
H 83 cm (32½ in)
Manufacturer: Fritz Hansen, Denmark

200 GIANDOMENICO BELOTTI
Sofa, *Homage to Chareau*
Wood and steel frame and cotton-covered cushion.
H 67 cm (26½ in). L 175 cm (69 in)
Manufacturer: Alias, Italy

201 EILEEN GRAY
Table, *Double X*
Polished chromium-plated tubular steel frame with lacquered gloss finish in black, grey or white.
H 72 cm (28 in). L 224 cm (88½ in).
W 82 cm (32½ in)
Manufacturer: Vereinigte Werkstätten, West Germany under licence from Aram Designs, UK

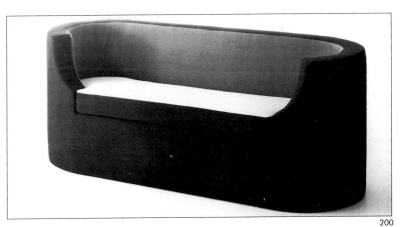

199

200

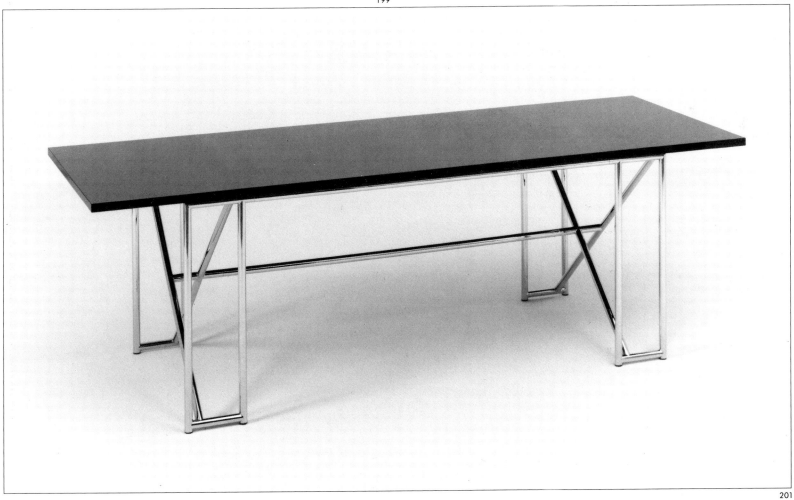

201

L I G H T I N G

Lighting design is still a relatively youthful activity; it has had no time to acquire the cultural baggage that furniture design, for example, brings with it. The chair is more than three thousand years old, the table even older. Inevitably archetypes have evolved, and most twentieth-century designs represent variations around them. But electric light is completely different. It is only just over a hundred years since Norman Shaw designed Cragside, the armament millionaire Lord Armstrong's spectacular Northumberland country house, and included the first-ever domestic installation of an electric lighting system. Since then lighting designers have had to make up the rules as they went along. In the early days they attempted to rely on precedent: deploying electric light in fittings patterned on candles, oil or gas fittings. Gradually a number of formal categories have evolved: wall lights, pendant fittings, floor-standing uplighters and so on. But this categorization has been completely overturned by the escalating pace of technological innovation.

In the last ten years the pace of technical change has been so rapid and so far-reaching that an entirely new design vocabulary for lighting has begun to appear. The sophistication and miniaturization of light sources have had two paradoxical effects. On the one hand, tiny low-voltage halogen fittings are now so efficient and visually unobtrusive that it is possible to design lighting systems in which the appearance of the fitting itself is of negligible importance. It virtually disappears, allowing the effect of the light to take over. On the other hand, new light sources, such as dichroic bulbs and miniature fluorescents, are so flexible and easy to use in electrical and technical terms, that many of the constraints have been removed from the design of lights. As a result virtually any form of fitting is possible. Thus, though the technical justifications are disappearing, some designers have been able to indulge in ever more flamboyant and showy fittings.

In many ways the most impressive new products are those which are designed with a sensitivity towards both sets of possibilities, at once addressing the formal problems of creating a means for the delivery of light, and at the same time being attuned to the requirements of the quality of light that they deliver. In general such fittings are the ones which deliver light in a mixture of different ways, allowing for both the gentle diffusion of light from an indirect source, and for the sparkle from direct light as well. The emphasis on aggressive delivery systems, such as ostentatious spotlights or over-elaborate adjustability, has faded, to be replaced by a new subtlety and gentleness. Since low voltage has made it possible to supply current to a source without external wires, formal refinements have concentrated on the integration of transformers into the fittings, and on the maximization of the tactile quality of switches and joints, as in Sapper's *Tizio* light (page 20).

202 HIROSHI MORISHIMA
Table lamp, *Wagami Andon*
Lamp encircled in a cone of Japanese handmade paper.
H 75 cm (29 1/2 in). W 55 cm (21 1/2 in)
Manufacturer: Time Space Art, Japan

204

203, 204 ASAHARA SIGHEAKI
Table lamp, *Luna*
With lacquered metal body and porcelain
diffuser. The reflecting disc has an
adjustable height and inclination. 50 W.
halogen lamp.
H 43 cm (17 in). W 15.5 cm (6 in)
Manufacturer: Stilnovo, Italy

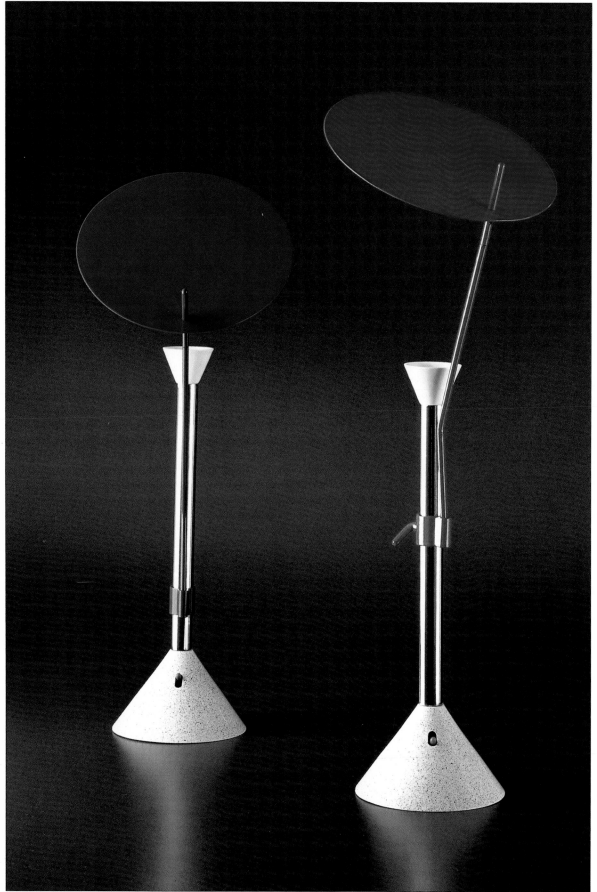

203

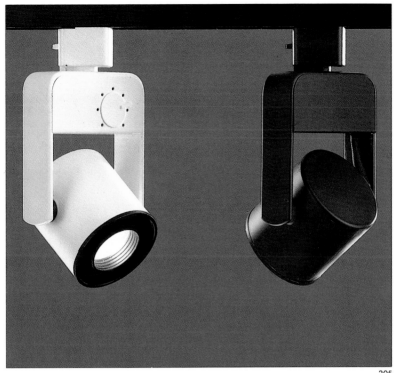

205

205 ANTHONY DONATO
Spotlight, *Dimatron 16*
Integral transformer and built-in dimmer
permits individual control from 100 per
cent to 15 per cent intensity on these
spots. The stepped baffle is die-cast,
painted aluminium.
H 19 cm (7½ in). L 7.5 cm (3 in). W 7.5 cm
(3 in)
Manufacturer: Lightolier, USA

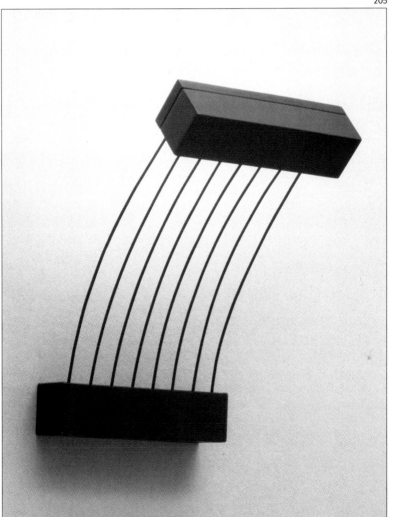

206

206 MITCHELL MAUK
Wall lamp, *Damocle*
Made in plastic material, the body diffuser
is held to the base with bent metal rods.
100W. halogen lamp.
H 33 cm (13 in). W 18 cm (7 in).
Overhang 20–51 cm (8–21 in)
Manufacturer: Artemide, Italy

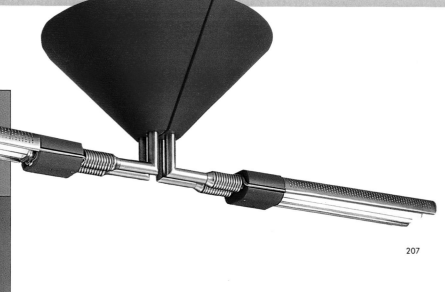

207

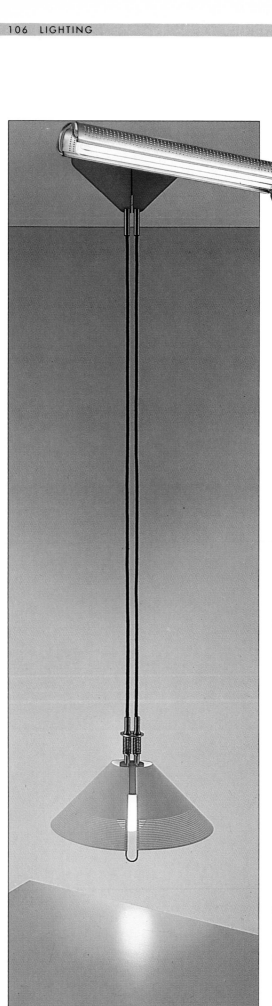

209

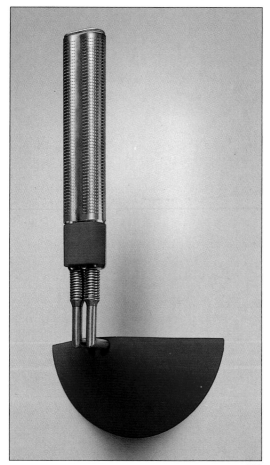

210

208

207 FERDINAND ALEXANDER PORSCHE
Ceiling lamp, *Plafone*
Ceiling-mounted version of the *Sintheto* system, with a high-gloss chromed metal stem and a base painted matt red, smoky or light grey. Takes two PL 11 miniature fluorescent bulbs.
L 72 cm (28¼ in). D 18 cm (7 in)
Manufacturer: Luci, Italy

208 FERDINAND ALEXANDER PORSCHE
Pendant lamp, *Soffitto*
Floor version of the *Sintheto* system, with a high-gloss chromed metal stem, a base painted red, smoky or light grey, red or yellow reflector, and a pearl grey diffuser. 100 W. halogen lamp, fitted with a dimmer.
H 186 cm (73¼ in)
Manufacturer: Luci, Italy

209 FERDINAND ALEXANDER PORSCHE
Wall lamp, *Parete H*
Wall version of the *Sintheto* system, with a high-gloss chromed metal stem, a base painted matt red, smoky or light grey, and a red or yellow reflector. 100 W. halogen lamp.
H 33 cm (13 in). D 18 cm (7 in)
Manufacturer: Luci, Italy

210 FERDINAND ALEXANDER PORSCHE
Wall lamp, *Parete PL*
Wall version of the *Sintheto* system, with a high-gloss chromed metal stem. Takes one PL 11 miniature fluorescent bulb.
H 44 cm (17¼ in). D 18 cm (7 in)
Manufacturer: Luci, Italy

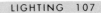

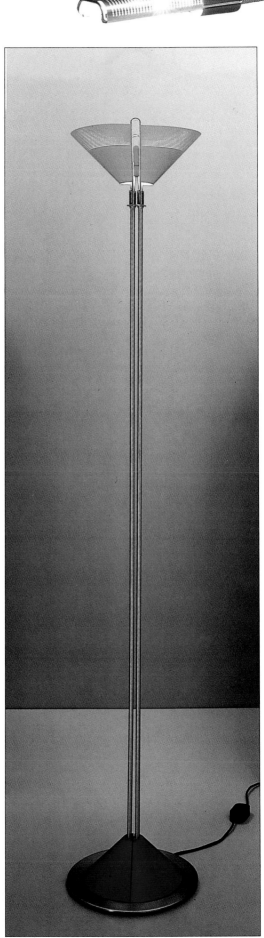

211 FERDINAND ALEXANDER PORSCHE
Floor lamp, *Terra*
Floor version of the *Sintheto* system, with a high-gloss chromed metal stem, a base painted matt red, smoky or light grey, and a red or yellow reflector. Takes two 100W. halogen bulbs.
H 186 cm (73¼ in)
Manufacturer: Luci, Italy

212 FERDINAND ALEXANDER PORSCHE
Floor lamp, *Lettura PL*
Floor version of the *Sintheto* system, with a high-gloss chromed metal stem and a base painted matt red, smoky or light grey. Takes two 11 W. halogen bulbs.
H 110 cm (43 in). D 70 cm (27½ in)
Manufacturer: Luci, Italy

211

212

213

214

215

● Ever since the 1930s, when George Carwardine perfected the Anglepoise adjustable desk light, using a system of jointed arms stressed by pairs of springs that pull in opposite directions, designers have struggled to devise a work lamp that can beat its elegant simplicity. Technologically, Richard Sapper's *Tizio* of 1972 (page 20) may be much more advanced, with its low-voltage halogen source, its built-in transformer which allows unsightly wires to be banished, and the metal arms of the light allowed instead to carry the current; but it does not have the effortless adjustability or the robustness of the Anglepoise.

Alberto Meda's lights for Luceplan are an attractive refinement on the Anglepoise theme, attenuating the adjustable arms to almost nothing and introducing an element of indirect light from the lamp. This is achieved by using in one case a coloured glass back for the reflector (plate 218), in the other a diffusing ring located in front of the light source (plate 215).

216 BRUNO GECCHELIN
Table lamp, *Beam*
Tungsten bulb light with diffusers.
Diffuser: H 20 cm (8 in). D 20 cm (8 in)
Manufacturer: Artemide, Italy

217 ANGELO MANGIAROTTI
Table lamp, *Ghost*
Blown-glass cylinders combined with low-wattage
tungsten lamp. 50W. halogen lamp.
H 30/33/45 cm (12/13/17¾ in). D 46/28/35 cm
(18/11/13¾ in)
Manufacturer: Skipper, Italy

216

213, 214 DIETER WITTE
Spotlights, *Trispot*
Adjustable spotlights in white plastic and metal. 20W.
halogen lamps.
L 180 cm (71 in)
Manufacturer: Osram, Italy

215 ALBERTO MEDA
Table lamp, *Jack*
Adjustable reading lamp – for table, wall or use with a
clamp. Metal parts in anodized aluminium, and three
interchangeable filters in different colours. 20W. halogen
lamp.
Base: L 52 cm (20½ in)
Table: L 48 cm (19 in)
Wall: L 41 cm (16 in)
Manufacturer: Luceplan, Italy

218 ALBERTO MEDA
Table lamp, *Berenice*
Adjustable reading lamp with metal body in anodized
aluminium. 20W. halogen lamp.
Base: L 45 by 45 cm (17¾ by 17¾ in)
Clamp: L 45 by 45 cm (17¾ by 17¾ in)
Wall: L 30 by 80 cm (12 by 31½ in)
Floor: L 80 by 30 cm (31½ by 12 in)
Manufacturer: Luceplan, Italy

217

218

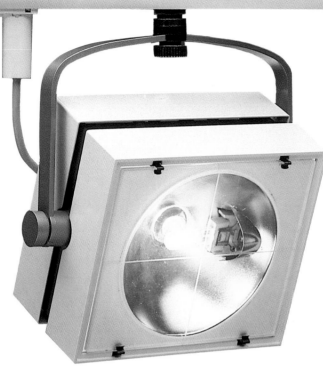

219

219 JULIAN POWELL-TUCK WITH CONCORD LIGHTING
Spotlight, *Powerhouse HQI*
Square spot or floodlight can be surface or Lytespan track-mounted. In die-cast aluminium. 70/150/300 500W. lamp.
H 27.5 cm (10¾ in). L 27.5 cm (10¾ in).
D 12 cm (4¾ in)
Manufacturer: Concord Lighting, UK

220 JULIAN POWELL-TUCK WITH CONCORD LIGHTING
Track, *Micro* and miniature spotlights, *Optics*
In extruded PVC with plated copper conductors, this is a low-voltage lighting system track.
Track: H 1.3 cm (½ in). L 100/150 cm (39/59 in). W 1.9 cm (¾ in)
Flood: H from track 11.5 cm (4½ in).
W of bulb 5.8 cm (2⅜ in).
Universal: H from track 14.5 cm (5¾ in).
D of bulb 3 cm (1¼ in).
Cube: H from track 14.2 cm (5⅝ in).
D of bulb 5.8 cm (2⅜ in).
Manufacturer: Concord Lighting, UK

● The deployment of ever more sophisticated light sources has had the side-effect of making over-designed though supposedly 'functional' spotlights seem needlessly ostentatious. A tiny low-voltage tungsten halogen source with a built-in reflector is capable of delivering as much or more light, more economically, than a bulky conventional spot, and threatens to replace in popularity large reflectors and polished chrome fittings.
Working with Concord's design team, the designer Julian Powell-Tuck has produced the *Optics Series* which clearly demonstrates the point. The differentiation between fitting and light source is absolutely minimal, the principal distinguishing features being the refined detailing of the joints, and the accessories used to maximize the potential of a high-performance product that is satisfyingly unobtrusive.

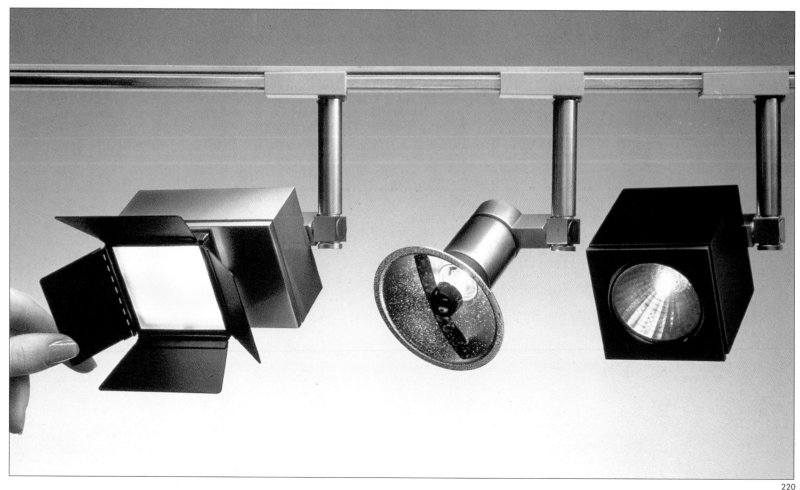

220

221

221 JULIAN POWELL-TUCK WITH CONCORD LIGHTING
Miniature spotlight, *Optic Universal*
Can also be surface-mounted, with permanent tensioning
to allow full rotation. Sealed low-voltage tungsten
halogen lamp. In die-cast aluminium.
H from track 14.5 cm (5¾ in). D of bulb 3 cm (1¼ in)
Manufacturer: Concord Lighting, UK

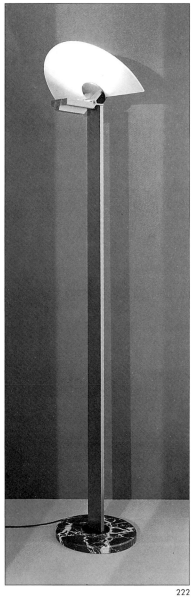

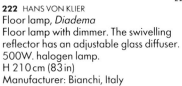

222

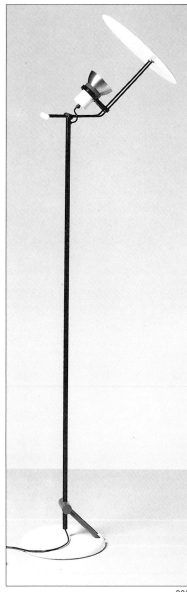

223

222 HANS VON KLIER
Floor lamp, *Diadema*
Floor lamp with dimmer. The swivelling reflector has an adjustable glass diffuser.
500W. halogen lamp.
H 210 cm (83 in)
Manufacturer: Bianchi, Italy

● Adjustability is perhaps not such an obvious requirement for a floor lamp as it is for a desk lamp. But Achille Castiglioni's *Grip* light for Flos intelligently combines a floor lamp with the potential for use over a desk – handy perhaps for those with desks too crowded to admit even the skimpiest of light sources. With its concentric ring joints, Castiglioni is using the idea of adjustment almost as much for visual as for functional reasons.

223 SCHLAGHECK & SCHULTES DESIGN/SCARLETT
Floor lamp, *Thalos*
In lacquered metal; is adjustable with a regulator. Available in black and blue, or white. 150W. halogen lamp.
H 190 cm (75 in). Base D 37 cm (14 in)
Manufacturer: Vereinigte Werkstätten, West Germany

224, 225 ACHILLE CASTIGLIONI
Floor lamp, *Grip*
Floor-standing lamp with an adjustable head for reading purposes. 40W. E14 spot bulb.
H 100 cm (39½ in)
Manufacturer: Flos, Italy

224

225

226

226 ERNESTO GISMONDI
Lighting system, *Pleiadi*
High-performance, low-energy
fluorescent tubes. Components interconnect
for angled compositions.
6.5 cm (2½ in) thick. Ceiling installation
trunnions L 12 cm (4¾ in)
Manufacturer: Artemide, Italy

227

227 ERNESTO GISMONDI
Lighting system, *System 133*
Integrated office lighting. An aluminium
body allows for controlled light emission
for the fluorescent light source.
H 10.9 cm (4¼ in). L 13.3 cm (5¼ in)
Manufacturer: Artemide, Italy

228

228 JULIAN POWELL-TUCK AND CONCORD
LIGHTING
Spotlight, *Optic Universal*
Surface-mounted, with permanent
tensioning to allow full rotation. In die-cast
aluminium, with tungsten halogen reflector
lamp.
H 14.5 cm (5¾ in). W 3 cm (1¼ in).
L 14.5 cm (5¾ in)
Manufacturer: Concord Lighting, UK

229, 230 RENÉ KEMNA
Lamps, *Sigla Collection*
Set of lamps, each with fixed base or
clamp with a flexible fibreglass arm that
enables the light to be adjusted in height
and projection. The dimmer switch in the
base has two settings.
Table lamp: H 60–70 cm (24–28 in).
L 10–70 cm (4–28 in)
Floor lamp: H 135–150 cm (53–59 in).
L 10–80 cm (4–31½ in)
Clamp: H 60–75 cm (24–29½ in).
L 10–70 cm (4–27½ in)
Manufacturer: Sirrah, Italy

229

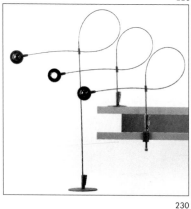

230

● René Kemna's work takes a different tack from the Anglepoise. He
has turned the structure of his *Sigla*
light into an anorexic, limitlessly flexible but stiff length of wire. By looping
it through a friction joint, it is possible
to position the light source at virtually
any point along the wire. The same
principle holds good for Kemna's
floor-standing version, and for his
desk lights, which are fitted either
with a clamp or a solid base. By contrast, De Pas, D'Urbino and Lomazzi's
counterbalanced 'up and over'
Valentina desk lamp (page 115)
looks gawky.

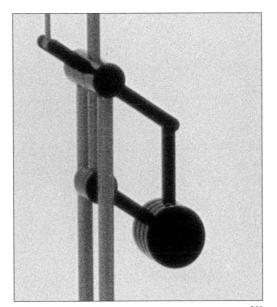

231

231–236 JONATHAN DE PAS, DONATO D'URBINO AND PAOLO
LOMAZZI
Table lamp, *Valentina*
In moulded polycarbonate and aluminium tubing, this
multi-directional lamp comes in a variety of colours. 50W.
halogen lamp.
H 20 cm (8 in). L 93 cm (36½ in)
Manufacturer: Valenti, Italy

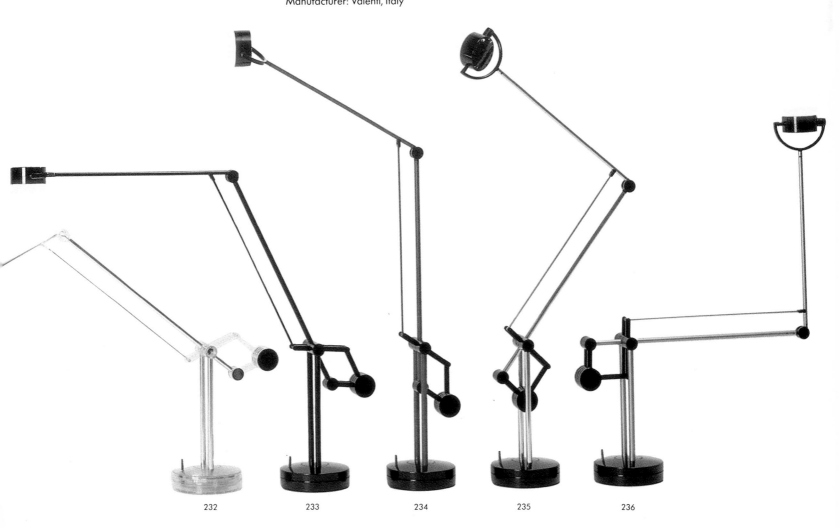

232   233   234   235   236

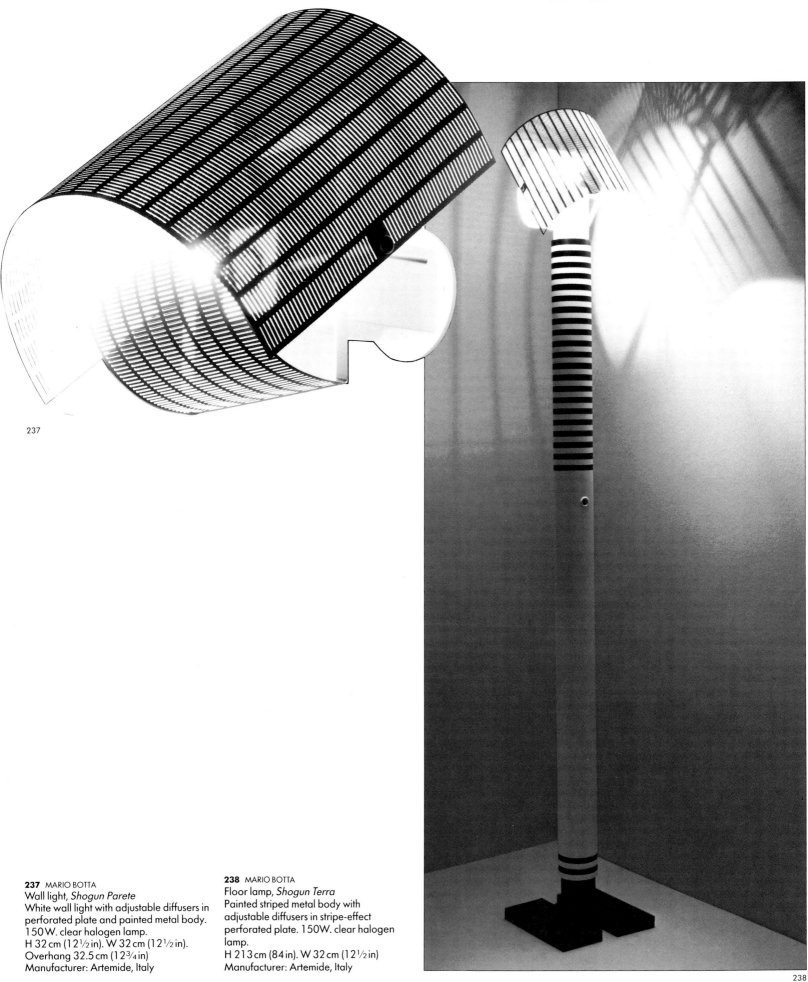

237

237 MARIO BOTTA
Wall light, *Shogun Parete*
White wall light with adjustable diffusers in
perforated plate and painted metal body.
150 W. clear halogen lamp.
H 32 cm (12 1/2 in). W 32 cm (12 1/2 in).
Overhang 32.5 cm (12 3/4 in)
Manufacturer: Artemide, Italy

238 MARIO BOTTA
Floor lamp, *Shogun Terra*
Painted striped metal body with
adjustable diffusers in stripe-effect
perforated plate. 150 W. clear halogen
lamp.
H 213 cm (84 in). W 32 cm (12 1/2 in)
Manufacturer: Artemide, Italy

238

239

239 MARIO BOTTA
Table lamp, *Shogun Tavolo*
Painted striped metal body with
adjustable diffusers in stripe-effect
perforated plate. Combined with 150W.
clear halogen lamp.
H 58.5–68.5 cm (23–27 in). W 32 cm
(12½ in)
Manufacturer: Artemide, Italy

240 MARTINE BEDIN
Table lamp, *Olimpia*
Available with natural or lacquered wood
base. In blue and green glass, with yellow
glass tube. 75 W. bulb.
H 24 cm (9½ in). 34 cm (13¼ in) square
Manufacturer: Memphis, Italy

● Mario Botta, the Swiss architect,
has already designed a number of
pieces of furniture that have attracted
considerable attention. His first lighting designs for Artemide use similar
materials, perforated and folded
sheet metal, and a simplified geo-
metry of shapes. The *Shogun* range
reflects the current predilection of
many designers for making one idea
stretch a long way: the basic form is
deployed as a table light, a floor light
and a wall light, in each incarnation
demonstrating a completely different
character, yet using exactly the same
basic elements.

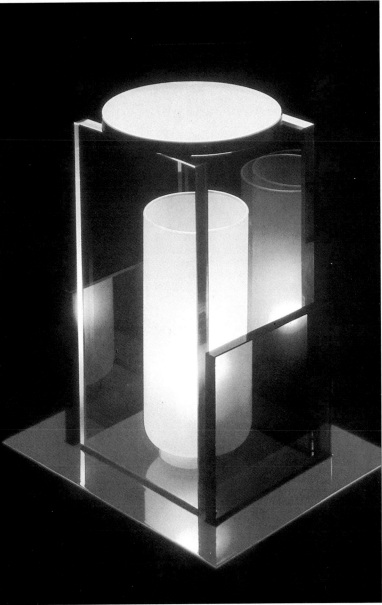

240

241

● Since they began their experiments with quartz halogen lights using cast glass diffusing shades in the late 1970s, Perry King and Santiago Miranda have emerged as two of the world's foremost lighting designers. King has said that their work attempts to recapture the atmospheric character of traditional lighting sources, with the quality of a guttering candle-flame; their two new lights for Arteluce, the *Triana* and the *Palio*, both show this approach. In each case the diffusing characteristics of the materials used to house the lamp are exploited to the full, creating a gentle, soft source of light. The addition of texturing by means of applied graphic ornament is a new departure, and one that King and Miranda's many imitators will no doubt take up before long.

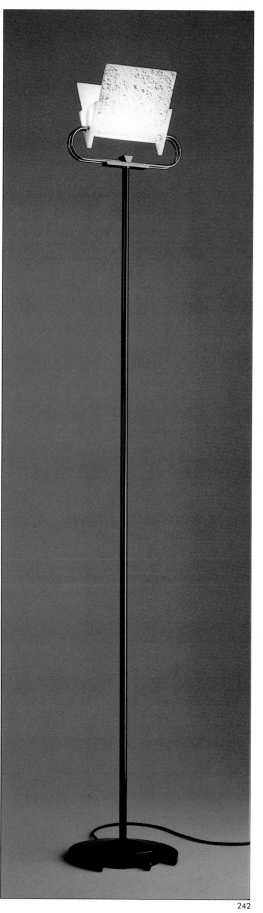

242

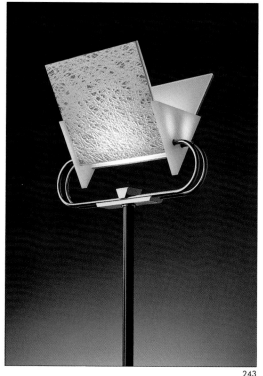

243

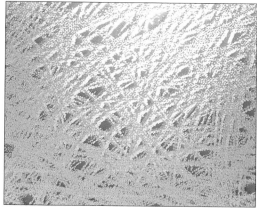

244

241 PERRY A. KING AND SANTIAGO MIRANDA
Table lamp, *Palio*
With glass diffuser and a polished aluminium or copper reflector. 100W. halogen lamp with dimmer.
H 40 cm (16 in)
Manufacturer: Arteluce, Italy

242–244 PERRY A. KING AND SANTIAGO MIRANDA
Floor lamp, *Triana*
Standing lamp giving direct light with dimmer. The diffusers are rectangular sheets of coloured glass. 500W. halogen lamp.
H 200 cm (80 in)
Manufacturer: Arteluce, Italy

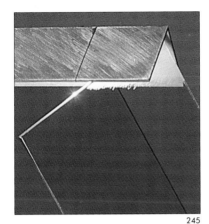

245, 246 THOMAS EISL
Desk light
Slate base supporting plate glass sides
and aluminium top. 50W. halogen lamp.
H 53 cm (21 in). L 43 cm (17 in). W 20 cm
(8 in)
Manufacturer: Thomas Eisl, UK

246

● The artist Thomas Eisl brings a
painterly eye to the lights he has
been designing in the last few years.
The most recent, produced in small
batches, combine a strong sense of
formal values with an intriguing level
of sophistication in their technical
aspects. He employs low-voltage
sources, allowing the constructivist
forms of his aluminium and timber
lamp (plate 247) to conduct the electricity. His other new light (plate 246)
uses metal tape as the conducting
material. In both cases, the lamp and
reflector housing are detachable
from their supports and can be re-
positioned at will.

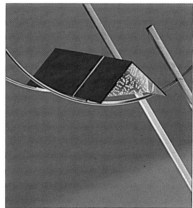

248

247, 248 THOMAS EISL
Desk light
Black-stained sycamore base with
aluminium rods. 50W. halogen lamp.
H 70 cm (27½ in). L 51 cm (20 in).
W 18 cm (7 in)
Manufacturer: Thomas Eisl, UK

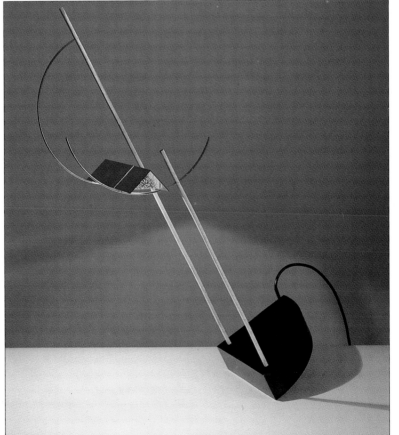

247

249, 250 TOBIA SCARPA
Floor lamp, *Butterfly*
Standing lamp with a dimmer providing screened and
diffused light, and an etched-glass diffuser. 300W.
halogen lamp.
H 205 cm (81 in)
Manufacturer: Flos, Italy

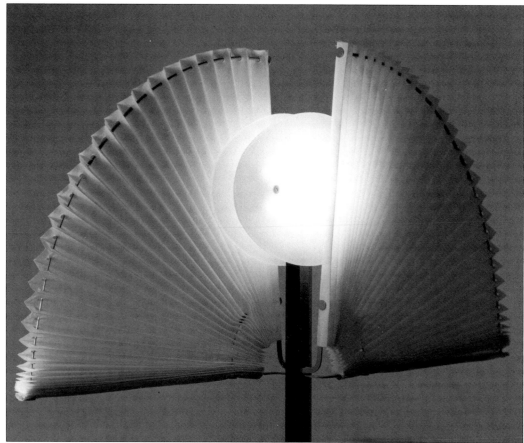

249

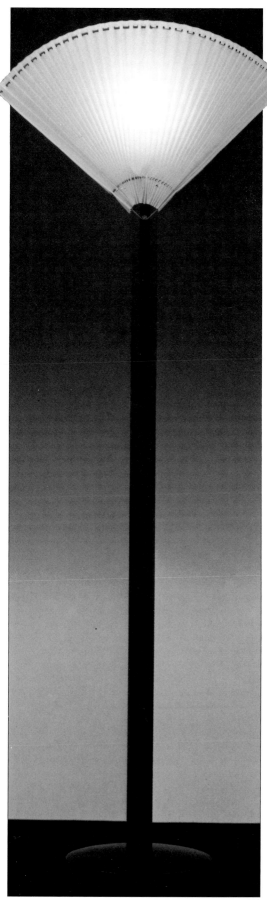

250

251, 253 PATRIZIA BELLONI
Table lamp, *Pendolo*
In lacquered white metal with a
swivelling screen, coloured black. 20W.
halogen lamp.
H 35 cm (14 in)
Manufacturer: Quattrifolio, Italy

252 ERNESTO GISMONDI
Wall lamp, *Stria*
The body of the lamp is polyester
reinforced with fibreglass, while the
protruding adjustable diffusers are white-
painted metal. 150W. opalin lamp.
H 38 cm (15 in). W 36 cm (14 in)
Manufacturer: Artemide, Italy

251

252

253

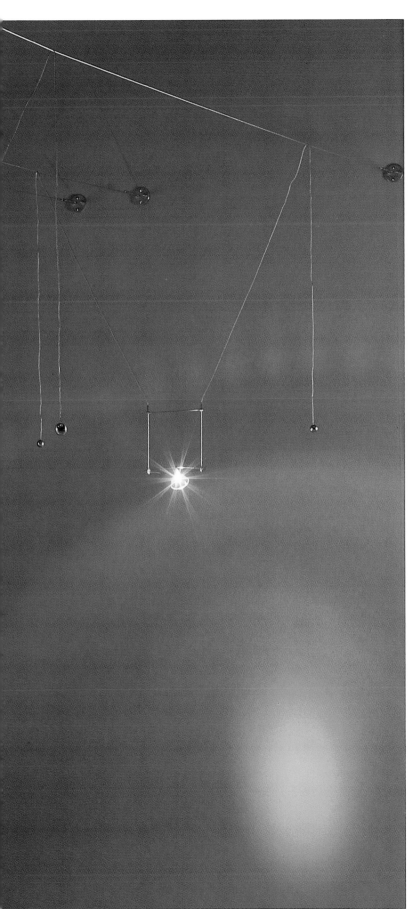

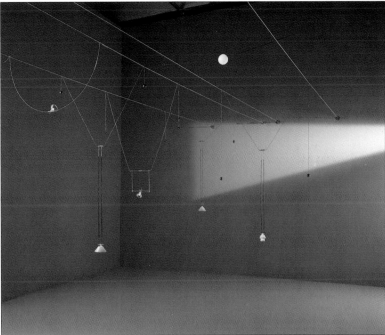

255

● The German Ingo Maurer's new design — 'installation' is probably a better word to describe it than 'fitting' — is mysteriously named the *YaYaHo*. It must rank among the most original pieces of lighting produced in the last twenty years — probably since the Castiglioni brothers thought, equally improbably, of cobbling together a fishing-rod, a bandsaw and a car headlamp to produce the world's first high-tech uplighter. Maurer combines high technology — electrical transformers, exotic miniature light sources — with an almost totemistic visual mood, denying the formal perfection of the machine-made object and instead allowing the purchaser to create his own design out of a number of parts.

The *YaYaHo* demands space, a big interior where there is room to manoeuvre. Four low-voltage cables are stretched across it, and carry a variety of what appear to be found objects; casually collected ornaments, balls, bells and discs, disposed according to mood. The actual location of each piece doesn't really matter — what's important is the magical overall effect.

254, 255 INGO MAURER
Pendant lights, *YaYaHo*
In glass, porcelain, ceramic, metal and plastic. This low-voltage cable system has two mounting parts and four different lighting elements. All the elements are movable, either vertically or horizontally. Two-pin halogen 20W. and 50W. lamps and 50W. reflectors.
Cables: L 6,000 cm (2,362 in)
Lighting elements: maximum D from string 50 cm (19½ in)
Manufacturer: Design M Ingo Maurer, West Germany

256

256 DENIS SANTACHIARA
Table lamp, *Maestrale*
Sculptured, cone-shaped object; the fan
flutters a fabric flag, illuminated by an
internal light.
H 56 cm (22 in)
Manufacturer: Tribu, France

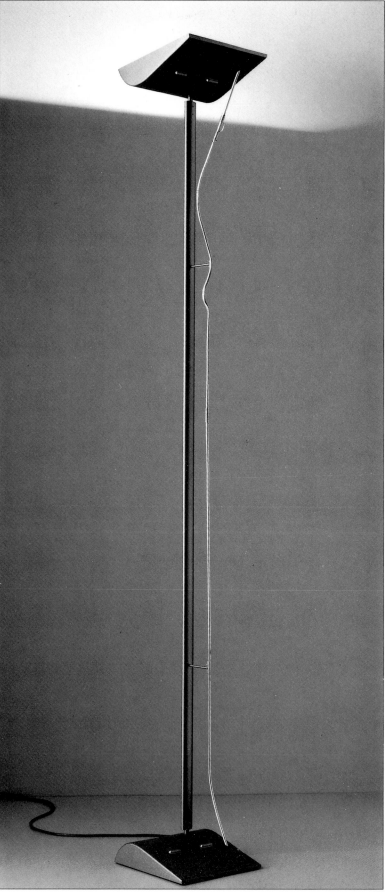

257

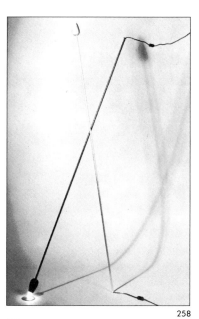

258

258 DENIS SANTACHIARA
Light, *Sparta*
Spear light intended to lean up against a
wall.
H 200 cm (78¾ in)
Manufacturer: Tribu, France

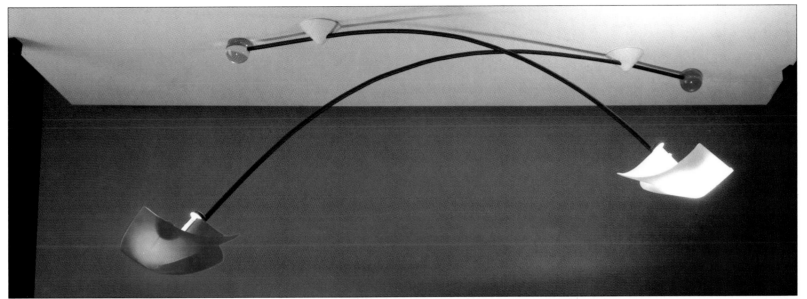

259

260

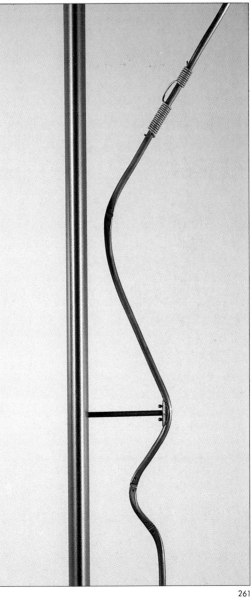

261

262

257, 260, 261 MATTHEW HILTON
Uplighter, *Walata*
Sculptural 500W. tungsten halogen uplighter, with stove-enamel finish. With a foot control dimmer and copper decorative detail.
H 190 cm (75 in)
Manufacturer: London Lighting, UK

259, 262 CARLO A. URBINATI-RICCI AND ALESSANDRO VECCHIATO
Ceiling lamp, *Plana Soffitto*
In lacquered metal and Murano glass. The support allows the lamp to revolve through 360°. The diffuser comes in blown acidified blue or white glass, while the counter-weight is a blue or white glass sphere. 300W. halogen lamp.
H 60/45 cm (24/18 in). L 120/90 cm (47/36 in)
Manufacturer: Foscarini, Italy

263 MASANORI UMEDA
Reading lamp, *Farfalla*
Angled lamp with painted metal supports
and head and lacquered plastic shade.
H 41.5 cm (16¼ in). W 40 cm (16 in).
L 20 cm (8 in)
Manufacturer: Daiko Electric, Japan

264 MASANORI UMEDA
Floor lamp, *Farfalla*
The angled lamp is adjustable from the
painted metal ball. Two-sided lacquered
plastic shade with shaped edge.
H 178 cm (70 in). W 48 cm (19 in)
Manufacturer: Daiko Electric, Japan

263

264

265 MARCO ZANUSO JR
Floor lamp, *Tula*
In metal and natural or sand-blasted glass. 750W. halogen lamp.
H 95 cm (37½ in)
Manufacturer: Carlo Moretti, Italy

265

266 MATTEO THUN
Table lamps, *Stillight Collection*
Left to right:

Reading lamp, *Zeronove Tobruk*
In painted steel with a shade in printed glass. 150W. halogen lamp.
H 20 cm (8 in). W 20 cm (8 in)

Table lamp, *Zerosette Zero Visibility*
In porcelain and glass, the shade is handmade glass over a PL11 Philips bulb.
H 35 cm (14 in). W 20 cm (8 in)

Reading lamp, *Dieci Spargi*
In black-painted steel with cupola shade in painted glass. 150W. halogen lamp.
H 20 cm (8 in). W 20 cm (8 in)

Table lamp, *Zerosei Guardiano Giovanni*
In red- and black-painted steel with printed glass shade. 300W. lamp with dimmer.
H 43 cm (17 in). W 21 cm (8½ in)

Reading lamp, *Zerootto Spargiotto*
In black-painted steel with printed glass shade. 100W. lamp.
H 35 cm (14 in). W 17 cm (7 in)

Table lamp, *Zerocinque Maddalena*
Black-painted steel base. Two 150W. lamps with dimmers.
H 47 cm (18½ in). W 25 cm (10 in)

Manufacturer: Bieffeplast, Italy

266

267

267 MAKOTO KOMATSU
Light
Stainless-steel mesh light.
H 35 cm (14 in). L 11 cm (4½ in). W 25 cm (10 in)
Prototype
Manufacturer: Makoto Komatsu, Japan

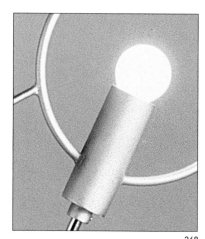

268

● Javier Mariscal and his collaborator Pepe Cortés represent one of the lively new currents emerging from Barcelona, a city now enjoying a design-led cultural revival. They are manufactured in modest quantities under the label of BD, a firm established in Barcelona in the late 1960s by a group of architects in order to put works into production that no manufacturer would adopt. Their lights have a playful, frivolous quality.

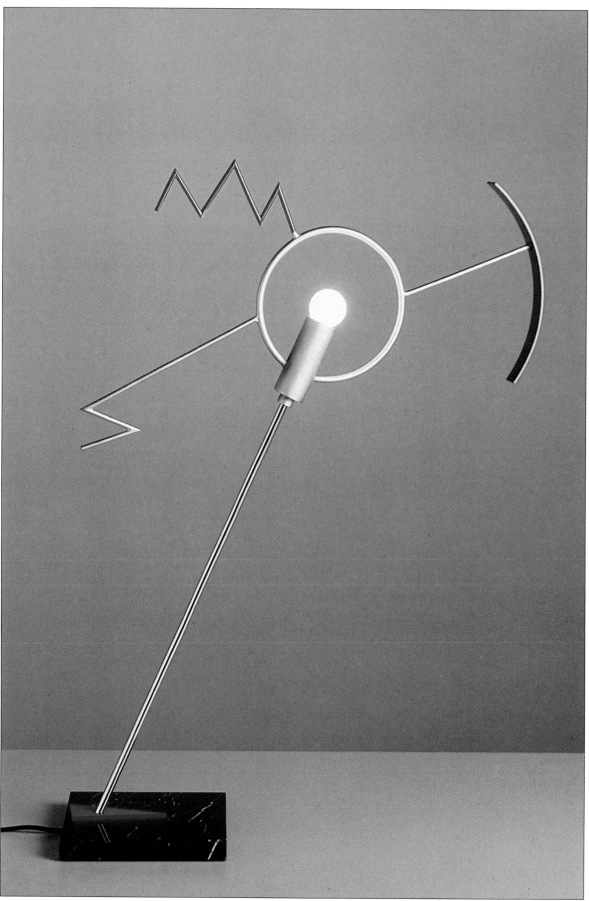

268–270 JAVIER MARISCAL
Table lamp, *Valencia*
In sanded steel, with matt nickelled
structure and painted red and blue
elements. The bright chrome steel frame is
supported on a black marble base. 25W.
lamp.
H 70 cm (27½ in). W 20 cm (8 in)
Manufacturer: BD, Spain

271, 272 JAVIER MARISCAL AND PEPE CORTÉS
Table lamp, *Garraf*
Metallized grey steel pyramid supported
on a black marble base with painted blue
metallic arms. 36W. fluorescent daylight
lamp.
H 110 cm (43 in). W 37 cm (14½ in).
L 119 cm (47 in)
Manufacturer: BD, Spain

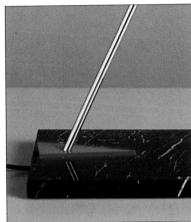

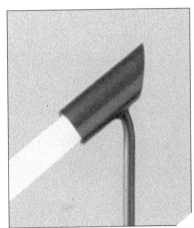

270   271

272

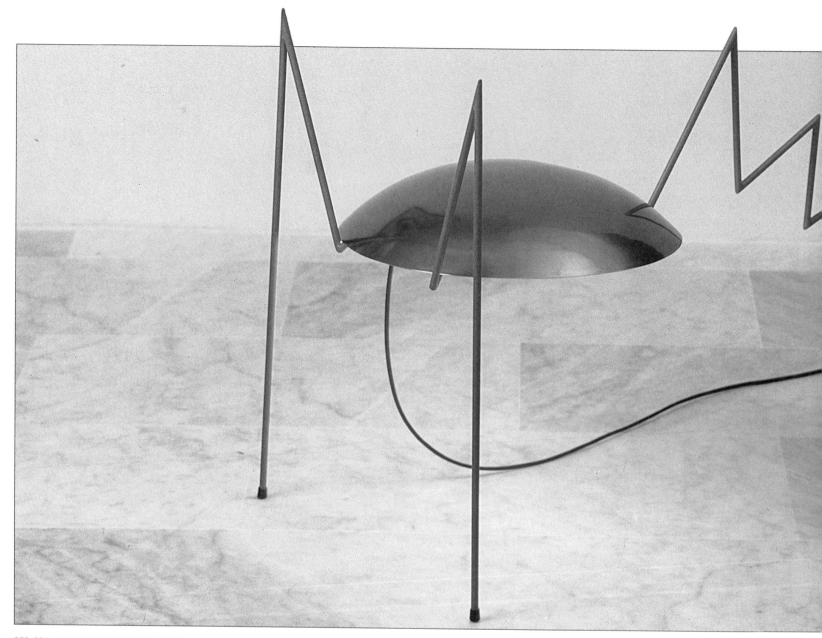

273, 274 JAVIER MARISCAL AND PEPE CORTÉS
Floor lamp, *Araña*
In polished epoxy-coated steel, with
tungsten lamp.
H 27 cm (10½ in). L 60 cm (23½ in).
W 20 cm (8 in)
Manufacturer: BD, Spain

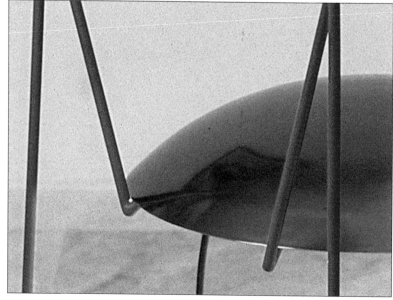

274

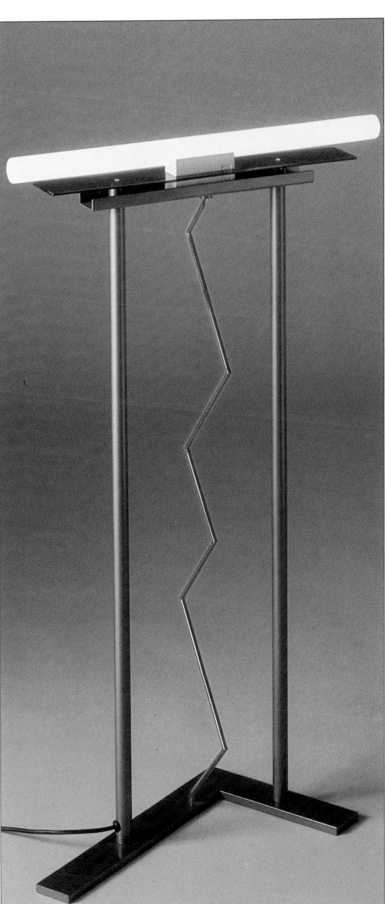

273

276

275 JAVIER MARISCAL AND PEPE CORTÉS
Low pedestal lamp, *Rocafort*
Metallized grey steel frame and base with
painted decoration. 60W. tungsten lamp.
H 83 cm (33 in). W 50 cm (20 in)
Manufacturer: BD, Spain

276 JAVIER MARISCAL AND PEPE CORTÉS
Floor lamp, *Olvidada*
In chrome steel, with three tungsten strip
lights.
H 84 cm (33 in). L 50 cm (19½ in).
W 23 cm (9 in)
Manufacturer: BD, Spain

275

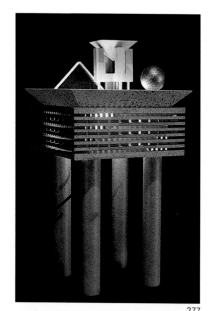

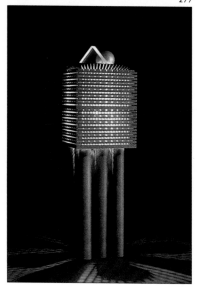

277

278

277 JAMES EVANSON
Table light, *Lightstruck*
From the *Lighthouse Collection*. In
lacquered wood with removable lucite
accessories in neon colours.
H 38 cm (15 in). W 23 cm (9 in). L 23 cm
(9 in)
Manufacturer: Art et Industrie, USA

278 JAMES EVANSON
Floor lamp, *Hi-Beam*
From the *Lighthouse Collection*.
In lacquered wood with removable
lucite accessories in neon colours.
H 53 cm (21 in). W 18 cm (7 in). L 18 cm
(7 in)
Manufacturer: Art et Industrie, USA

279 JAMES EVANSON
Lamps, *Lighthouse Collection*
In lacquered wood with removable lucite
accessories in neon colours.
Manufacturer: Art et Industrie, USA

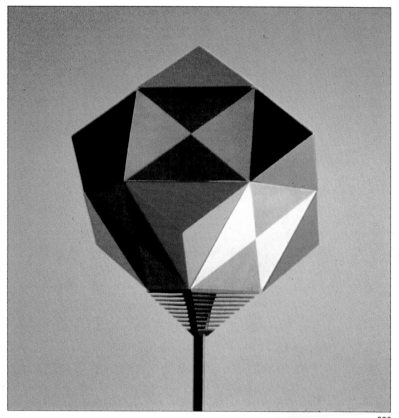

280

281

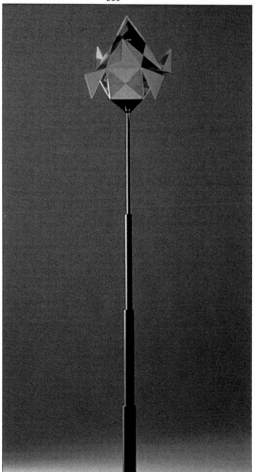

282

283

● To employ origami as the basis for a light shade is peculiarly appropriate in Japan, where there is in any case a highly developed tradition of using paper to make shades. Kitaoka's floor-standing fitting brings colour and variety to lighting.

280–283 SETSUO KITAOKA
Floor lamp
Floor light with basic cube-shaped head has adjustable coloured leaves that open up. The stalk graduates in thickness.
H 1,800 cm (708½ in)
Prototype

TABLEWARE

It is possible to see contemporary tableware in terms of a series of tensions: between form and surface treatment, between art and utility, and between craft and design. While these factors are also at work in the creation of most of the other pieces shown in this book, in few areas are such tensions so clearly expressed as in ceramics and glass.

On grounds of economy some ceramics manufacturers are quite prepared to use a single product, and decorate it in different ways. Some are even ready to buy in a semi-finished product, and treat its surface to their own specifications. Clearly in such cases form has been entirely subordinated to surface pattern.

It is also possible to place products on a scale that moves from straightforward utility at one end, to pure art at the other. The revival of interest in the craft approach, particularly in Britain and America, has created a curious new category of artefact, exemplified by the vase in which it is impossible to keep flowers, and the jug which will not pour water. Ultimately wrong-headed though these extremes may be, they can sometimes make for rich explorations of form. Yet strangely, the purely functional can often outmatch them in poetry.

The same crafts revival is behind the schism between designers and makers. Too often craft pieces depend simply on the quality of their execution, rather than on an assessment of the way in which that workmanship is used.

The most convincing works are those which contrive a synthesis between the poles in each of these three tensions: which are both usable and formally conceived, which blur the distinctions between form and surface, and which put both designer and maker to work. Interestingly this is a direction in which those members of the Memphis group who have turned their attention to glass and ceramics are moving: they are producing plates, vases and glass intended for limited production in craft-oriented workshops.

The skills of glassmakers must be nurtured, and they depend on the establishment of enterprises committed to the long-term production of pieces of quality. Hence the concentration of such manufacturers in certain areas of the world, such as northern Italy, Finland, or, indeed, Japan. More and more, they cross-fertilize each other, swapping designers.

Perhaps more so than with other categories of design, the design of tableware remains an area dominated by the personality of individual designers rather than by broader stylistic trends.

284 LELLA AND MASSIMO VIGNELLI AND DAVID LAW
Dinnerware
Complete dinner set in stoneware, available in various
matt and gloss colours.
Dinner plate: D 27.3 cm (10¾ in)
Salad plate and bowl: D 19.1 cm (7½ in)
Cup: H 8.6 cm (3⅜ in)
Saucer: D 15.2 cm (6 in)
Manufacturer: Sasaki Crystal, Japan

285

● Borek Sipek, a Czech-born designer now working in Germany, has taken the example set by Ettore Sottsass's designs for the master craftsmen of the Murano glass work-shops to good effect with his relation-ship with the Glashütte Süssmutt. The glass bears more than a passing resemblance to that of Memphis, too.

285 BOREK SIPEK
Bowl, *Broadway Collection*
Handmade green glass supported on a clear glass stand.
H 11.5 cm (4½ in). D 28.5 cm (11 in)
Manufacturer: Glashütte Süssmuth, West Germany

286 BOREK SIPEK
Vase, *Broadway Collection*
Handmade glass, from a series; a vase within a vase.
H 23.5 cm (9 in). D 14.5 cm (5½ in)
Manufacturer: Glashütte Süssmuth, West Germany

286

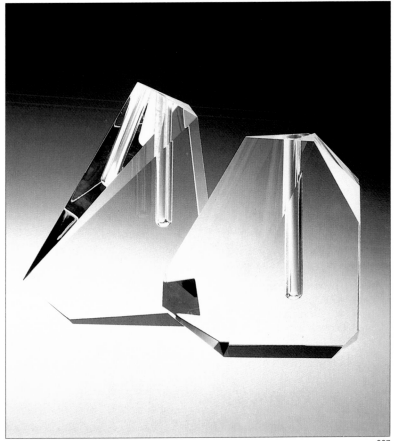

287

287 FUMIO SASA
Vases, *Apollo*
Crystal vases – clear glass, cast, cut and polished.
H 18/21 cm (7/8 in). W 17.5/19 cm (7/7½ in)
Manufacturer: Hoya, Japan

288

288 BOREK SIPEK
Cheese dish, *Broadway Collection*
Covered cheese dish in handmade clear glass with green handle.
H 16 cm (6½ in). D 26 cm (10 in)
Manufacturer: Glashütte Süssmuth, West Germany

289

290

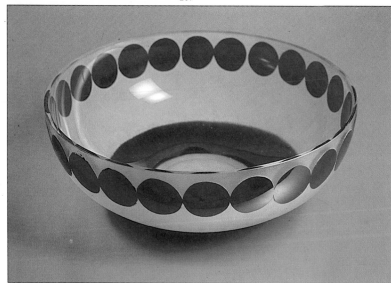

291

289–292 HIDETOSHI NOZAWA
Bowls, *Ai*
Selection of clear glass bowls, cased in
cobalt-blue-tinted glass, sandblasted and
then polished.
H 12/20 cm (5/8 in). D 24/40 cm
(9½/16 in)
Manufacturer: Nigara, Japan

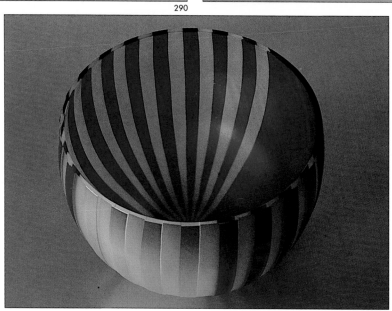

292

293

294

295

296

293 HORST BARTELS
Decanter and glasses, *Taiga-Wodka-Set*
Set of glasses and decanter in crystal.
H of decanter 36 cm (14 in)
Manufacturer: Rastal, West Germany

294 AKIRA SHIRAHATA
Vases
Crystal vases – clear glass, blown, cut and polished.
H 21.7/32.2 cm (8½/12¾ in). W 14 cm (5½ in)
Manufacturer: Hoya, Japan

295 SMART DESIGN
Dinnerware
In Melamine and styrene plastic, including plates, bowls and servers.
Dinner plate: D 25 cm (10 in)
Salad bowl: H 13–15 cm (5-6 in).
D 25–30 cm (10–12 in)
Salad server: L 29–34 cm (11½–13½ in).
W 9–11 cm (3½–4¼ in)
Manufacturer: Copco, USA

296 SABURO FUNAKOSHI
Vases, *Capsule–Star '85*
Crystal vases – clear glass, blown, cut and polished.
H 19/22/25 cm (7½/8½/10 in).
W 11.5 cm (4½ in)
Manufacturer: Hoya, Japan

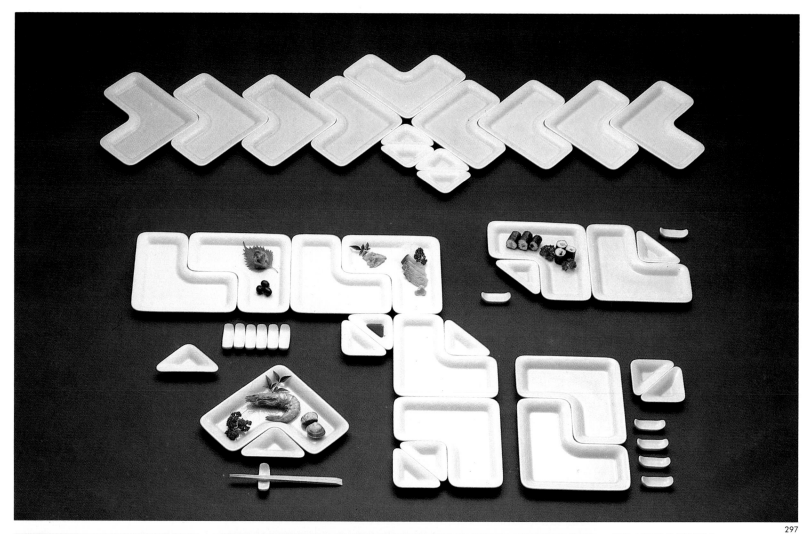

297

298

297, 298 MASAHIRO MORI
Party Trays
Interlocking porcelain trays.
24 cm (9½ in) square
Manufacturer: Hakusan Porcelain, Japan

299 ACHILLE CASTIGLIONI
Cruet set
Oil and vinegar set with personal salt
castor, made in crystal with electro-plated
stainless-steel base, handle and tops, and
stand.
Vinegar cruet: H 18.5 cm (7¼ in). D 6 cm
(2½ in)
Oil cruet: H 23.5 cm (9¼ in). D 7.5 cm
(3 in)
Salt castor: H 6 cm (2½ in). D 4.5 cm
(1¼ in)
Cruet stand: L 16.5 cm (6½ in). W 9 cm
(3½ in)
Manufacturer: Alessi, Italy

299

300 MART VAN SCHIJNDEL
Vase, *Delta*
Frosted glass in clear and opal white,
handmade and signed.
H 23 cm (9 in). W 19 cm (7½ in). D 19 cm
(7½ in)
Manufacturer: Martech, The Netherlands

300

301 FREI OTTO
Pitchers
Ceramic pitchers designed for the
'Golden Eye' exhibition at the Cooper-
Hewitt Museum.
Prototypes

301

302

303

304

306

304 SERGIO ASTI
Vases
Glass, available in several sizes and
colours, and made by several processes.
H 26.5/31.5 cm (10½/12½ in). D 14 cm
(5½ in)
Manufacturer: Nason & Moretti, Italy

305, 306 SERGIO ASTI
Boxes and cups
Glass sweet boxes in several sizes and
colours made by different processes, with
or without lids.
H 9.8/10 cm (3⅞/4 in). D 14.5/18 cm
(5¾/7 in)
Cone-shaped box: D 10 cm (4 in)
Cylinder-shaped box: D 14.5 cm (5¾ in)
Manufacturer: Nason & Moretti, Italy

307 SERGIO ASTI
Boxes
Glass with coloured bases, with or without
lids.
H 7/11 cm (2¾/4½ in). D 10.5/22.5 cm
(4¼/9¼ in)
Manufacturer: Nason & Moretti, Italy

305

302 SERGIO ASTI
Boxes
Glass, with or without lids, in a range of
colours and sizes.
H 11 cm (4¼ in). D 25 cm (10 in)
Manufacturer: Nason & Moretti, Italy

303 SERGIO ASTI
Ashtrays
Stacking ashtrays in several sizes and
colour combinations.
D 14/19 cm (5½/7½ in)
Manufacturer: Nason & Moretti, Italy

307

308

309

310

308 ROBERT A.M. STERN
Pitcher
Straight-sided pitcher in plated silver.
H 25.5 cm (10 in)
Manufacturer: Swid Powell Design, USA

309 ROBERT A.M. STERN
Salt and pepper set
In plated silver.
H 7.5 cm (3 in)
Manufacturer: Swid Powell Design, USA

310 GIOTTO STOPPINO
Tableware, *Tholos Collection*
Boxes, ashtrays, pencil-holders and
paper-weight industrially produced in
marble. The surfaces are lathe-engraved.
H 4.5 cm–9.5 cm (1½ in–3¾ in).
D 6 cm–16.5 cm (2½ in–6½ in)
Manufacturer: Casigliani, Italy

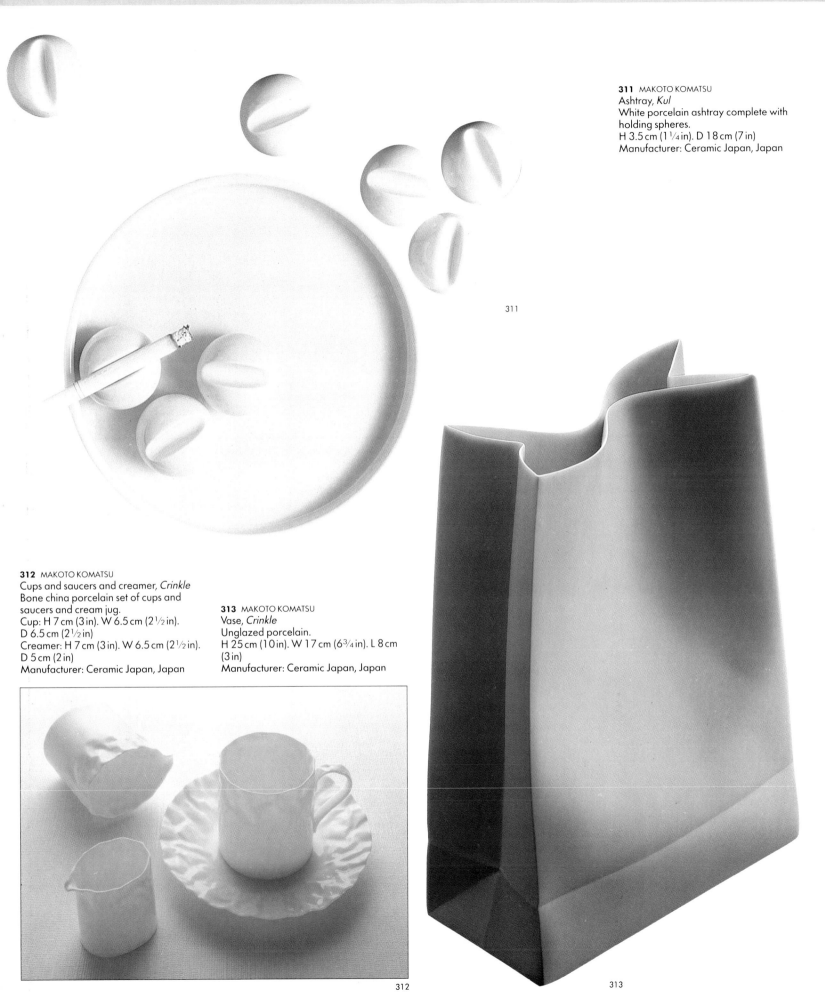

311 MAKOTO KOMATSU
Ashtray, *Kul*
White porcelain ashtray complete with
holding spheres.
H 3.5 cm (1 ¼ in). D 18 cm (7 in)
Manufacturer: Ceramic Japan, Japan

311

312 MAKOTO KOMATSU
Cups and saucers and creamer, *Crinkle*
Bone china porcelain set of cups and
saucers and cream jug.
Cup: H 7 cm (3 in). W 6.5 cm (2 ½ in).
D 6.5 cm (2 ½ in)
Creamer: H 7 cm (3 in). W 6.5 cm (2 ½ in).
D 5 cm (2 in)
Manufacturer: Ceramic Japan, Japan

313 MAKOTO KOMATSU
Vase, *Crinkle*
Unglazed porcelain.
H 25 cm (10 in). W 17 cm (6 ¾ in). L 8 cm
(3 in)
Manufacturer: Ceramic Japan, Japan

312

313

314

315

316

317

316 NANNY STILL McKINNEY
Bowls, *Snow Dew*
Wavy-edged crystal in a variety of sizes.
H 12/14/17 cm (4³/₄/5¹/₂/6³/₄ in).
W 15/18/24 cm (6/7/9¹/₂ in)
Manufacturer: Rosenthal, West Germany

317 TAPIO WIRKKALA
Glasses, *Pallas*
Handmade crystal, in a variety of sizes.
Capacity 4/14/22/28/36/38 cl
(1¹/₂/5/8/10/13/13¹/₂ oz)
Manufacturer: Iittala, Finland

314 MAKOTO KOMATSU
Glasses, *Shiwa*
Range of clear glasses.
H 8.2/10.8/8.5 cm (3¹/₄/4¹/₄/3¹/₄ in)
Manufacturer: Kimura, Japan

315 MAKOTO KOMATSU
Glassware, *Kami*
Tumblers, pitcher and ice bucket in clear
glass.
Tumbler: H 10 cm (4 in). W 7.5 cm (3 in).
L 8.5 cm (3¹/₄ in)
Pitcher: H 20 cm (8 in). W 8 cm (3¹/₄ in).
L 8 cm (3¹/₄ in)
Ice bucket: H 10 cm (4 in). W 12 cm
(4³/₄ in). L 12 cm (4³/₄ in)
Manufacturer: Kimura Glass, Japan

318 VALTO KOKKO
Vases, *Otso*
Handmade crystal.
H 18.5/20/25 cm (7¹/₄/8/10 in)
Manufacturer: Iittala, Finland

319, 321 JORMA VENNOLA
Glasses, *Kaveri*
Handmade opal and cobalt blue crystal
on plastic stems.
Capacity 22/24 cl (8/8¹/₂ oz)
Manufacturer: Iittala, Finland

320 JORMA VENNOLA
Glasses, *Claudia*
Clear hand-blown glasses with sandblasted
bases.
Capacity 5/14/18/22/28 30 cl
(1¹/₂/5/6¹/₂/8/10/10¹/₂ oz)
Manufacturer: Iittala, Finland

318

319

321

320

● The Finnish glassworks of Iittala has long been one of the world's leading centres for contemporary glass. Its traditions go back to Aalto in the 1930s; in the post-war years it has continually employed some of Finland's most talented designers of both hand-blown and cut glass, as well as mass-produced glassware. Gunnel Nyman, in the brief years between the end of the war and her early death in 1948, created a distinctive folded and cut style for glass vessels. Tapio Wirkkala worked exclusively for Iittala from 1947 until the mid-1950s, and regularly thereafter right up until his death in 1985.

322

323

324

325

326

322 ETTORE SOTTSASS JR
Plate, *Indivia*
Salad plate, decorated white ceramic.
D 21 cm (8½ in)
Manufacturer: Memphis, Italy

323 ETTORE SOTTSASS JR
Plate, *Ruggola*
White ceramic dinner plate with raised
white and flat black decoration.
D 30 cm (12 in)
Manufacturer: Memphis, Italy

324 ETTORE SOTTSASS JR
Plate, *Lettuce*
White ceramic dinner plate with flat black
and raised white decoration.
D 30 cm (12 in)
Manufacturer: Memphis, Italy

325 ALDO CIBIC
Tea set, *Cabbage, Pepper, Radish*
Ceramic teapot, cup and sugar bowl with
black decoration.
Teapot: H 19 cm (7½ in)
Cup: H 10 cm (4 in)
Sugar bowl: H 7 cm (3 in)
Manufacturer: Memphis, Italy

326 MARTINE BEDIN
Vase, *Cucumber*
Ceramic.
H 30 cm (12 in)
Manufacturer: Memphis, Italy

327 MARCO ZANINI
Bowl, *Broccoli*
Ceramic fruit bowl, decorated in three
different shapes and colours.
D 35 cm (14 in)
Manufacturer: Memphis, Italy

328 MARIA SANCHEZ
Ashtray, *Squash*
Ceramic ashtray, in three different primary
colours.
15 cm (6 in) square
Manufacturer: Memphis, Italy

327

328

● Barbara Radice, Memphis's spokeswoman, dismisses suggestions that the movement is in some way an arts and crafts revival. As she sees it, the industrial revolution put an end to that option finally and permanently. 'On the one hand, so-called handi-craft has survived as the depository of certain traditional values, for the production of handmade, one-of-a-kind articles — more and more estranged from innovation. On the other hand, craft skills have developed as a specialized stage of industrial design, as an experimental area open to new models that mass pro-duction cannot deal with because of its rigid technical and production structure. Memphis have never even dreamed of opting for one path or the other.' Another member of Memphis, Andrea Branzi, is blunter still. 'Memphis utilize the building technology of both industry and craft — the difference between them is irrelevant — with the aim of sparking new experiences capable of renewing language.'

Memphis maintain that all their work, with the exception of certain hand-blown Murano glassware pro-duced a couple of years ago, is intended for industrial production; but there is a certain disingenuous-ness to this stance. In their recent collections Memphis have shown an increasing emphasis on ceramics — partly, no doubt, because of the limited investment that such com-paratively small-scale works require. And there is really little to choose between, say, Aldo Cibic's cups and saucers, and the vigorous studio ceramics of the English.

● Strong, saturated colours and bold free ornament in the work of both Martine Bedin (page 153) and Nathalie du Pasquier demonstrate that Memphis still have not run out of steam.

329

329, 330 NATHALIE DU PASQUIER
Vase, *Carrot*
Ceramic.
H 30 cm (12 in)
Manufacturer: Memphis, Italy

331 NATHALIE DU PASQUIER
Bowl, *Cauliflower*
Ceramic fruit bowl.
D 29 cm (11½ in)
Manufacturer: Memphis, Italy

332 NATHALIE DU PASQUIER
Bowl, *Onion*
Ceramic fruit bowl.
L 30 cm (12 in). W 25 cm (10 in)
Manufacturer: Memphis, Italy

330

331

332

333 MICHELE DE LUCCHI
Plate, *Tomato*
White ceramic serving plate with black,
yellow and red decoration.
L 28 cm (11 in). W 32 cm (12½ in)
Manufacturer: Memphis, Italy

334 MICHELE DE LUCCHI
Plate, *Celery*
White ceramic serving plate with
decoration.
L 42 cm (16½ in). W 32 cm (12½ in)
Manufacturer: Memphis, Italy

335 GEORGE SOWDEN
Tray, *Potato*
Ceramic with metal handles.
D 31 cm (12 in)
Manufacturer: Memphis, Italy

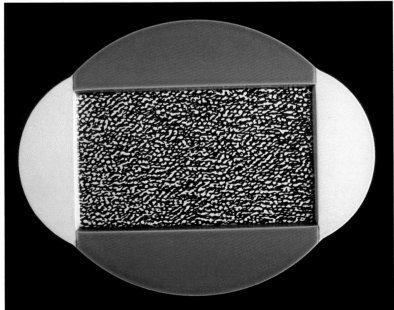

334

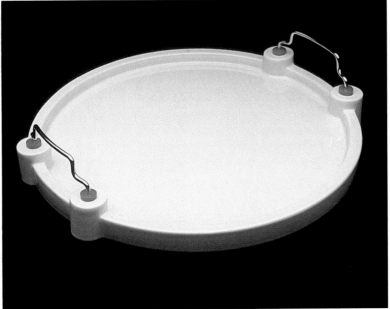

335

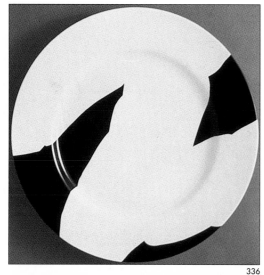

336

337

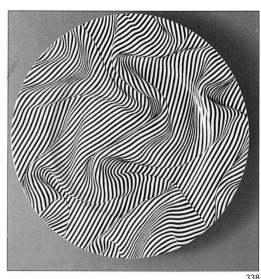

338

339

340

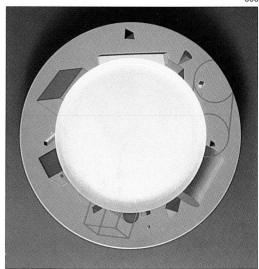

341

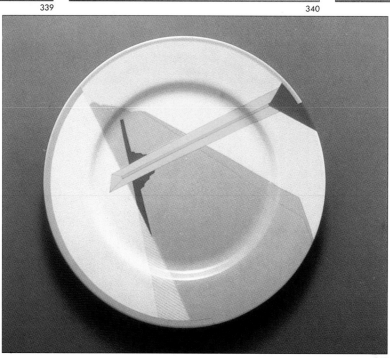

342

336 ROBERT AND TRIX HAUSSMANN
Plate, *Broken*
White porcelain with black decoration.
D 30.5 cm (12 in)
Manufacturer: Swid Powell Design, USA

337 ROBERT AND TRIX HAUSSMANN
Plate, *Stripes White on White*
Fine-striped white porcelain, which looks
like folds of fabric.
D 30.5 cm (12 in)
Manufacturer: Swid Powell Design, USA

338, 343 ROBERT AND TRIX HAUSSMANN
Plate, *Stripes Black on White*
Cleverly striped porcelain plate looks like
folds of fabric.
D 30.5 cm (12 in)
Manufacturer: Swid Powell Design, USA

339 STEVEN HOLL
Plate, *Planar*
Porcelain with decorated black border
and pale turquoise centre.
D 30.5 cm (12 in)
Manufacturer: Swid Powell Design, USA

340 STEVEN HOLL
Plate, *Linear*
White porcelain with blue line motifs.
D 30.5 cm (12 in)
Manufacturer: Swid Powell Design, USA

341 STEVEN HOLL
Plate, *Volumetric*
Porcelain with decorated turquoise
border and plain white centre.
D 30.5 cm (12 in)
Manufacturer: Swid Powell Design, USA

342 JAVIER BELLOSILLO
Plate, *Ruin*
Porcelain decorated with geometric
shapes in blue, orange, yellow and black.
D 30.5 cm (12 in)
Manufacturer: Swid Powell Design, USA

● Launched in 1984 by Nan Swid and Addie Powell, both formerly with Knoll International, Swid Powell market glass and ceramics designed by America's architectural stars. The company makes large claims, comparing its commitment to quality with Saarinen's Cranbrook, the Bauhaus and the Vereinigte Werkstätten. To this end, it has recruited fresh talents. Venturi, Isozaki and Meier are now joined by Hollein, the talented Austrian architect, by Bellosillo and by Holl. In addition Tigerman and Meier have produced new work. But this approach is not without difficulties. Unlike the Memphis collection, in which designers have the scope to create a piece from scratch, exploring with manufacture and form as well as surface decoration, Swid Powell's ceramics rely very much on decorating one standard product. Nevertheless, remarkable inventiveness has been brought to bear on such a modest problem: designers such as Hollein have singlemindedly addressed the form of the plate, rather than applying stylistic preconceptions.

343

344 JAVIER BELLOSILLO
Dinnerware, *Figure*
Porcelain, orange and ochre jagged design crossed with stripes of blue.
Plate: D 30.5 cm (12 in)
Small plate: D 23.5 cm (9¼ in)
Cup: H 5.1 cm (2 in). D 7.6 cm (3 in)
Saucer: D 9.5 cm (3¾ in)
Manufacturer: Swid Powell Design, USA

344

345 HANS HOLLEIN
Dinnerware, *Festival*
Plate, cup and saucer in white porcelain
decorated in three varying intensities of
grey.
Plate: D 30.5 cm (12 in)
Small plate: D 23.5 cm
(9¼ in).
Cup: H 5.1 cm (2 in).
D 7.6 cm (3 in)
Saucer: D 9.5 cm
(3¾ in).
Manufacturer:
Swid Powell
Design, USA .

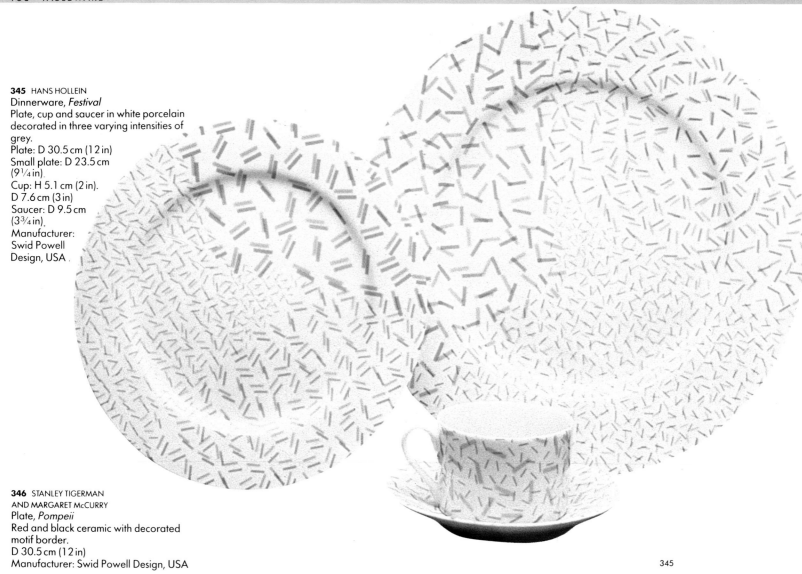

346 STANLEY TIGERMAN
AND MARGARET McCURRY
Plate, *Pompeii*
Red and black ceramic with decorated
motif border.
D 30.5 cm (12 in)
Manufacturer: Swid Powell Design, USA

345

346

347

347 STANLEY TIGERMAN
AND MARGARET McCURRY
Plate, *Tigerpause*
Red porcelain decorated with black paw
prints.
D 30.5 cm (12 in)
Manufacturer: Swid Powell Design, USA

348

350

349

348 HANS HOLLEIN
Dinnerware, *Kaleidoscope*
Plate, cup and saucer in white ceramic
decorated with stripes of red and green.
Plate: D 30.5 cm (12 in)
Small plate: D 23.5 cm (9¼ in)
Cup: H 5.1 cm (2 in). D 7.6 cm (3 in)
Saucer: D 9.5 cm (3¾ in)
Manufacturer: Swid Powell Design, USA

349, 350 RICHARD MEIER
Dinnerware, *Signature*
White porcelain with design in black or
red lines.
Plate: D 30.5 cm (12 in)
Small plate: D 23.5 cm (9¼ in)
Cup: H 5.1 cm (2 in). D 7.6 cm (3 in)
Saucer: D 9.5 cm (3¾ in)
Manufacturer: Swid Powell Design, USA

T E X T I L E S

Design is now being presented as the last hope for ailing textile industries in many parts of Western Europe, hit by Far Eastern imports, Third World weavers, and the increasing domination of the market by bigger and bigger manufacturers. Surplus capacity has allowed small design-led businesses to produce textiles with a freshness and originality that differentiates them from their competitors.

One commentator once characterized British textile design as entirely the product of the garden, and it is certainly true that traditional patterns have relied heavily on naturalistic forms since the eighteenth century, when technical developments first allowed for the commercial production of repetitive patterns on fabric. Many major manufacturers now rely on their archives of designs built up over the years. Stylized representations of nature have become the traditional means of introducing texture and pattern into domestic interiors.

No entirely convincing 'modern' alternative to naturalism in textiles has yet emerged. In the 1950s and 1960s, contemporary art movements, such as Miró's Surrealism or the geometric abstractions of Op Art, were the inspirations for textile designers. The two Memphis-associated designers, George Sowden and Nathalie du Pasquier, have both attempted to put their particular brand of new colour sensibility to work on fabrics and textiles. The increasing interest of decorators in minimalism in the 1980s has produced a new crop of textiles that rely for their impact on texture and finish, effects achieved partly by the composition of the fabrics, and partly by the way in which they are treated. Shifts in colour sense have been reflected in using new furniture fabrics on old designs to give them a longer lease of life.

351 JUNICHI ARAI
Fabric
100 per cent polyester fabrics in a range of bright colours
achieved by using metal plates.
Manufacturer: Junichi Arai, Japan

352

353

352 ANNA FRENCH DESIGN
Furnishing fabric, *Angry Arthur*
100 per cent cotton with regular abstract
design. From the *Skylights Collection*.
W 137 cm (54 in)
Manufacturer: Margo International, UK

353 ANNA FRENCH DESIGN
Furnishing fabric, *Candles in the Rain*
100 per cent cotton with stripes of
abstract geometric shapes. From the
Skylights Collection.
W 137 cm (54 in)
Manufacturer: Margo International, UK

354 MARK ROCHESTER
Fabric, *Devonscape*
100 per cent cotton fabric in subtle print
of apricots, blues and greens.
W 137 cm (54 in)
Manufacturer: Warner Fabrics, UK

354

355, 356 ANNA FRENCH DESIGN
Furnishing fabric, *Jumping Jack*
100 per cent cotton with abstract
geometric design. From the *Skylights
Collection.*
W 137 cm (54 in)
Manufacturer: Margo International, UK

357 ANN LARSSON-KJELIN
Furnishing fabric, *Swing It!*
Collection featuring seven different fabrics
all woven in 100 per cent cotton or wool.
W 150 cm (60 in)
Manufacturer: Marks-Pelle Vävare,
Sweden

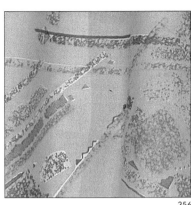

356

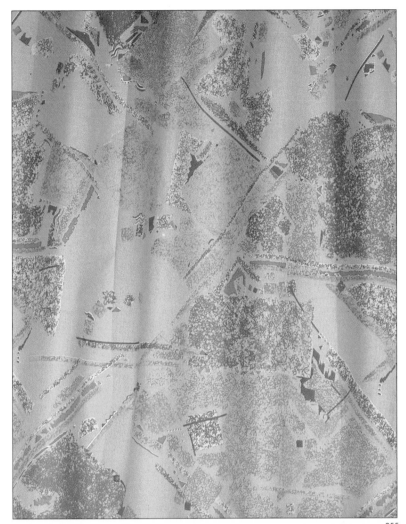

355

357

358

358–360 MONICA HJELM
Furnishing fabrics, *Movie Collection*
Range of curtain and household fabrics
woven in cotton/polyester and acrylic/linen.
W 150 cm (60 in)
Manufacturer: Marks-Pelle Vävare,
Sweden

360

359

361

● The enduring popularity of the style of the traditional English country house goes a long way
toward explaining the success of the Osborne &
Little (page 169) and Designers Guild ranges of
printed fabrics — and not just in Britain. Tradition is a
loaded word in this context — the Designers Guild in
particular use textile designers to create fabric
which has no direct precedents, but does evoke the
vocabulary of floral themes and undemanding
colours associated by many with the country house
of the past.

361 CAROLINE GRAY
Fabric, *Laurel*
One of five designs from the *Trees Collection*. Stencils of
giant leaves screen-printed using oil pastels in muted tones.
W 137 cm (54 in)
Manufacturer: Designers Guild, UK

362

363

● At one time Japan's textile designers had to go to Europe for recognition of their work. Firms such as Marimekko still rely on a Japanese input to their products, but Japan itself is now much more able to make use of the talents of its designers, in textiles as in other areas. This is particularly true since the rise in prominence of its fashion industry: such well-known houses as Issey Miyake have provided outlets — in the case of Junichi Arai, for his work in cotton and other fabrics.

364

362, 364, 365 JUNICHI ARAI
Fabrics
Designs in hand-woven cotton; one undyed (plate 365), the others in black/grey.
Manufacturer: Junichi Arai, Japan

363 JUNICHI ARAI
Fabric
100 per cent polyester fabrics in a range of bright colours achieved by using metal plates.
Manufacturer: Junichi Arai, Japan

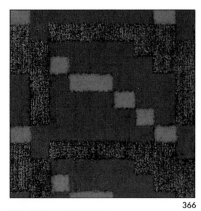

366

366, 367 MARC VAN HOE
Fabric, *Ornament Collection*
Geometric step-patterned design in spun rayon and cotton velvet in red, green and blue.
W 140 cm (55 in)
Manufacturer: Ter Molst, Belgium

367

368 ROBERTO CASPANI
Carpet, *Frammenti*
Hand-knotted, made on a horizontal loom with pure woollen yarn and cotton: the warp is of cotton, the weft of hemp. 40,000 Ghiordes knots per square metre.
L 375 cm (147 in). W 250 cm (98 in)
Manufacturer: Elio Palmisano Edizioni Tessili, Italy

368

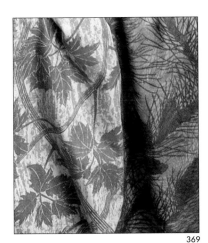

369

369, 370 OSBORNE & LITTLE
Fabrics, *Darkwood Collection*
Four large-scale leafy designs silhouetted against a textured-effect background of bark, lichen and flaking walls. In sixteen colourways.
W 140 cm (55 in)
Manufacturer: Osborne & Little, UK

370

● Japanese handmade paper might not, strictly speaking, be defined as a textile at all. Yet the subtlety of effect, the careful use of texture and surface, that Hiroshi Morishima has been able to give to his roll screens, without doubt ennoble the material.

371 HIROSHI MORISHIMA
Wagami roll screen
Screens in handmade Japanese paper.
Manufacturer: Time Space Art, Japan

371

373

374

372, 373, 375 FUJIO ISHIMOTO
Fabric
Pink and red squared design based on
crayon sketches.
Manufacturer: Marimekko, Finland

374 FUJIO ISHIMOTO
Fabric
Geometric multi-coloured design based
on crayon sketches.
Manufacturer: Marimekko, Finland

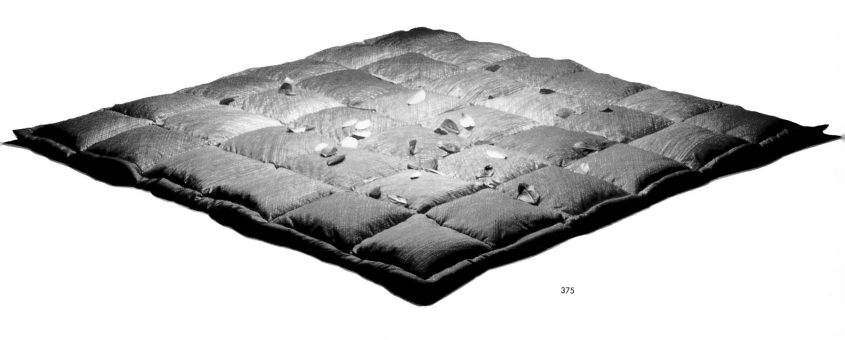

375

376

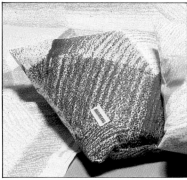

377

378

376 FUJIO ISHIMOTO
Fabric
Squared crayon-like design in browns
and black.
Manufacturer: Marimekko, Finland

377, 378 FUJIO ISHIMOTO
Fabric
Geometric design, filled in with crayon-
like colourings in shades of green, blue
and yellow.
Manufacturer: Marimekko, Finland

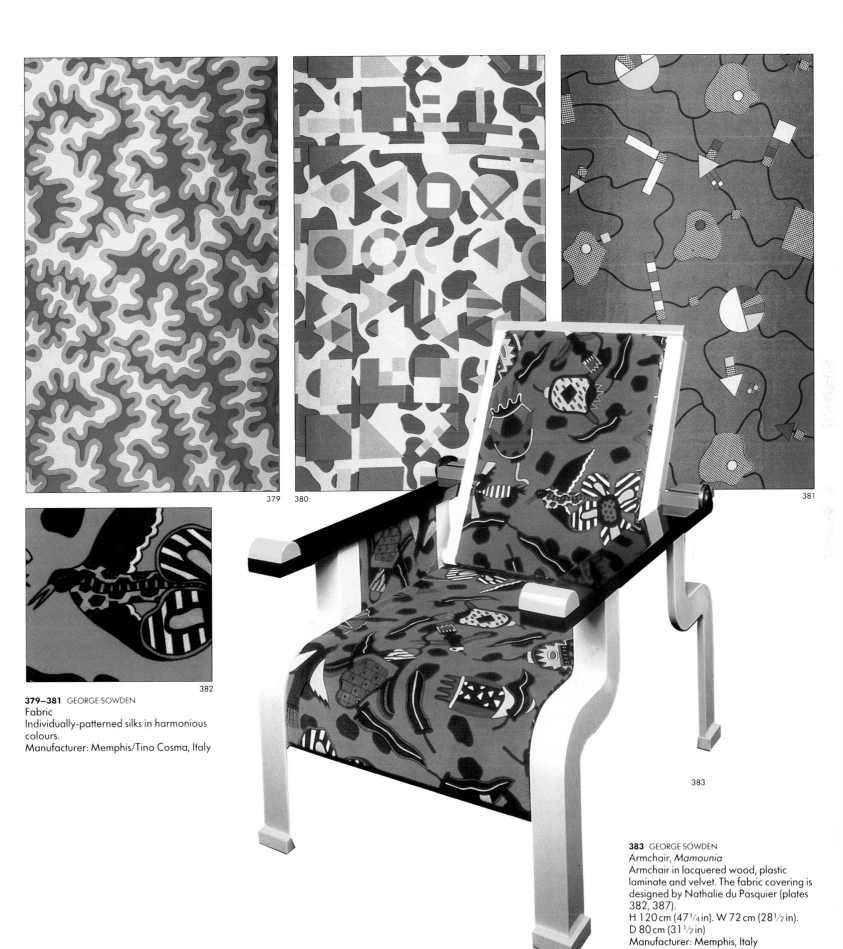

379 380

381

382

379-381 GEORGE SOWDEN
Fabric
Individually-patterned silks in harmonious colours.
Manufacturer: Memphis/Tino Cosma, Italy

383

383 GEORGE SOWDEN
Armchair, *Mamounia*
Armchair in lacquered wood, plastic laminate and velvet. The fabric covering is designed by Nathalie du Pasquier (plates 382, 387).
H 120 cm (47¼ in). W 72 cm (28½ in). D 80 cm (31½ in)
Manufacturer: Memphis, Italy

384, 385 GEORGE SOWDEN
Fabrics
Individually patterned silks in harmonious colours.
Manufacturer: Memphis/Tino Cosma, Italy

386 NATHALIE DU PASQUIER
Fabric
Brightly-patterned cotton – colourful motifs on a white background.
Manufacturer: Esprit, USA

387 NATHALIE DU PASQUIER
Fabric
Velvet patterned with flowers and birds in reds, pinks and mauves.
Manufacturer: Harriet Selling, Italy

388 NATHALIE DU PASQUIER
Fabric
Brightly-patterned polyester.
Manufacturer: Esprit, USA

389 NATHALIE DU PASQUIER
Fabric
Black and white checked silk overlaid with colourful geometric motifs.
Manufacturer: Memphis/Tino Cosma, Italy

390 NATHALIE DU PASQUIER
Fabric
Patterned polyester in greys, mauve and yellow.
Manufacturer: Esprit, USA

391 NATHALIE DU PASQUIER
Fabric
Mauve animals on plain blue silk overlaid with zigzag stripes.
Manufacturer: Memphis/Tino Cosma, Italy

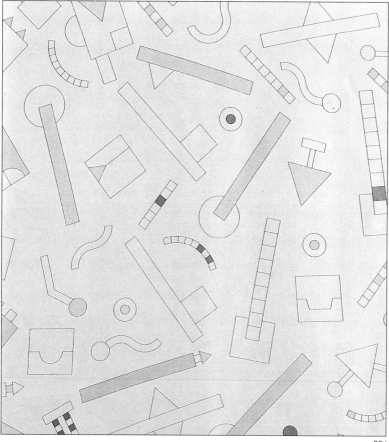

384

385

386

387

388

389

390

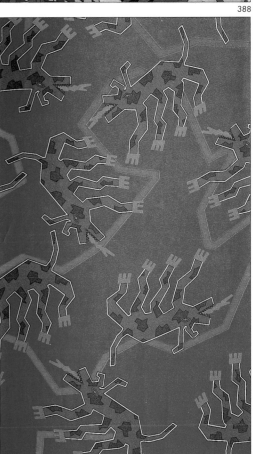

391

392

393

● Once they have escaped from the functional constraint of the floor, the window or the upholstered armchair, textiles take on an exotic new life as works of art, in which texture, structure, form and colour are seen as more important than function and durability. In Britain, with its notorious prejudice against manufacturing industry stretching back to Ruskin and Morris, wall hangings, though intrinsically useless, are often considered in some undefined way superior to the useful.

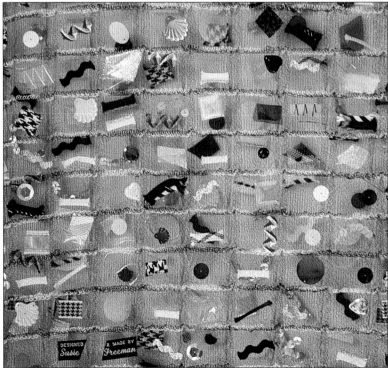

394

392, 393 MAISA TIKKANEN
Wall hangings, *Broken Red* and *Broken Blue*
Appliquéd squares of felted wool, multi-coloured or in shades of blue.
H 150 cm (59 in). L 200 cm (79 in)

394, 397 SUSIE FREEMAN
Wall hangings
Double-layer hangings in nylon monofilament and lurex astroyarn with knitted pockets containing braid, sequins, ribbon.
62 cm (24½ in) square
One-off

395

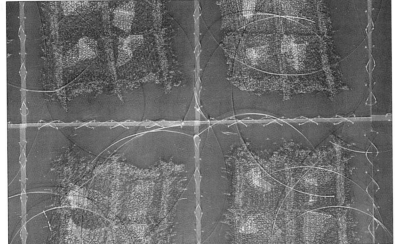

396

395 MICHAEL BRENNAND-WOOD
Wall hanging, *On the Way to a Little Way*
Tapestry in wood, wire, acrylics, thread
and fabric.
H 223.5 cm (88 in). W 320 cm (126 in)
One-off

396 SUSIE FREEMAN
Wall hanging
Detail of laminated iridescent wall piece
with pockets knitted in foil, laminated in
plastic and stitched with monofilament.
One-off

398 SUSIE FREEMAN
Fabric, *Pearly Queen*
Nylon monofilament with knitted pockets
containing braid, ribbon, beads, sequins,
yarn and paper.
One-off

397

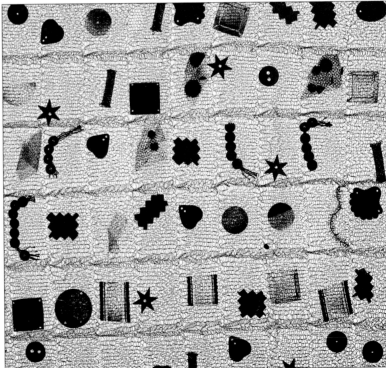

398

P R O D U C T S

Product design has in the past been a pragmatic affair. It has not had the philosophical underpinning of aesthetic or moral principle which has differentiated architecture from simple building. Instead, those who design products have tended to rely on an *ad hoc* adoption of the prevailing aesthetic vocabulary. In the nature of things, this vocabulary has tended to be shaped by architecture and architects, still the primary form givers, although this role has also now been adopted by engineers in the air and space industries and even by those who manufacture weapon systems. Both these areas — weapons and aero-space — have far more resources available to them than the architects of mere buildings; it is not surprising then to find designers adopting some of the more seductive of their imagery.

The crisis in the architectural community, the widespread loss of faith in the moral certainty of simple-minded functionalism, has taken a while to percolate through to product design. In many cases, product designers have gone on working in the same rationalist mode as they always have, putting everything from washing machines to radios in basically the same boxes, and ignoring the expressive possibilities of design. But the changing climate could not fail to affect them in the end, given that so many of the underlying assumptions of product design had come from those pioneers of modernism whose architectural theories were coming in for criticism. At the same time, technological advances have tended to substitute miniaturized microprocessor circuits for mechanical moving parts, thereby removing many of the functional constraints that had previously underpinned the formal types for various products. Many designers have begun to show a greater interest in the symbolic and expressive potential of products, leading them to look for alternatives to monochrome uniformity.

It is now taken for granted that a Japanese tape-recorder, for example — once considered miraculous, now a commonplace of electrical wizardry — will function well. There is no longer any need for designers to style a product in such a way as to reassure the consumer that it works efficiently. Instead, products are styled to look like playful toys, maximizing the potential for pleasure in manipulating their working parts. Pastel colours, highly tactile controls and eccentric typography have taken the place of brushed aluminium, aggressively textured knobs and a profusion of dials. The latter were once used to suggest precision and reliability: now that reassurance will often be off-putting to the increasingly sophisticated, visually attuned consumer. Many products look more playful, such as Sharp's ice-cream-coloured TV sets (plate 419). A wider range of colours and more expressive shapes are being deployed in the attempt to create more suggestive and saleable products.

399 RON ARAD
Hi-fi system
Hi-fi system in an outer covering of concrete. Includes
speakers, amplifier and deck.
Record player: H 7.5 cm (3 in). W 46 cm (18 in). D 38 cm
(15 in)
Manufacturer: One-Off, UK

400

• There is nothing particularly functional about the technocratic styling of the average audio system. Matt black, or even the teak-and-brushed-chrome look that preceded it, are decorative frills just like the ghetto-blaster flash or post-modern pastel.

Ron Arad has exposed the trick in a shocking way, presenting his hi-fi system — by encasing it in jagged concrete from which bits of reinforcing steel protrude — like some chunk from a half-demolished tower block. That the result looks so startling reveals the extent of our continuing if primitive enthralment by the 'miracle' of stereophonic sound: a high-precision box still reassures us that we will get a high-performance product.

But Arad takes a different view. 'The components these days are so sophisticated that you can do anything with them; they don't need a special box to protect them.' He buys the electronics for his systems from the large manufacturers, makes up special moulds, encases the fragile circuits in a waterproof resin, and casts the concrete around them.

400 RON ARAD
Hi-fi system
Hi-fi system in an outer covering of concrete. Includes speakers, amplifier and deck.
Record player: H 7.5 cm (3 in). W 46 cm (18 in). D 38 cm (15 in)
Speakers: H 89 cm (35 in). W 20 cm (8 in). D 20 cm (8 in)
Pre-amp with power amp: H 20 cm (8 in). W 30.5 cm (12 in). D 25 cm (10 in)
Manufacturer: One-Off, UK

401

401 GRAHAM THOMSON OF BRAND NEW
INDUSTRIAL DESIGN
Designer Range Stereo Headphones
Lightweight headphones with two-way
rotation and left and right identification in
Braille as well as lettering. A range of
three, for video and TV listening as well as
for stereo sound, they are simply adjusted
by moving the earpieces up and down the
headband.
H 16.5 cm (6½ in). W 6.4 cm (2½ in).
L 19 cm (7 in)
Manufacturer: Ross Electronics, UK

402, 403 GRAHAM THOMSON OF BRAND NEW
INDUSTRIAL DESIGN
Radio
Three-band radio, either home mains or
battery-operated. The controls, apart
from the on-off switch, are hidden behind
the facia. Available in four colours.
H 15 cm (6 in). L 22.4 cm (8¾ in). W 6.4 cm
(2½ in)
Manufacturer: Ross Electronics, UK

● Radios have been in production
for quite a while, but their use has
changed dramatically. Once the
radio occupied a position at the
centre of the home; later, it was the
turn of the TV set until the advent of
video and the multi-set household.
Now, according to Brand New, the
designers of Ross's portable radio,
people typically own several radios
too, and use one in each room.
Portability is thus not particularly
important. Nor is there much point in
celebrating the tuning equipment:
Brand New believe that, once tuned
to a particular station, users seldom
make further adjustments, simply
turning the set on to and off the
station of their choice — hence the
hinged flap, and the prominence
given to the on-off switch in their
design. It is an emphasis which was
first given to the Brionvega radio
developed by Marco Zanuso and
Richard Sapper in the late 1960s.
Brand New however have given the
Ross radio some fashionable 1950s
'retro' embellishments.

402

403

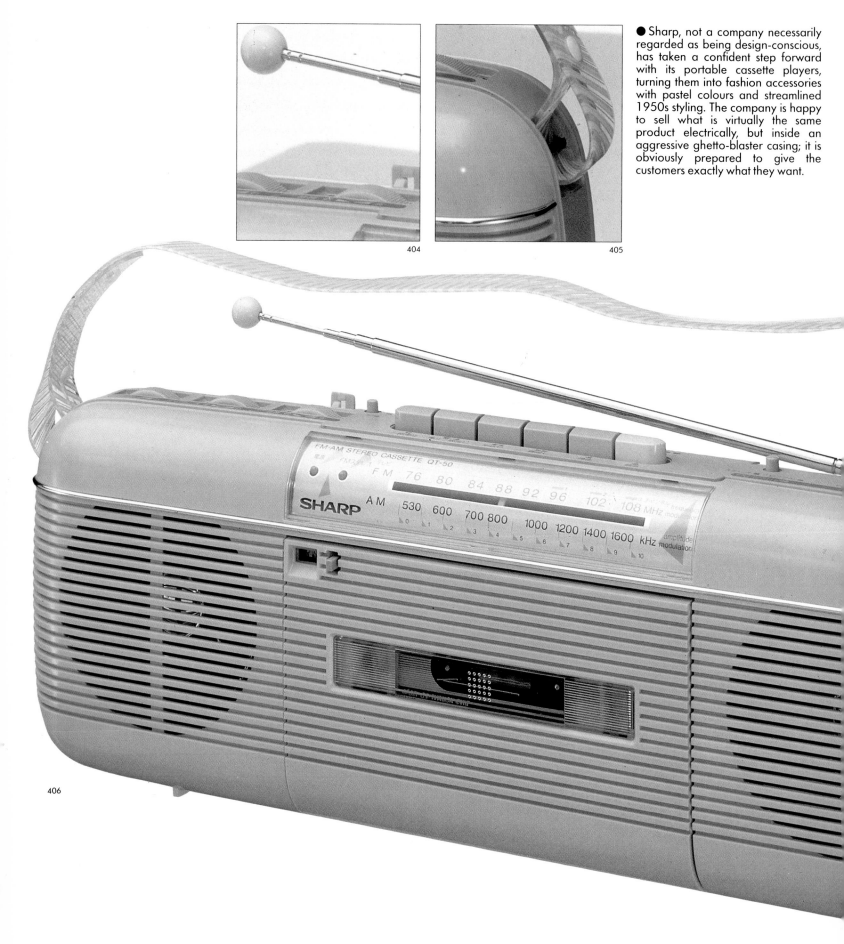

● Sharp, not a company necessarily regarded as being design-conscious, has taken a confident step forward with its portable cassette players, turning them into fashion accessories with pastel colours and streamlined 1950s styling. The company is happy to sell what is virtually the same product electrically, but inside an aggressive ghetto-blaster casing; it is obviously prepared to give the customers exactly what they want.

404

405

406

407

404–406 SHARP DESIGN SECTION
Cassette recorder, *QT-50*
Portable cassette recorder with capsule-like design comes in a range of ice-cream colours and has stereo sound for both radio and cassettes.
H 40.2 cm (15¾ in). W 13.7 cm (5⅜ in). D 8.1 cm (3⅛ in).
Weight: 2 kg (4 lb 6½ oz) including batteries
Manufacturer: Sharp, Japan

407 SONY DESIGN SECTION
Cassette player, *Sports Walkman*
Splashproof cassette tape player, designed for outdoor use.
L 9.65/9.77 cm (3¾/3⅞ in). W 3.58/3.76 cm (1⅜/1½ in).
D 1.16/1.17 cm (⅜/⅜ in). Weight 290/320 g
(10¼/11¼ oz) including batteries
Manufacturer: Sony, Japan

408 KAZUO KAWASAKI
Speaker system, *Culipeus*
Self-polarizing electrostatic speaker system. In plywood and faced with a lacquered finish, the speaker units are covered with dyed polyurethane foam.
H 135 cm (53 in). W 45 cm (17¾ in). D 43 cm (17 in)
Manufacturer: Maruichi Selling, Japan

409

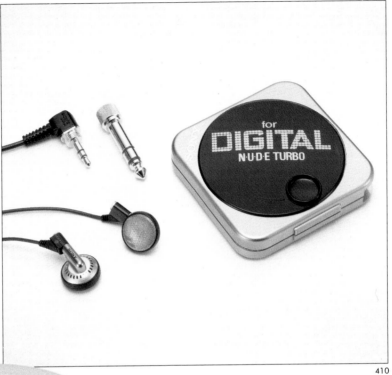

410

● 'Turbo', 'digital' and 'sports' have become crucial talismanic words, no longer found solely on the backs of cars but transferred to the context of miniature audio equipment, packaged here by Sony with typical Japanese flair.

409–411 SONY DESIGN SECTION
Headphones, *Nude Turbo 12*
Compact headphones in plastic and metal for cassette players, available in a fashionable range of colours.
Headphone: D 13.5 cm (5¼ in)
Manufacturer: Sony, Japan

411

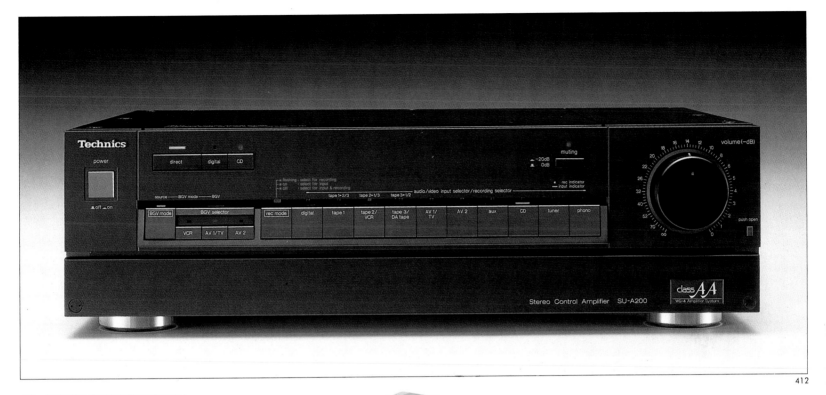

412

412 MATSUSHITA ELECTRIC DESIGN SECTION
Amplifier, *SU-AZ00*
Stereo control amplifier in aluminium.
H 12.5 cm (5 in). W 43 cm (17 in). L 36 cm (14 in)
Manufacturer: Matsushita Electric, Japan

● The compact disc player uses technology originally developed by Philips, who first sought high-quality sound transmission without risk of damage for video discs. Miniaturization of the equipment has posed a challenge for audio manufacturers, who have yet to develop a convincing identity for this new product — as Sony did with the *Walkman*, for example, right at the start. Technics, with its tradition of restrained technological imagery, has attempted the task by applying a discreet elegance.

413 MATSUSHITA ELECTRIC DESIGN SECTION
Compact disc player, *SL-XP7*
Portable compact disc player case in die-cast plastic.
H 58 cm (23 in). W 137 cm (5½ in).
L 15 cm (6 in)
Manufacturer: Matsushita Electric, Japan

413

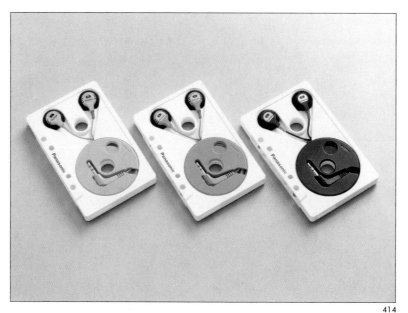

414

● Sony's development of the *Walk-man* was a brilliant move, boosting flagging sales by 'inventing' the combination of a miniature recorder with lightweight headphones. The original *Walkman* did not even record. Sony treated it as a piece of jewellery, meant to be worn conspicuously, with tactile controls and spongy orange headphones.

Since then all Sony's competitors have made cosmetic graphic additions. Toshiba have gone further than most, frankly turning their version into a fashion accessory. The same product comes in a choice of nursery colours, with decorative shapes for the controls.

414 PANASONIC
Cassette headphones, *EAH Z18*
Ultra-light headphones stored in a cassette-style case. They can be kept in the cassette box compartment of a recorder/player. Available in three colours.
Weight 4.5 g (⅛ oz)
Manufacturer: Panasonic, Japan

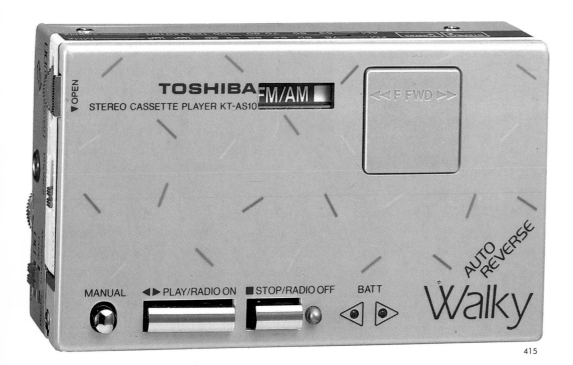

415

415–417 TOSHIBA DESIGN DEPT
Walky Headphone Stereo Cassette Player
Slim-line cassette and radio player available in a variety of finishes.
L 11.85/11.85/11.6/11.6/10.35/12.4 cm ($4\frac{5}{8}$/$4\frac{5}{8}$/$4\frac{1}{2}$/$4\frac{1}{2}$/$4\frac{1}{8}$/$4\frac{7}{8}$ in).
W 7.8/8.35/8.35/8.5/8.7/8.8 cm ($3\frac{1}{8}$/$3\frac{1}{4}$/$3\frac{1}{4}$/$3\frac{3}{8}$/$3\frac{3}{8}$/$3\frac{1}{2}$ in).
D 3.55/3.55/2.95/3.05/3.2/4.1 cm ($1\frac{3}{8}$/$1\frac{3}{8}$/$1\frac{1}{8}$/$1\frac{1}{8}$/$1\frac{1}{4}$/$1\frac{5}{8}$ in).
Weight 290/295/255/250/200/310 g ($10\frac{1}{4}$/$10\frac{1}{4}$/9/$8\frac{3}{4}$/$7\frac{1}{8}$/$10\frac{7}{8}$ oz)
Manufacturer: Toshiba, Japan

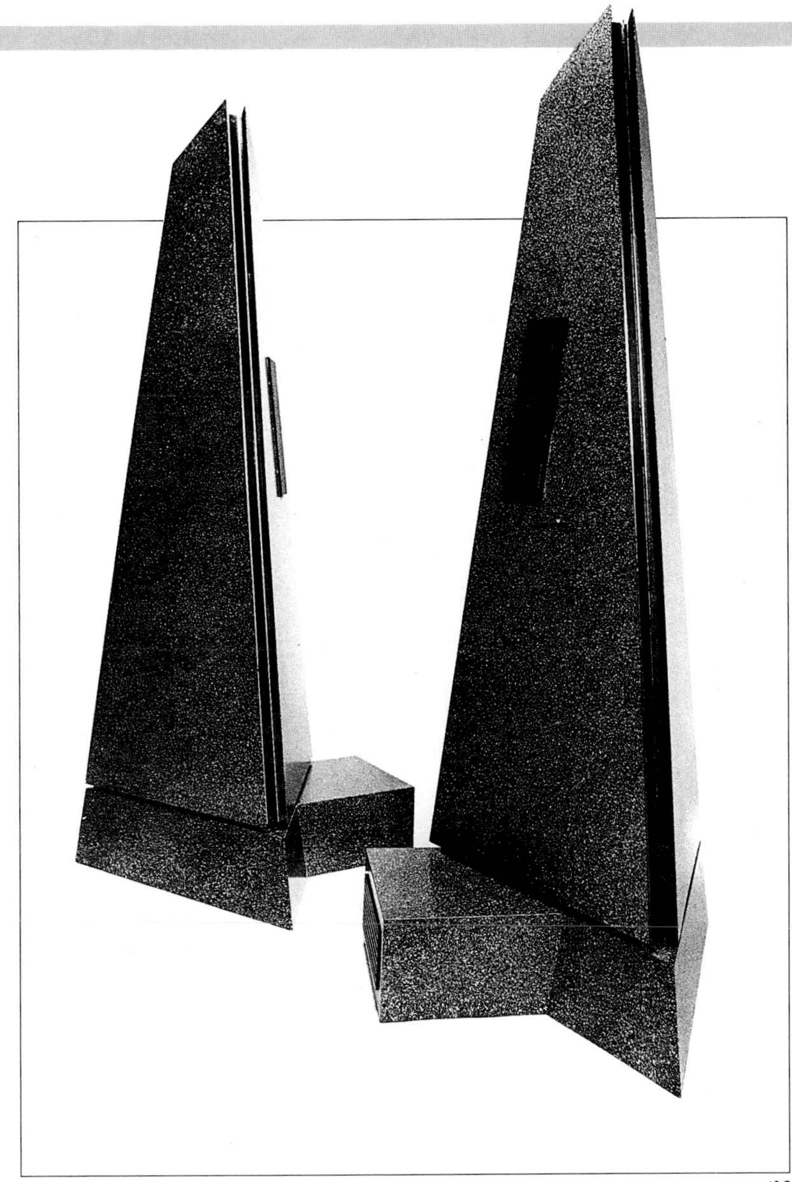

418

418 SIMON CONDER
Loudspeakers, *Amadeo*
In medium-density fibreboard, these speakers are shaped to produce the best sound; less volume at the top and more volume at the wider base. The grille is set at a 30° angle to the back wall.
H 150 cm (59 in)
Manufacturer: Amadeo, UK

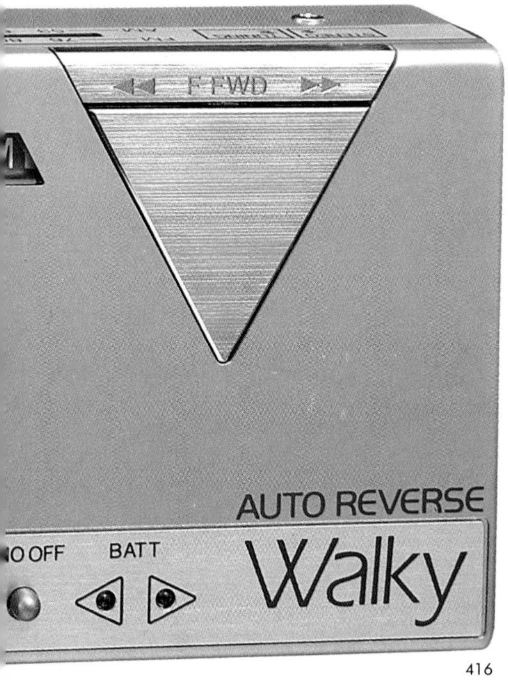

416

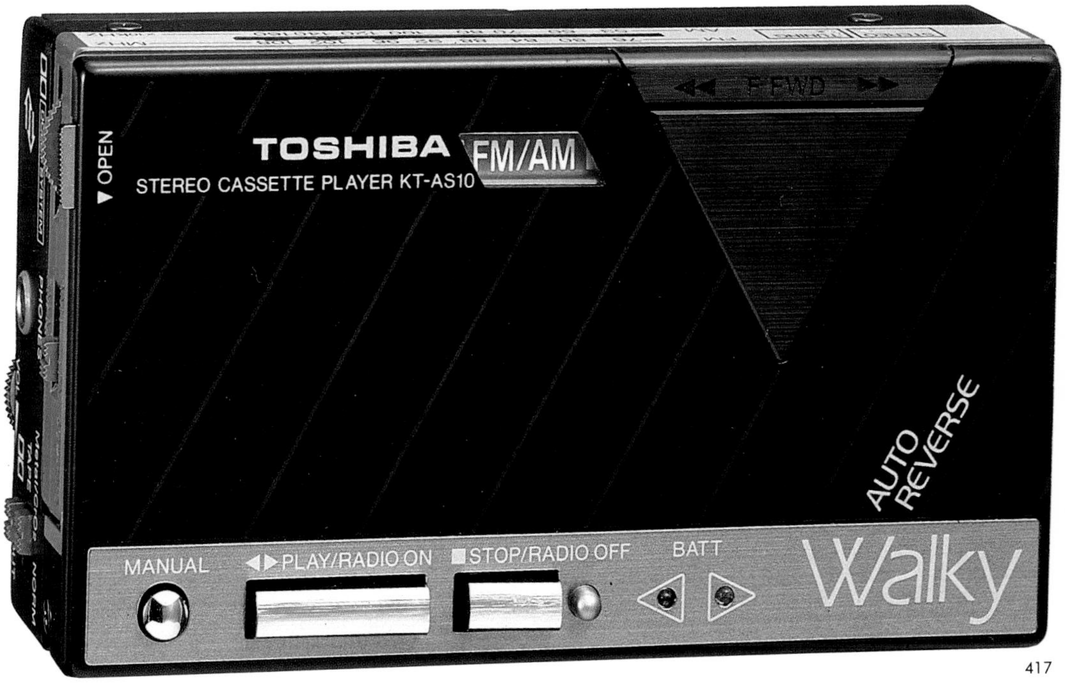

417

419

● The toy-like quality of Sharp's products is especially pronounced in their portable colour TV sets, small enough to fit into a coat pocket. Once Japanese goods were deemed cheap but unreliable compared with their Western competitors, and therefore had to be styled to look technocratic and efficient. Now performance is taken for granted, allowing the designer room for manoeuvre.

419 SHARP DESIGN SECTION
TV, 4C-P1
Colour TV, for use with batteries or to plug in to the mains.
Comes either with a stand or a hand carrier and is
available in a range of five colours.
Screen size: 10 cm (4 in)
Manufacturer: Sharp, Japan

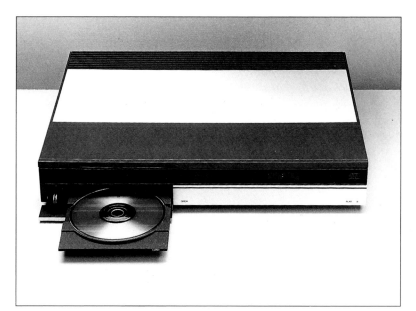

420

420 BANG & OLUFSEN
Compact disc player, *Beogram CD 50*
Part of a wider system, this player can be used by itself. It has its own remote control unit, and comes in an aluminium cabinet.
H 7.5 cm (3 in). W 42 cm (16½ in).
D 32.5 cm (13 in)
Manufacturer: Bang & Olufsen, Denmark

421

421 BANG & OLUFSEN
Compact disc player, *Beogram CDX*
Incorporating many important features, including laser technology, and housed in an aluminium cabinet.
H 7.5 cm (3 in). W 42 cm (16½ in).
D 31 cm (12 in)
Manufacturer: Bang & Olufsen, Denmark

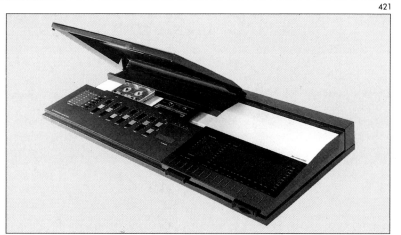

422

422 BANG & OLUFSEN
Music centre, *Beocentre 4000*
Two cassette decks and a tuner/amplifier in a metallic grey cabinet.
H 9.5 cm (3¾ in). W 64 cm (25 in).
D 33 cm (13 in)
Manufacturer: Bang & Olufsen, Denmark

423 HEINZ JUNGER
TV, Loewe Art 1
Large flat-screen red TV in wooden case.
H 95.5 cm (37½ in). D 46.5 cm (18 in).
W 64.5 cm (25 in)
Manufacturer: Loewe Opta, West
Germany

● Bang & Olufsen of Denmark realized early in their history that their only chance of survival in the highly competitive world of audio equipment was to commit themselves to distinctive design as well as to technological excellence. Initially they produced only radios, but have subsequently moved into record players and TV sets; they are now matching the Japanese and Dutch with their own versions of every technological improvement, such as the compact disc player (see page 189).

Bang & Olufsen use a number of designers, but all their products exhibit that starkly beautiful genre of Danish design that comes close to being Japanese in its intensity. Jakob Jensen produced the earlier rectilinear designs, and his work is still used by the company; but the new *MX 2000* TV set, the most impressive of the new products, is designed by David Lewis. Available in a variety of colours, it reduces all distractions from the screen image to a minimum. Lewis has moved on from Jensen's technocratic rectilinear style, to give electrical products a more sculptural form.

424 BANG & OLUFSEN
TV, MX 2000
Flat-screen TV in red or black case, with covered control panel designed for floor use.
Screen size: 50.8 cm (20 in)
Manufacturer: Bang & Olufsen, Denmark

● Seiko have taken the opposite tack from Sharp with their miniature TV set, choosing to ignore the playful possibilities of the product and instead adopting a relatively serious matt black casing.

423

424

425

426 MATSUSHITA ELECTRIC DESIGN SECTION
TV, *Alphatube Monitor TH28-DM03*
Monitor-style TV, with flat screen and grey
exterior.
Screen size 71 cm (28 in)
Manufacturer: Matsushita Electric, Japan

427 MASAYUKI KUROKAWA
Tape cutter, *Metal Wave*
Stainless-steel desk-top tape cutter
H 6 cm (2½ in). L 20 cm (8 in). W 11 cm
(4½ in)
Manufacturer: Daichi, Japan

426

425 SEIKO DESIGN SECTION
TV, *My Channel*
Pocket-size, portable, battery-operated
TV in plastic, with built-in alarm clock.
H 11.3 cm (4½ in). W 7.2 cm (3 in).
L 2.1 cm (¾ in)
Manufacturer: Hattori Seiko, Japan

427

● Enzo Mari is one of those Italian designers for whom, paradoxically, the very act of designing is problematic. When invited to take part in 1972 in the 'Italy: The New Domestic Landscape' exhibition at the New York Museum of Modern Art, he refused to create an environment, choosing instead to make a political 'anti-design' statement in the space allotted to him, and claiming that 'The only correct undertaking for "artists" is that of language research — that is, critical examination of the communication systems now in use.' He explained his continued practice of design with difficulty: 'The profession to which I belong must rely solely on formal quality for its patronage and hence for its survival.' Mari has nonetheless worked for Bruno Danese's company since it was founded, producing many exquisite household objects of formal excellence but minimal social content of the kind that he appears to be advocating. However, these apparent inconsistencies are no reason to decry the quality of his work, typified here by his most recent set of moulded glass products.

430

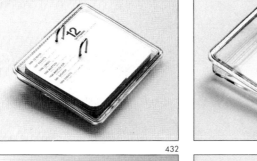

429

428–438 ENZO MARI
Desk set, *Salina*
In moulded glass, either transparent or frosted: paper-holder, pencil-holder, table calendar, tray and ashtray. Desk pad in leather and felt, and paper-knife in polished steel.
Paper-holder: H 12.5 cm (5 in). L 18.5 cm (7¼ in). W 14 cm (5½ in)
Pencil-holder: H 4 cm (1½ in). L 18.5 cm (7¼ in). W 29 cm (11½ in)

428

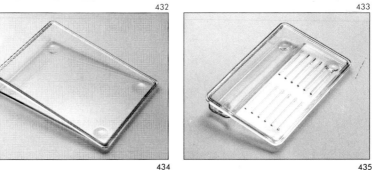

432

433

434

435

436

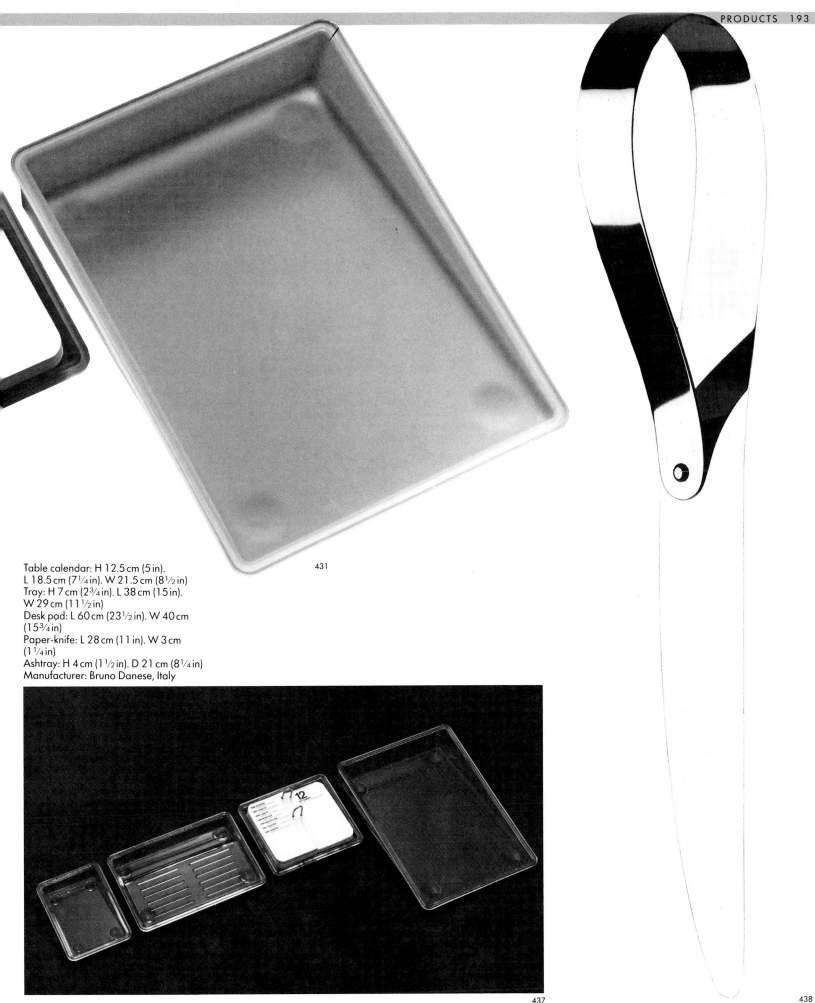

431

Table calendar: H 12.5 cm (5 in).
L 18.5 cm (7¼ in). W 21.5 cm (8½ in)
Tray: H 7 cm (2¾ in). L 38 cm (15 in).
W 29 cm (11½ in)
Desk pad: L 60 cm (23½ in). W 40 cm
(15¾ in)
Paper-knife: L 28 cm (11 in). W 3 cm
(1¼ in)
Ashtray: H 4 cm (1½ in). D 21 cm (8¼ in)
Manufacturer: Bruno Danese, Italy

437

438

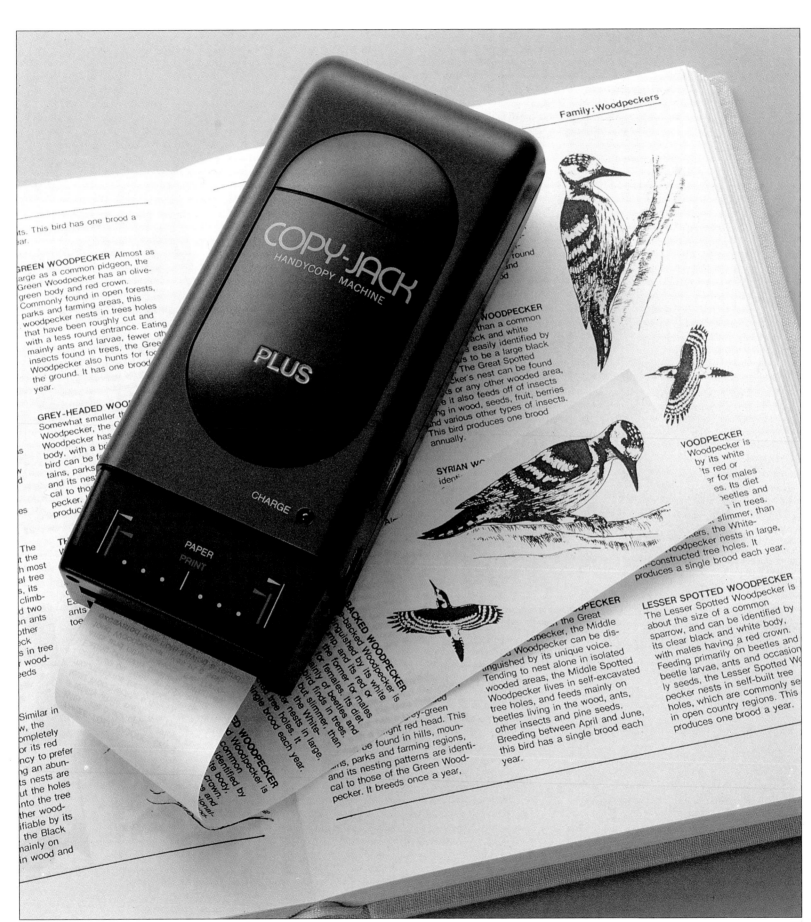

439 PLUS DESIGN SECTION
Photocopier, *Copy-Jack*
Hand-held, powered by a rechargeable battery.
H 17.2 cm (6¾ in). W 7.1 cm (2¾ in). L 4.7 cm (2 in)
Manufacturer: Plus, Japan

440 MARIANNE BRANDT
Ashtray
Two-piece ashtray in polished brass or stainless steel.
H 5.5 cm (2¼ in). D 11 cm (4½ in)
Manufacturer: Alessi, Italy

440

● The habit of re-editioning classic modern furniture has spread into other areas of design. Marianne Brandt's ashtray, now manufactured for the first time, by Alessi, was designed in the 1920s when she was teaching at the Bauhaus.

● The Plus Corporation has specialized in turning supposedly mundane items of equipment into covetable consumer goods. It draws on the Japanese tradition of highly imaginative packaging, creating pocket cases for miniature scissors or other accessories (page 205) to command premium prices. A matching set exploits the magpie instincts that lurk in many grown-up children (page 186). Plus's products all have a toy-like quality. Its newest product, however, the *Copy-Jack*, goes beyond refined finish and intelligent use of colour. The size of a pocket camera, it can produce photocopies on a continuous strip of paper. It was an instant success when launched in early 1986, with sales of fifty thousand in two months. The styling, clearly influenced by the *Olympus XA* series, has a lot to do with that.

441

443 MICHIKO CHIKANO
Pencil/pen set, *P's Bar*
Set of five: ballpoint pens, pencil and marking pen in a carrying case. The case top also acts as a stand for use on a desk. Available in a variety of colours.
Case: H 12.6 cm (5 in). W 6.4 cm (2½ in). L 1.6 cm (⅝ in)
Manufacturer: Plus, Japan

441, 442 MOGGRIDGE/ID TWO
Telephone, *Telenova 1*
Grey plastic slim-line desk telephone.
Manufacturer: Telenova, USA

442

443

444

444 PDD LTD
Exect 100 Portable Computer
The portable computer case is made from three aluminium
extrusions. It folds up to protect the screen and keyboard.
H 4.4 cm (1 ½ in). L 29.7 cm (11 ¾ in). W 22.7 cm (9 in)
Manufacturer: Dawn Systems, UK

● One of the Italian electrical appliance company Zanussi's designers, Andries van Onck, once described the millions of so-called 'white goods' — refrigerators, washing machines and ovens — as a 'Niagara of white cubes falling over Europe', adding, 'We don't want those things to be ugly cubes, do we?'

Roberto Pezzetta's work for Zanussi — a company now owned by Electrolux of Sweden, but still one of the best-known mass-market names in Europe — illustrates one set of solutions to the design problem. Pezzetta concentrates most of his attention on those parts of the machine to be touched by users, radiusing the edges, treating the control panels carefully, and thus imparting character to what would otherwise be simple-minded cubes.

445

● A delayed effect of the break-up of the world's tele-communications monopolies, from British Telecom to Bell and AT&T, has been the proliferation of consumer-oriented telephone equipment. The initial reaction against total standardization of products — from the time when telephones were treated more as pieces of scientific equipment than as consumer items — was a descent into kitsch: telephones shaped like Coke cans, and models of Mickey Mouse. Now things have settled down, and a large number of electronics equipment manufacturers, for the first time easily able to reach consumer markets, are beginning to use design. Antti Nurmesniemi's handset for Fujitsu demonstrates the trend.

446

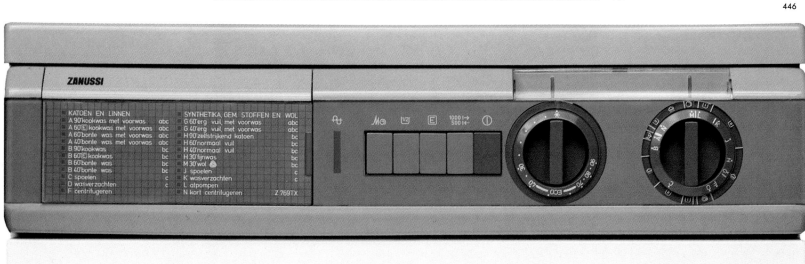

447

445, 446 ROBERTO PEZZETTA
Washing machines
Control panels from co-ordinated ranges
of household electrical equipment.
Manufacturer: Zanussi Elettrodomestici,
Italy

447, 448 ANTTI NURMESNIEMI
Antti Telephone
Slim-line push-button telephone in a
variety of colours.
Manufacturer: Fujitsu, Japan

448

449 CANON
Camera, *Canon T80*
Single-lens reflex 35 mm camera.
14.1 cm (5½ in) by 10.2 cm (4 in) by
5.47 cm (2⅛ in). Weight 605 g (21½ oz)
Manufacturer: Canon, Japan

449

● Kenneth Grange is a founder member of the Pentagram design consultancy. Apart from such large-scale projects as the styling for British Rail's high-speed passenger train, he has worked for a long period for the Wilkinson razor company — originally a firm which manufactured swords. His work on safety razors has helped the company to meet the growing challenge from international competition in a crowded market. By making a conventional razor an object that is a pleasure to handle, Wilkinson are able to counter the cost advantages of cheaper, throw-away products.

450

450 KENNETH GRANGE
Kompakt Razor
Made in polypropylene, this razor carries spare blades in the handle.
H 11.6 cm (4½ in). L 2.8 cm (1 in). W 4 cm (1½ in)
Manufacturer: Wilkinson Sword, UK

451 KENNETH GRANGE
Profile Razor
The bonded blade system incorporates a sophisticated mechanism for picking up and disposing of blades. Made from high-density polystyrene.
H 12.6 cm (5 in). L 2.5 cm (1 in). W 3.9 cm (1½ in)
Manufacturer: Wilkinson Sword, UK

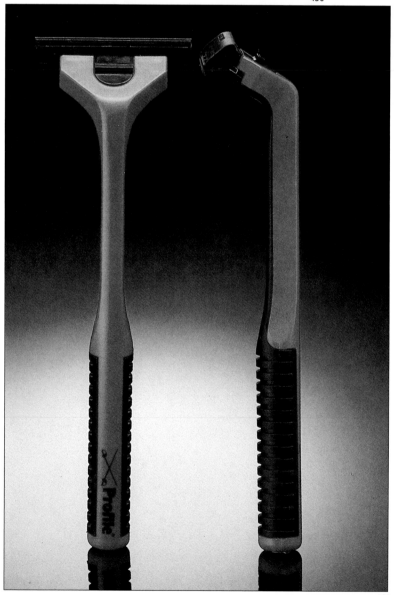

451

452 BLACK & DECKER
Vacuum cleaner, *Dustbuster*
This self-charging vacuum cleaner mounts on the wall beside a normal plug ready for re-charging when not in use.
L 44 cm (17¼ in). W 16 cm (6¼ in). D 12 cm (4¾ in)
Manufacturer: Black & Decker, USA

453, 454 BLACK & DECKER
Cordless drill/screwdriver
Complete in a carrying case with screws and drill bits, when not in use it can be left permanently on charge in its case. The drill has forward and reverse functions.
L 36 cm (14 in). W 31 cm (12¼ in). Handle 8 cm (3¼ in)
Manufacturer: Black & Decker, USA

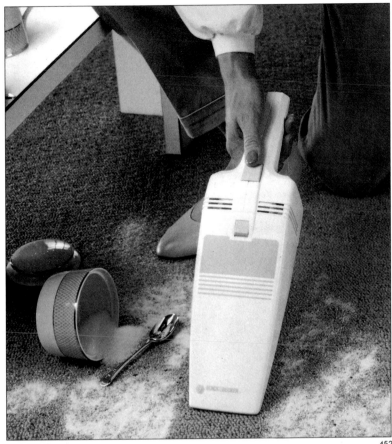

452

453

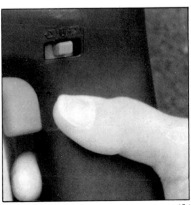

454

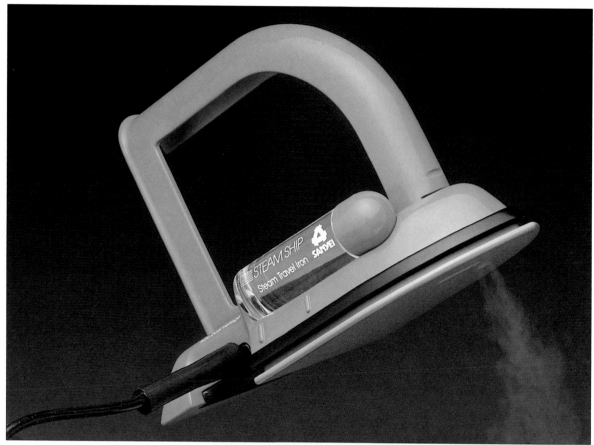

455

455, 456 SMART DESIGN
Iron, *Steam Ship Travel Iron*
The iron has a polycarbonate shell and
handle and a non-stick coated metal sole
plate.
H 11 cm (4½ in). L 19.5 cm (7¾ in).
W 5 cm (2 in)
Manufacturer: Sanyei America, USA

456

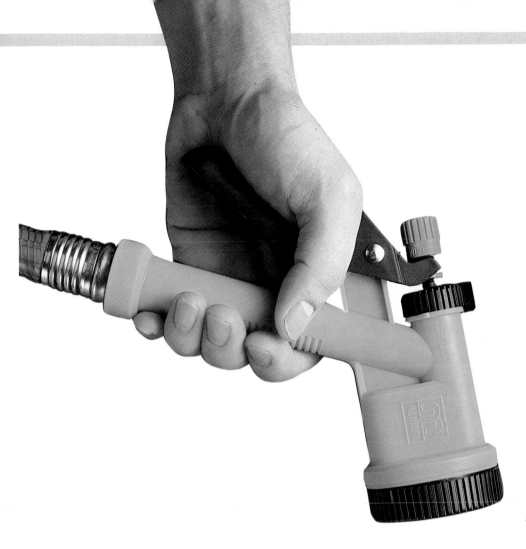

457

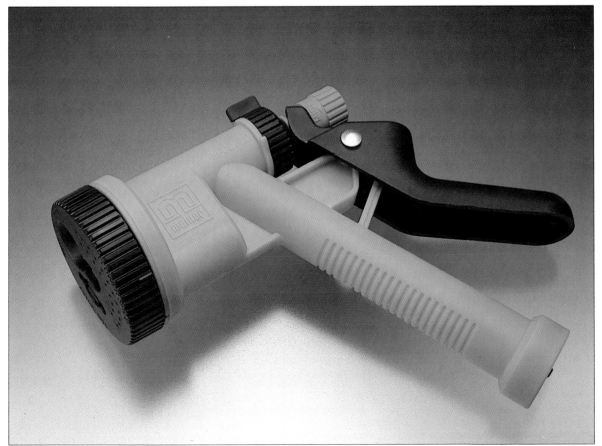

458

457, 458 JEFFREY KAPEC AND KAZUNA TANAKA
Aqua gun
Water spray gun in polypropylene. Easy-to-hold pistol grip with variable water control.
H 14 cm (5½ in). L 17 cm (6 in). W 2.5 cm (1 in)
Manufacturer: Melnor Industries, USA

459

459 CITIZEN DESIGN DEPT
Vega Vivi Digital Watch
Digital quartz watch on two-tone strap.
Manufacturer: Citizen, Japan

460 PORSCHE DESIGN
Watch, *Ultra Sport*
Sports watch with black face.
Manufacturer: Porsche Design, Austria

460

461 PLUS DESIGN SECTION
Scissors, *Pic and Nic*
Set comprising small scissors and paper-
knife, in stainless steel with plastic caps.
Scissors: L 7.8 cm (3 in)
Paper-knife: L 8.5 cm (3¼ in)
Manufacturer: Plus, Japan

462 RICHARD SATHERLEY
Travelling Steam Iron
H 5.7 cm (2¼ in). W 7.5 cm (3 in).
L 18.3 cm (7¼ in)
Prototype
Manufacturer: Dymension Models, UK

461

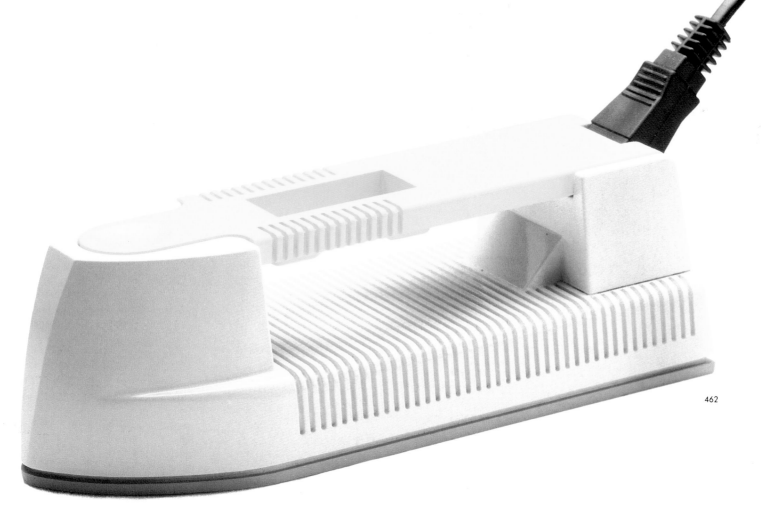

462

● The Swiss Watch Company — generally known as Swatch — is an illuminating example of a European company which has successfully fought the flood of cheap Far Eastern competition into its traditional market.

Though it was the English entre-preneur Clive Sinclair who produced the world's first throw-away-priced quartz watch in the early 1970s, the Japanese quickly followed, and seized dominance of the world mass market for watches from the Swiss. Traditionally-minded Swiss manu-facturers made what they regarded as the only possible response and clung on to the premium end of the market, producing highly priced, conservatively styled pieces. Swatch on the other hand saw such moves as short-sighted, and instead capitalized on the transformation wrought by the Japanese, turning watches into dis-posable fashion items and producing a stream of different designs. These they have marketed with wit and subtlety, sustaining design input so that ever newer watches continue to reach the shops, and relying on consumers' fickleness: once tired of the matt black Swatch or the Haring graffiti Swatch, they keep coming back for more.

464

463–465 SWATCH
Watches
Quartz watches with plastic faces and
straps. The internal working parts remain
the same but the designs of the faces
(either large or small) change every six
months with the latest fashions.
Manufacturer: Swatch, Switzerland

465

466

467

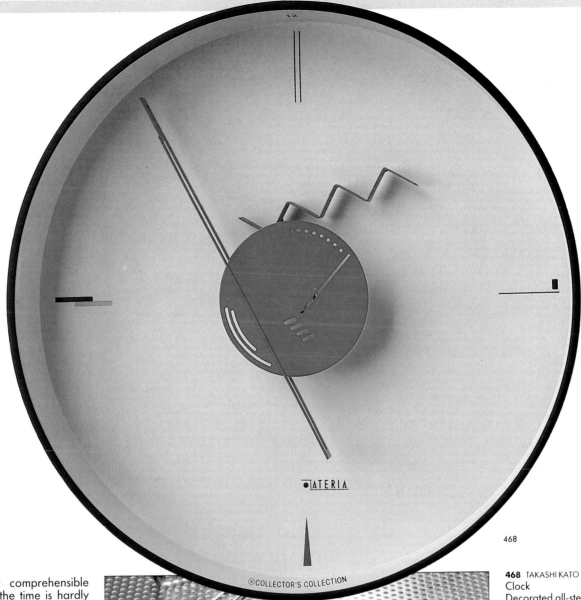

468

● Imparting easily comprehensible information about the time is hardly the point of this series of clocks. They do however demonstrate the ease with which Japanese designers have appropriated historical traditions, from constructivism to Memphis, to their own decorative ends.

466 TAKASHI KATO
Clock
Steel with a curved yellow face and orange base, joined with a swivelling rod, allowing the face to be moved into a variety of positions. Battery-powered.
H 28.5 cm (11¼ in). W 12.5 cm (4⅞ in)
Manufacturer: Ateria, Japan

467 TAKASHI KATO
Clock
One of a selection of clocks in a variety of colours with plastic faces and steel stands on which the head pivots.
H 35 cm (13¾ in). W 16.2 cm (6⅜ in)
Manufacturer: Ateria, Japan

468 TAKASHI KATO
Clock
Decorated all-steel wall clock with circular face and central pivot holding one hand. Marked on the central pivot for the hour hand.
Diameter 21.3 cm (8⅜ in). Depth 5.2 cm (2⅛ in)
Manufacturer: Ateria, Japan

469 TAKASHI KATO
Clock
Clock with solid steel base and enclosed plastic top, exposing face and hands.
H 10.4 cm (4⅛ in). D 8.7 cm (3⅜ in)
Manufacturer: Ateria, Japan

469

470

470 MICHAEL KOMAR
Kettle, *Highline*
Microchip jug kettle in white with blue lid and wide spout.
H 26 cm (10¼ in). W 10.8 cm (4½ in)
Manufacturer: T.I. Russell Hobbs, UK

471–473 ROBERT VENTURI
Tray, *Campidoglio*
Stainless-steel tray mechanically
engraved with galvanic gold-plating.
L 46 cm (18 in). W 38 cm (15 in)
Manufacturer: Alessi, Italy

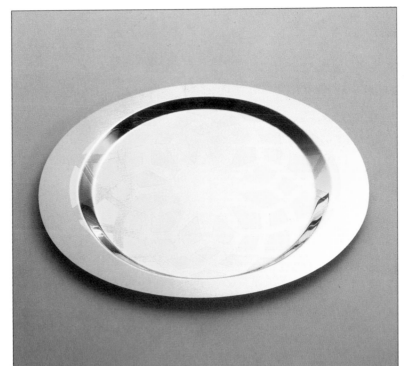

471

472

473

● The long-established Alessi Company has recently invested ever greater efforts in engaging stars of architecture and design to endow the most mundane of household objects with formal significance. Sometimes the result has considerable success, as with Michael Graves's bird-equipped kettle, a post-modern riposte to Richard Sapper's modernist design of 1984 (also for Alessi). Robert Venturi is the architect recently appointed to construct a new extension to the National Gallery in London in Trafalgar Square. He has resorted to the pattern used by Michelangelo on the floor of his Campidoglio piazza in Rome in an attempt to add significance to his tray for Alessi (page 211).

474

474, 476 MASSIMO MOROZZI
Pasta set
Stainless-steel pasta cooker, with an outer
saucepan, inner perforated holder and lid
with knob. Each compartment has two
heat-proof handles.
H 30 cm (12 in). D 23 cm (9 in). Capacity
5 litres (11 pts)
Manufacturer: Alessi, Italy

475 MICHAEL GRAVES
Kettle
Stainless-steel kettle with blue polyamide
handle and red whistle in the shape of a
bird.
Capacity 2.27 litres (4 pints)
Manufacturer: Alessi, Italy

475

476

477

477 IVAN CHERMAYEFF AND MILTON GLASER
Toy boxes
In papier-mâché and fabric, for the
'Golden Eye' exhibition at the Cooper-
Hewitt Museum.
Prototypes

478 MASAYUKI KUROKAWA
Gas rice-cooker
In enamelled steel and painted aluminium,
this enclosed rice-cooker has a bright
yellow plastic release button.
H 25.5 cm (10 in). Internal D 29.5 cm
(11½ in). External D 32.5 cm (12¾ in)
Manufacturer: Paloma Industries, Japan

478

● The Golden Eye is a studio and information centre in India, organized by the Indian designer Rajiv Sethi. With the help of government and private funds, he has imported a number of American and European designers to supply the ideas for pieces capable of production by Indian craftsmen and artisans and likely to find a Western outlet. The motivation is partly economic, but it is also a cultural enterprise. Craftsmen who once made artefacts for temples and for themselves, are now increasingly dominated by the demands of the tourist trade, producing what Sethi calls 'the ethnic bric-a-brac and junk that India is now known for'. When swords were still the weapons of battle, inlaid damascene work could make them things of beauty. Now much of such ornament is simply kitsch; so Frei Otto, the celebrated German architect, has designed a range of cutlery for the damascene workers to make. Ettore Sottsass has designed knives, and Ivan Chermayeff and Milton Glaser a set of toy boxes.

479 ETTORE SOTTSASS JR
Knives
Steel, with shaped blades and handles, designed for the 'Golden Eye' exhibition at the Cooper-Hewitt Museum.
Prototypes

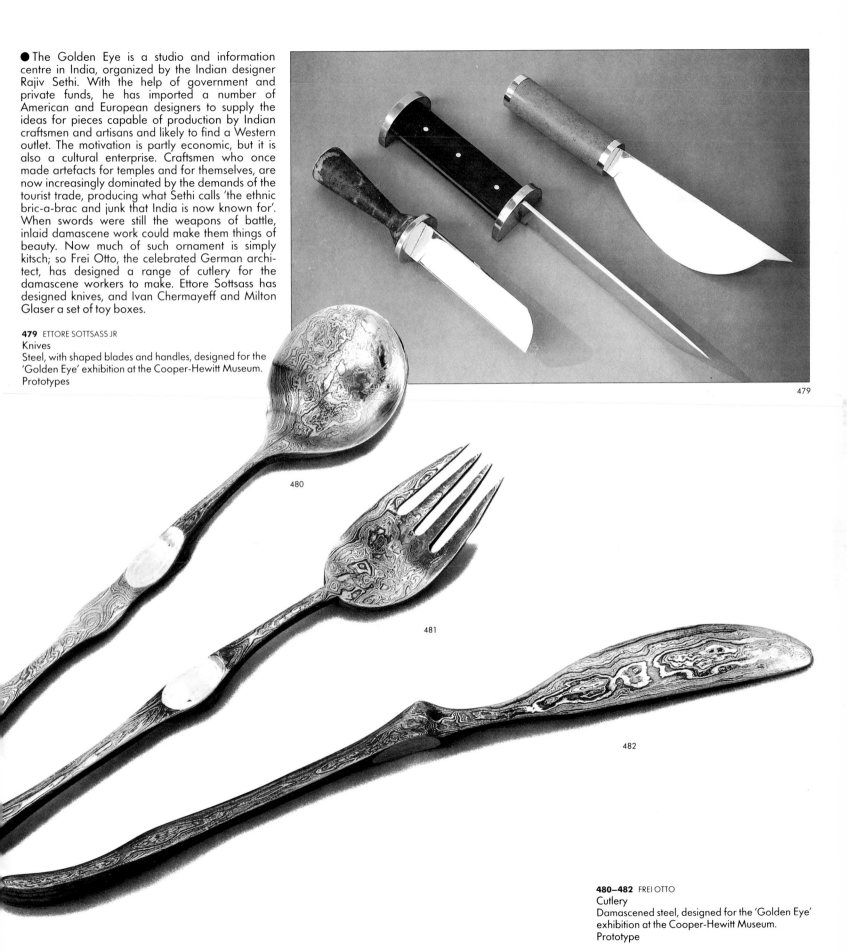

479

480

481

482

480–482 FREI OTTO
Cutlery
Damascened steel, designed for the 'Golden Eye' exhibition at the Cooper-Hewitt Museum.
Prototype

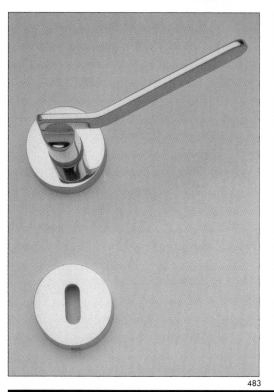

483

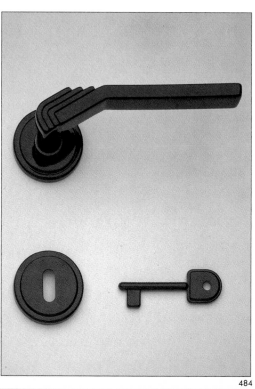

484

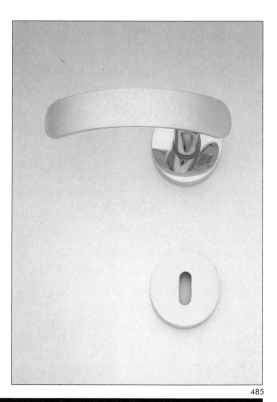

485

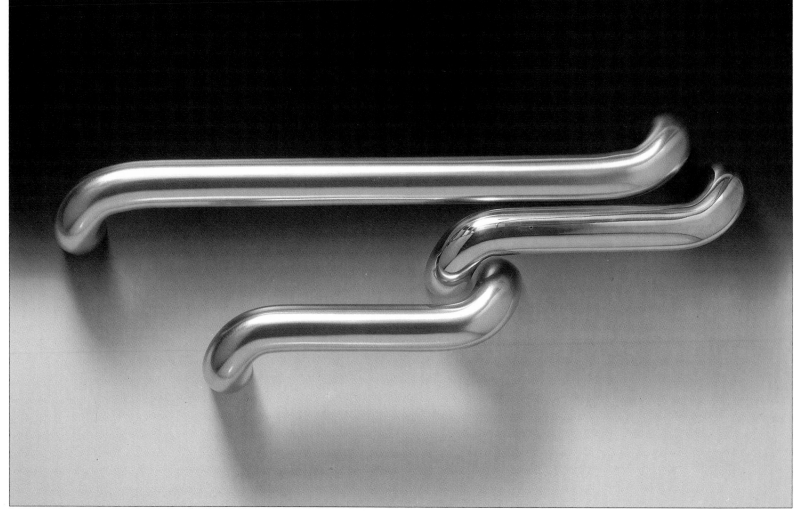

486

487

488

489

483 ACHILLE CASTIGLIONI
Door furniture, *Cinque C*
Brass with round base plate and lever
handle.
Handle: L 12.5 cm (5 in)
Plate: D 4.5 cm (1¾ in)
Manufacturer: Fusital, Italy

484 SOTTSASS ASSOCIATI
Door furniture, *H 38 R8*
In cast brass with black finish. Available
with all fitments including keys.
Handle: L 13.1 cm (5¼ in).
Plate: D 4.5 cm (1¾ in)
Manufacturer: Fusital, Italy

485 VICO MAGISTRETTI
Door furniture, *Quattro M*
Brass with round base plate and curved
lever handle.
Handle: L 13.1 cm (5¼ in)
Plate: D 4.5 cm (1¾ in)
Manufacturer: Fusital, Italy

486 ALAN TYE DESIGN
Door furniture, *Allgood Modric Quaver*
Anodized aluminium and polished brass,
available in a large range of colours and
finishes. The handles can be fixed either
back-to-back or singly.
Handle: L 15.2/22.8/30.5 cm (6/9/12 in)
Plate: D 2 cm (¾ in)
Manufacturer: G & S Allgood, UK

487 ANDRIES AND HIROKO VAN ONCK
Door furniture, *Tokio*
Brass with chrome or epoxy finish. The
nylon button covering the fixing hole acts
as a bumper when the door opens.
L 7 cm (3 in). W 4 cm (1½ in)
Manufacturer: Olivari, Italy

488 ANDRIES AND HIROKO VAN ONCK
Door furniture
Lever door-handle on circular base and
keyhole in chrome finish.
Handle: L 12.3 cm (4¾ in).
Plate: D 4.3 cm (1¾ in)
Manufacturer: Olivari, Italy

489 ANDRIES AND HIROKO VAN ONCK
Door furniture
Die-cast brass lever door-handle and
keyhole.
Handle: L 12.3 cm (4¾ in).
Plate: W 4 cm (1½ in). L 14.3 cm (5⅝ in)
Manufacturer: Olivari, Italy

490 JEFFREY KAPEC AND KAZUNA TANAKA
Ultra-safe thermostatic and pressure
balance shower valve. Designed for totally
safe operation, to guard against
accidental scalding or shock.
17.1 cm (6¾ in) square
Manufacturer: T & S Brass and Bronze
Works, USA

490

491

491, 493 DAVIDE MERCATALI AND PAOLO
PEDRIZZETTI
Tap/mixer, *HI-FI*
One-hole washbasin mixer with pop-up
plug and single control lever. In brass, it
comes in two finishes, chrome or
coloured.
H 12.7 cm (5 in). L 13 cm (5 in). D 5 cm (2 in)
Manufacturer: Flli Fantini, Italy

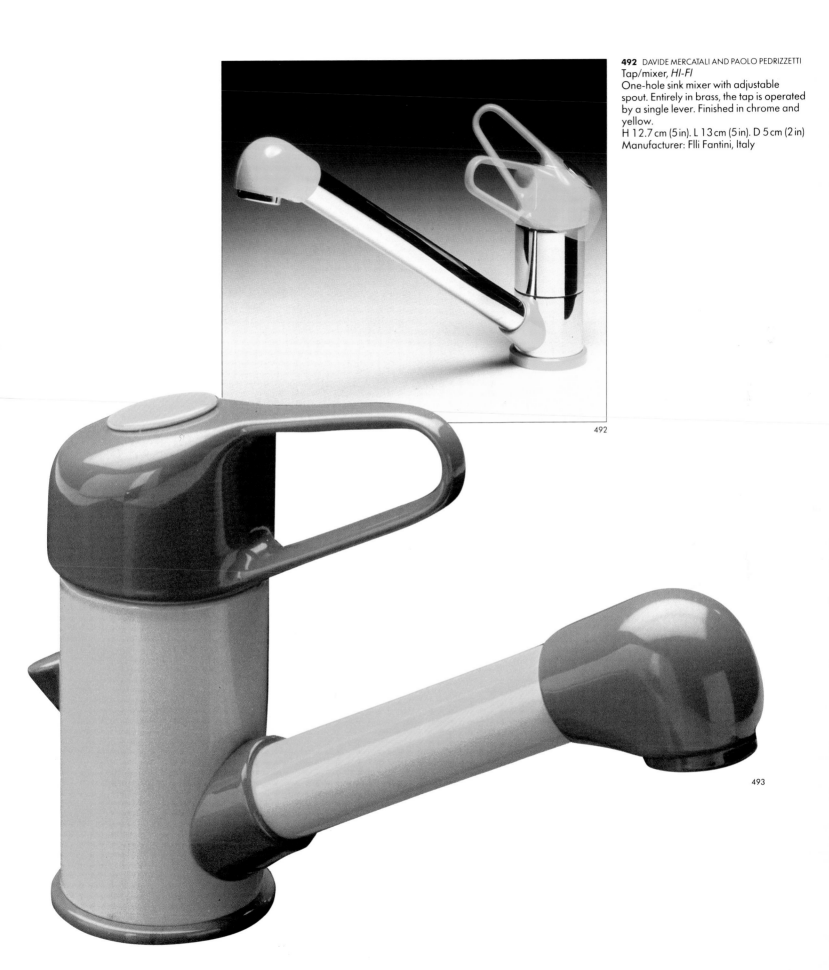

492 DAVIDE MERCATALI AND PAOLO PEDRIZZETTI
Tap/mixer, HI-FI
One-hole sink mixer with adjustable
spout. Entirely in brass, the tap is operated
by a single lever. Finished in chrome and
yellow.
H 12.7 cm (5 in). L 13 cm (5 in). D 5 cm (2 in)
Manufacturer: Flli Fantini, Italy

492

493

494

494 ACHILLE CASTIGLIONI
Coat-stand, *Servomanto*
In tubular steel.
H 194 cm (76 in). D 48 cm (19 in)
Manufacturer: Zanotta, Italy

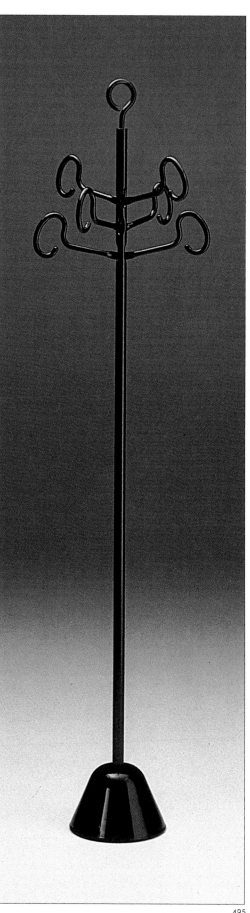

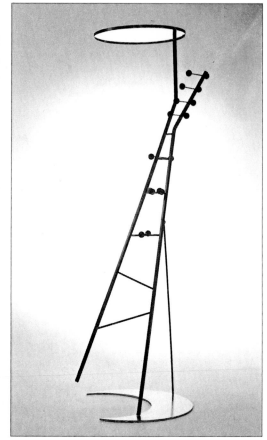

496

495 JONATHAN DE PAS, DONATO D'URBINO AND PAOLO LOMAZZI
Coat-stand, *Parrucca*
In inox steel and enamelled tubing, this clothes hanger
rotates.
H 171 cm (67 in)
Manufacturer: Cast Design, Italy

496 CARLO FORCOLINI
Coat-stand, *Bukowski's Holiday*
Black-painted metal coat-stand with crescent-shaped
base.
H 197 cm (77½ in). D 68 cm (26¾ in)
Manufacturer: Alias, Italy

BIOGRAPHIES

The figures following each entry refer to the illustrations in which the designer's work is represented.

A

ABDENENGO is an Italian fashion designer who began designing furniture in 1985 with a simple metal chair for Bieffeplast, and went on to produce a matching table. *(112)*

TINA AMMANNATI is an Italian interior and furniture designer. She has collaborated with **GIANPIER VITELLI** since 1960 in their Milan studio, producing interior designs and furniture, mainly for Brunati. *(5)*

RON ARAD was born in 1951 in Israel. He studied architecture at the Architectural Association, London, graduating in 1979. After working for a firm of London architects, he founded the design company One-Off Ltd in 1981. He has exhibited in London, Milan and Tokyo, and designs furniture, products and interiors. *(121, 399, 400)*

JUNICHI ARAI is a Japanese textile designer and manufacturer specializing in sculptural, heavily textured fabrics. He has supplied Issey Miyake and Comme des Garçons, among other leading Japanese designers. *(351, 362–365)*

SERGIO ASTI is an Italian architect who has designed the furnishings and interiors of several flats, shops and exhibitions. He has lectured and exhibited extensively, and has sat on a number of award juries since he completed his studies at the Milan Politecnico in 1953. *(92, 93, 145, 148, 149, 302–307)*

B

FRED BAIER is a British furniture designer. He graduated from the Royal College of Art, London in 1975, and has worked as an independent designer and maker ever since. His work is in the collection of several municipal art galleries, as well as regional and national arts bodies. He does consultancy work with architects and furniture companies in the UK and abroad. *See also* **CHRIS ROSE**. *(187)*

HORST BARTELS, a German artist and craftsman in glass, was born in Haldensleben in 1941. From 1965 until 1981 he worked as a graphic designer, and from 1981 onward started to produce glasswork which has been exhibited around the world, including at the Corning Museum of Glass in the USA, in Tokyo, Madrid and New York. *(293)*

MARTINE BEDIN was born in Bordeaux, France, in 1957. She studied architecture in Paris, and in 1978 was awarded an Italian scholarship and worked at the Superstudio in Florence. She has been working with **ETTORE SOTTSASS** since 1980, designing lamps and furniture for Memphis since 1981, and has been a freelance industrial designer since 1982. She also teaches design at the École Camondo, Paris. *(240, 326)*

MARIO BELLINI was born in Milan, Italy, in 1935 and graduated in architecture in 1959. He works in architecture and industrial design for firms such as Artemide, B & B Italia, Cassina and Rosenthal. Since 1965 he has been a consultant with Olivetti SpA on electronic machines. Recently he has produced a new office seating range for Vitra. He has won several awards including the Compasso d'Oro in 1962, 1964, 1970, 1979 and 1981. His works are included in the collection of the Museum of Modern Art, New York. He became editor of *Domus* magazine in 1986. *(19, 105, 106)*

PATRIZIA BELLONI was born in Milan, Italy, in 1960. She studied architecture there, has worked in the architectural studio Sirigatti, and has completed the design of a number of light fittings for the firm of Quattrifolio. *(251, 253)*

JAVIER BELLOSILLO is a graduate of the Madrid School of Architecture and the Architectural Association, London. He has been a visiting professor at the Syracuse School of Architecture, Rhode Island School of Design and Cornell School of Architecture, USA. *(342, 344)*

GIANDOMENICO BELOTTI was born in Bergamo, Italy in 1922. He studied sculpture with Mario Marini and later moved to Milan, where he attended the Brera Academy's Secondary School of Fine Arts. After studying architecture at the University of Milan, he worked with Novate Milanese and Sesto San Giovanni in Milan and began to undertake independent designs. Since then he has worked for private companies and public institutions, where his interests and research centred on urban planning and industrial design. In 1979 he began work with Alias, creating the *Odessa* or *Spaghetti* chair among numerous other projects. *(200)*

ERNST BERANEK is an Austrian architect and designer, born in 1931. He has designed a number of pieces of furniture for Thonet Vienna. *(88)*

GEMMA BERNAL was born in Barcelona, Spain and trained at the School of Industrial Design there before working as an independent designer, in collaboration with **RAMON ISERN**, for such manufacturers as Disform, Gruppo T, Garcia Garai and Fellex. *(66)*

ULRICH BOEHME, a German architect and furniture designer, was born in 1936 at Rostock. He studied architecture at the Technical University of Stuttgart. Since 1973 he has worked as a consultant for Gebrüder Thonet in partnership with **WULF SCHNEIDER**. *(30, 31)*

MARIO BOTTA, architect, was born in 1943 in Mendrisio, Switzerland. He attended Milan Art School, then graduated in architecture from the University of Venice. He gained practical experience in Le Corbusier's studio, then established his own architectural practice in Lugano in 1969. He has completed a number of private houses and commercial buildings in Switzerland generally categorized as 'rationalist'. Since 1982 he has also designed furniture for Alias. *(115–119, 237–239)*

MARIANNE BRANDT was born in Chemnitz, then in East Prussia, in 1893 and died in 1983. She studied painting and sculpture at Weimar and joined the Bauhaus in 1923, working with Laszlo Moholy-Nagy in the metal workshop, where she produced a number of light fittings.

When Hannes Meyer took over the running of the Dessau Bauhaus, she left to work for Walter Gropius in Berlin on furniture and interior design. *(440)*

ANDREA BRANZI was born in Italy. He is both a designer and an editor. He has consistently been a representative of the radical tendency in Italian design, championing design as a broad cultural activity rather than simply as a device to encourage increased consumption. In 1966, with **PAOLO DEGANELLO**, Gilberio Corretti and **MASSIMO MOROZZI**, he was involved in the establishment of the then avant-garde group, Studio Archizoom. He has been an active member of the Studio Alchymia, the Milan-based group whose designs have created pieces that are closer to artworks than to conventional pieces of design. Since 1981 he has been involved with the Memphis group, collaborating with **ETTORE SOTTSASS**. *(155)*

MICHAEL BRENNAND-WOOD was born in Britain in 1952. He was educated at Bolton College of Art and Manchester and Birmingham Polytechnics in textile design, and is a lecturer at Goldsmiths' College, University of London. Brennand-Wood's work has explored the sculptural possibilities of textiles as an art form. His work is in the collections of the Crafts Council, London, the Gallery of Western Australia and the National Museum of Modern Art, Kyoto. *(395)*

MARCEL BREUER, the Hungarian-born American architect and designer, was born in Pecs in 1902 and died in 1981. He trained at the Bauhaus, and became a teacher there himself after graduating. It was during this period that Breuer designed the items of tubular steel furniture which were to be his most striking works. The question of who first designed a cantilevered steel tube chair will never be satisfactorily answered – Breuer, Mies and Mart Stam all had claims to that distinction. Certainly Breuer's was the most elegant. After the Nazi seizure of power, Breuer came to Britain, where he worked as an architect and designed a number of pieces of furniture, mainly in plywood. From Britain Breuer moved to America, following Gropius, working as an architect, planner and educator. *(196, 198)*

C

JEAN-PIERRE CAILLÈRES trained as an architect at the École des Beaux Arts, Paris. He has worked as an architect and town planner on a number of large-scale schemes in the French new towns. Since 1980 he has worked as an independent architect, as well as designing limited-edition furniture. *(10, 11, 74, 146)*

GASPARE CAIROLI is an Italian designer, born in Meda in 1952. After graduating he worked for Cassina and B&B Italia. In 1983 he started his own studio with Elisabetta Donzelli, working in industrial and graphic design. In 1958 he produced a range of folding metal furniture for Seccose. *(52, 53)*

ROBERTO CASPANI was born in 1951 in Casale Cero, Italy. He was educated at the Accademia di Brera, Milan, and in architecture at the Milan Politecnico. *(368)*

ACHILLE CASTIGLIONI was born in Milan, Italy, in 1918. He began designing with his brothers Livio and Pier

Giacomo Castiglioni. Today he is internationally known for his furnishings and lighting, and for his mass-produced objects in the field of radio-telecommunications. In addition to working as a designer, he is an architect and university lecturer. He has received seven Compasso d'Oro awards; six of his pieces are in the Museum of Modern Art, New York. *(224, 225, 299, 483, 494)*

IVAN CHERMAYEFF was born in the USA and educated at Harvard University. He is a graphic designer and artist, and a partner in the New York-based design consultancy of Chermayeff and Giesmar. He has worked on a number of poster and corporate-identity projects, notably for Mobil. *(477)*

MICHIKO CHIKANO is a Japanese industrial designer with the Plus Corporation, which originally specialized in stationery but has now moved on to produce a wide range of consumer goods. *(443)*

ALDO CIBIC is an Italian designer, born in 1955 in Schio. After studying at the Milan Politecnico, Cibic worked as an interior designer in Vicenza. He has been associated with the Memphis group since it was started. *(325)*

SIMON CONDER, a British architect and designer, was educated at the Architectural Association and the Royal College of Art, London. He has specialized in interior design and the development of furniture and hi-fi equipment. *(418)*

SEBASTIAN CONRAN was born in Britain in 1955 and educated as an industrial designer at the Central School of Art and Design, London. He worked as a designer for Wolf Olins and Habitat–Mothercare before establishing an independent design consultancy specializing in industrial design and product identity. *(120)*

PEPE CORTÉS was born in Barcelona, Spain in 1945. He collaborated on numerous projects, including lights, furniture and interiors with **JAVIER MARISCAL**. *(271–276)*

D

PAOLO DEGANELLO was born in Este, Italy, in 1940. He studied in Florence and from 1963 to 1974 worked as a town planner for the Florence municipality. In 1966 he founded, with **ANDREA BRANZI**, Gilberio Corretti and **MASSIMO MOROZZI**, the then avant-garde group, Studio Archizoom. In 1975, with Corretti, Franco Gatti and Roberto Querci, he founded the Collettivo Tecnici Progettisti. He has taught widely, including at Florence University and the Architectural Association, London, and has published several books and articles. He has designed products for Marcatré, Driade and Cassina and has taken part in many international exhibitions and competitions. *(102–104, 108, 143, 144)*

ERIK DE GRAAFF is a Dutch craftsman and furniture designer, now resident in Britain. *(188)*

MICHELE DE LUCCHI was born in Ferrara, Italy, in 1951. He studied first in Padua and then at Florence University, where he founded the Gruppo Cavat, which produced avant-garde and radical architecture projects, films,

texts and happenings. He obtained his degree in architecture from Florence University in 1975 and subsequently became assistant professor to Adolfo Natalini at the Faculty of Architecture there, as well as at the International Art University of Florence. In 1978 he left teaching and moved to Milan, where he began a close collaboration with **ETTORE SOTTSASS**. He worked and designed for Studio Alchymia, Milan, until the establishment of the international group Memphis in 1981. For Memphis he designed and carried out some of its best-known products. In 1979 he became a consultant for Olivetti Synthesis in Massa and in 1984 for Olivetta SpA in Ivrea. Under the supervision of Sottsass he designed Olivetti's *Icarus* office furniture. At the same time, with Sottsass Associati, he designed both the interior decoration and the image of more than 50 Fiorucci shops in Italy and abroad. A series of his household appliances for Zirmi was shown at the Milan Triennale of 1979, while at the Triennale of 1983 he exhibited a prefabricated holiday house in plastic material. Currently he is designing for a wide range of important furniture manufacturers: among others, Acerbis, Artemide, Vistosi, RB Rossana, Fontana Arte and Bieffeplast. *(29, 160, 161, 163, 333, 334)*

JONATHAN DE PAS was born in Italy in the 1930s. He studied in Milan, and in the mid-1960s, with **PAOLO LOMAZZI** and **DONATO D'URBINO**, he set up a studio specializing in architecture and interior design. The three of them have exhibited widely since 1970 and have received many awards. Their work is in several major museums. *(141, 142, 231–236, 495)*

SIMON DESANTA was born in 1952 in West Germany. He trained at the Weilefelt School of Design, and established himself as a freelance designer in 1976. Two of his chairs are currently manufactured by Rosenthal. *(111)*

ANTHONY DONATO is an American designer who was educated in industrial design. He is currently Design Director of Lightolier Inc. *(205)*

NATHALIE DU PASQUIER was born in France in 1957. She moved to Italy in 1979 and shortly afterwards came in contact with the Memphis group. She began working with textiles and later moved on to furniture and graphics as well. She is a freelance designer who lives and works in Milan. She often collaborates with **GEORGE SOWDEN**. *(164–167, 329–332, 386–391)*

DONATO D'URBINO was born in Italy in the 1930s. *See also* **JONATHAN DE PAS** and **PAOLO LOMAZZI**. *(141, 142, 231–236, 495)*

E

THOMAS EISL was born in Austria in 1947 and has lived in England since 1969. He was educated at the Central School of Art and Design, London, graduating in fine art in 1977. Since 1981 he has been designing lights, mainly one-offs. *(245–248)*

JAMES EVANSON is an American, born in 1946. He trained as an architect at the Pratt Institute, New York, and the Art Center College of Design, New York, and has worked as an artist exploring the boundaries between art and design. *(277–279)*

F

JOCHEN FLACKE was born in Germany in 1950. He served an apprenticeship as a joiner before completing an interior design course, and works as an independent furniture designer, notably for Rosenthal. *(51)*

CARLO FORCOLINI was born in Como, Italy, in 1947. He studied at the Institute of Graphic Arts, the Secondary School of Fine Arts, Brera, and the Academy of Fine Arts at Brera, Milan. From 1970 to 1974 he designed for the Amar Collection, and in 1976 he began working with **VICO MAGISTRETTI**. In 1978 he moved to London, and a year later he helped to found Alias SRL, which began production of the Broomstick Collection designed by Magistretti and of the *Spaghetti* chair designed by Giandomenico Belotti. In 1980 he founded Alias UK, for distribution of Alias products under their own brand name in the UK. *(496)*

GIANFRANCO FRATTINI, an architect and designer of exhibitions, interiors and furniture, was born in Padua, Italy, in 1926. He studied architecture at the Milan Politecnico, graduating in 1952. He worked as an assistant to Gio Ponti until 1957, when he left to establish his own studio. Since then he has worked for the majority of the major Italian furniture and lighting manufacturers, including Cassina, Artemide and Arteluce – for whom he designed the *Boalum* coiled tube light. He is the winner of eight Compasso d'Oro awards and has exhibited his work in museums throughout Europe and America. *(22, 23, 28)*

SUSIE FREEMAN was born in Britain in 1957 and was educated as a textile designer and maker at Manchester Polytechnic and the Royal College of Art, London. Her work is in the collections of the Crafts Council, London, the Victoria & Albert Museum, London, and the Whitworth Art Gallery, Manchester. *(394, 396–398)*

ANNA FRENCH DESIGN is run by **ANNA FRENCH**, Design Director of Margo International Fabrics Ltd. There she conceives her collections with the help of freelance designers with whom she frequently collaborates. *(352, 353, 355, 356)*

DAN FRIEDMAN, born in America in 1946, was educated at the Carnegie Institute of Technology, Pittsburgh, the Hochschüle für Gestaltung, Ulm, and the Allgemeine Gewerbeschule, Basel. He has taught art and design at Yale University School of Art and Architecture, and the State University of New York, Purschase. He has been an independent artist and designer since 1975. *(172)*

KAZUKO FUJIE, a Japanese interior and furniture designer, was born in Toyama in 1947. She graduated in 1967 from the junior college attached to the Musashino Fine Arts University, specializing in industrial design. Between 1969 and 1977 she worked in the Miyawaki architectural office, before setting up her own practice. Her principal projects include furniture for Keio University's old and new libraries. *(191–193)*

SABURO FUNAKOSHI was born in Ishikawa, Japan, in 1931. He graduated from Tokyo University of Arts, Department of Crafts, and has spent much of his career as a designer working for the Hoya Glass Corporation.

His work has been exhibited at numerous international exhibitions, and is in the permanent collections of the Japanese National Museum of Modern Art, the Hokkaido Museum, the Corning Museum of Glass, New York, and the Philadelphia Museum. *(296)*

G

BRUNO GECCHELIN is an Italian architect, born in Milan in 1939. He studied architecture at the Milan Politecnico and began his professional career in 1962, since when he has worked with many major companies. *(216)*

WALTER GERTH, who is German, trained as an aircraft engineer then turned to sculpture. He has worked as an independent industrial designer since 1968, producing furniture, glass, ceramics and consumer goods. *(24, 101)*

ERNESTO GISMONDI is an Italian lighting designer and entrepreneur, and the owner of Artemide SpA, for whom he has designed several lights. It was Gismondi's patronage which helped to finance the Memphis group, of which he is a director. Artemide has recently acquired the Alias Company. *(226, 227, 252)*

GIUGIARO DESIGN is run by **GIORGIO GIUGIARO**. He was born in Italy in 1938. After studying briefly at the Academy of Fine Arts in Turin he was apprenticed to Fiat, leaving to work as a stylist for Bertone. In 1968 he established his own car design studio, ItalDesign, working on such important models as the Fiat Panda and the Golf for Volkswagen. In recent years he has established an additional studio to design products, furniture, cameras and watches and even pasta. *(58)*

MILTON GLASER was born in the USA. He is an artist, designer and writer. Initially he worked with Push Pin Studios, but then went into independent practice, creating a number of memorable posters, packaging schemes and newspaper designs. His clients have included Sony and Olivetti; perhaps his best-known campaign was 'I Love NY'. Most recently he has worked for Oliver Goldsmith's American supermarket chain. *(477)*

THOMAS LEAR GRACE, sculptor and designer, was born in Pittsburgh, Pennsylvania in 1959. His installations have been exhibited at the Dallas Museum of Art. *(177–180)*

KENNETH GRANGE is a British designer, born in 1929. He trained as a technical illustrator during his national service in the British Army, and has worked as an assistant in various architectural offices. In 1971 he founded the Pentagram design consultancy with Fletcher Forbes and Gill and the architect Theo Crosby. Grange has worked primarily as an industrial designer, producing cameras for Kodak, parking meters for Venner, food mixers for Kenwood and pens for Parker. In 1983 his work was the subject of a special exhibition at the Boilerhouse Project at the Victoria and Albert Museum, London. *(450, 451)*

MICHAEL GRAVES was born in the USA in 1934. He is Schrimer Professor of Architecture at Princeton University, and is the architect of the Newark Museum and the Whitney Museum. He has received many awards for his architectural works, and has been widely exhibited. His paintings and murals are in several major

museums. He has designed furniture for Memphis and Sunar, and products for Alessi. *(475)*

CAROLINE GRAY is a British designer, born in 1957. She graduated from West Surrey College of Art and Design in 1979 and since then has worked as a freelance designer, designing printed textiles for fashion houses in Milan and Paris. She has also designed furniture fabric collections in Sweden and Finland, and has worked in association with the Designers Guild since 1981. *(361)*

EILEEN GRAY was born in Ireland in 1879 and died in 1976. She trained at the Slade School, London, and moved to Paris in 1907, making wood and lacquer furniture in her own atelier there from about 1920. She then took up architecture, and with Jean Badovici designed the famous villa E 1027 at Roquebrune. She was a member of the UAM along with René Herbst, Pierre Chareau, Jean Prouvé, Robert Mallet-Stevens, Le Corbusier and others. *(201)*

H

PENTTI HAKALA was born in 1949 in Saarijärvi, Finland. He graduated in furniture design in 1983. His work has been selected by the Finnish Design Council, and his chairs have been exhibited at the Museum of Applied Arts in Helsinki. *(87)*

ROBERT AND TRIX HAUSSMANN studied architecture in Zürich and began a practice together in 1967, on a variety of projects including restoration work and interior design. Robert Haussmann has taught at the Swiss Institute of Technology. Trix Haussmann has exhibited at the Studio Marconi, Milan. *(336–338, 343)*

SIMO HEIKKILÄ was born in 1943 in Helsinki, Finland. He studied at the Finnish Academy of Applied Arts, graduating in 1967. After a period spent as an assistant in the Marimekko design department, he established his own design studio. From 1975 he has taught at the Helsinki University of Industrial Art. Heikkilä collaborated with Yrjo Wiherheimo on furniture for Vivero in 1980. His works are in the permanent collections of the Victoria and Albert Museum, London, the Kunstindustrmuseet, Oslo, the Museum of Applied Arts, Helsinki and the Museum für Kunst und Gewerbe, Hamburg. He was the winner of the Finnish State Industrial Design Award in 1985. *(17, 18)*

MATTHEW HILTON, born in 1957, is a British designer. He studied furniture design at Kingston Polytechnic and then worked with the product design consultancy CAPA for five years, on a variety of high-technology products. He started as an independent furniture and interior designer in 1984, producing a number of lights as well as pieces of furniture. *(257, 260, 261)*

MONICA HJELM was born in Sweden in 1945 and attended the High School of Arts, Crafts and Design, Gothenburg from 1965 to 1969. Since 1969 she has worked as a designer for Marks-Pelle Vävare AB and is now responsible for the product development of curtain and cotton fabrics. She has designed curtains, mast-woven and printed cotton fabrics, plaids in wool and furnishing fabrics. *(358–360)*

JOCHEN HOFFMANN was born in Germany in 1940. He studied industrial design from 1962 to 1966 at the

Hochschule für Bildende Kunste in Braunschweig and graduated in industrial design. He worked for Firma Hans Kaufeld Polstermöbel in Bielefeld until 1970, and since then has worked as a freelance designer. *(65)*

STEVEN HOLL is an American architect and designer. He trained in architecture at the University of Washington, and went on to design a number of private houses. He has started a company called Pamphlet Architecture, publishing architectural research, and has taught at the Pratt Institute and the Parsons School of Design. *(339–341)*

HANS HOLLEIN was born in Vienna, Austria, in 1934. Since 1967 he has taught at the Academy of Art, Düsseldorf, and since 1976 at the College of Applied Arts, Vienna. He has exhibited widely and has been commissioned to design a large number of buildings. *(345, 348)*

JAMES HONG was born in 1948 in Vallejo, California. He graduated in architecture from the University of California at Berkeley, and worked for Gae Aulenti in Italy. He has been an instructor at Parsons School of Design since 1981, and is a designer of interiors and one-off furniture pieces. *(176)*

ISAO HOSOE was born in Tokyo, Japan, in 1942. He studied in Tokyo until 1967, and collaborated with Alberto Rosselli until 1974 in Milan. In 1981 he founded the Design Research Centre in Milan. He has received major prizes and has exhibited and written widely. *(14, 15)*

I

RAMON ISERN was born in Barcelona, Spain in 1944 and trained as an industrial designer. Since graduating he has worked with **GEMMA BERNAL** for, among others, the furniture manufacturers Disform, Gruppo T, Garcia Garai and Fellex. *(66)*

FUJIO ISHIMOTO was born in Shikoku, Japan, in 1941. He studied graphic design at the Tokyo National University of Art, then moved to Helsinki in 1970, after working for the Japanese textile house of Ichida. Until 1974 he designed for Decembre, a Marimekko sister company, working among other things on the Marimekko range of canvas bags. He is now a member of the Marimekko design team, mainly involved with interiors and fabrics. His works have been exhibited around the world, and he has also become involved with costume and set design with the Finnish National Opera. *(372–378)*

J

ELIZABETH BROWNING JACKSON, the American artist and designer, was educated at San Francisco Art Academy, the University of New Mexico, Albuquerque, and Capella Gardin, Sweden. *(174)*

ARNE JACOBSEN, Danish architect and designer, was born in Copenhagen in 1902 and died in 1971. He was educated at the School of Architecture of the Academy of Arts, Copenhagen. After working briefly in the office of Copenhagen's city architect, Jacobsen set up in

private practice in 1930. He was Professor of Architecture at the Copenhagen Academy of Arts from 1956. Jacobsen was known for both his architecture – which was in the purist Scandinavian modern manner, typified by his buildings for St Catherine's College, Oxford, and the SAS Hotel in Copenhagen – and his furniture, mainly in the form of moulded plywood bent into organic-looking shapes. *(199)*

JOUKO JARVISALO was born in 1950 in Varkaus, Finland. He has worked both as an interior architect and as a freelance designer. Since 1983 he has worked in an interior design office, designing home and office furniture for Artek, Asko, Arsel, Laukaan Puu and Inno. *(59, 60)*

HEINZ JUNGER was born in Germany in 1931. He trained as a graphic designer, and spent six years with Blaupunkt, working on the design of consumer electronics. He has worked for Loewe Opta since 1962, since 1966 as head of the design department. *(423)*

K

KAIROS is an architectural and design partnership founded by three Italian designers in 1980, specializing in industrial design and development, architecture and interiors. They have produced furniture for B & B Italia. Kairos consists of **MASSIMO BONETTI**, born in Turin in 1940, an engineering graduate of Padua University, **GIUSEPPE MANENTE**, born in Mestre in 1947, trained as an architect and designer at Venice University, and **ABRAMO MION**, born in Venice in 1951. *(36, 37)*

JEFFREY KAPEC, an American designer, graduated in industrial design from the Pratt Institute, New York, in 1972. Since 1980 he has worked in partnership with **KAZUNA TANAKA**. *(457, 458, 490)*

TAKASHI KATO is a Japanese industrial designer based in Tokyo, who has recently specialized in designing clocks for Ateria. *(466–469)*

KAZUO KAWASAKI was born in Japan in 1949. He graduated in art and industrial design from Kanazawa University in 1972, and worked for Toshiba on the design and development of audio equipment until 1979. He has had an independent practice as a designer since 1979 and is a lecturer at Kanazawa University. He was the winner of the Silver Prize of the Japan Design Forum in 1983. *(25, 408)*

RENÉ KEMNA was born in Zwolle, Holland, in 1956. He graduated in industrial design from Delft Polytechnic in 1981 and is now a teacher at Delft. He is established as an independent designer working in Holland and Italy, particularly in the field of lighting. *(229, 230)*

PERRY A. KING was born in London in 1938 and studied at the School of Industrial Design, Birmingham. He later moved to Italy to work as a consultant to Olivetti SpA, designing among other things the *Valentine* typewriter in collaboration with **ETTORE SOTTSASS**. He started to work with **SANTIAGO MIRANDA** on a project called Unlimited Horizon, an exploration of the elements that make and divide private and public spaces. At the same time they

began working on typeface design for Olivetti, and one of their dot matrix founts was adopted by the European Computer Manufacturers' Association. For the last 10 years he and Miranda have worked together from their office in Milan, where they are active in the fields of industrial design, furniture and interior design, lighting design and graphics. Their graphic work includes posters and catalogues for Olivetti and corporate-image programmes for a number of firms. Together with G. Arnaldi they have designed light fittings for Arteluce/Flos and have recently been working on office furniture, the design of power tools for Black & Decker and a design programme for the identification and control elements of the new Olivetti machines. Recently, they have moved into the area of furniture design, with the *Airmail* seating range for Marcatré. Their work has received several awards and has been exhibited in Italy and abroad. *(241–244)*

RODNEY KINSMAN was born in Britain in 1943. He studied at the Central School of Art, London, and received the NDD and Central School Diploma in Furniture Design. In 1966 he formed OMK Design Ltd, a design group offering consultancy to furniture manufacturers. It began a limited production of its own designs in 1967. The recipient of numerous awards, Kinsman has had his work widely published and exhibited. *(123)*

SETSUO KITAOKA, born in 1946, is a Japanese designer who works in Tokyo. He has designed a number of pieces of furniture including storage, screens and tables as well as lights. *(68, 69, 71, 72, 280–283)*

VALTO KOKKO is Finnish, born in 1933, and is head of Iittala's visual department. He worked for Iittala initially on the design of lighting fixtures, then turned his attention to packaging, film-making and the design of household glass. In 1980 his *Otso* glasses were selected for the permanent collection of the Museum of Modern Art, New York. *(318)*

MICHAEL KOMAR is a British product designer. He trained in industrial design at North Staffordshire Polytechnic, graduating in 1981, and has worked as an industrial designer for Russell Hobbs since then on a series of consumer electrical appliances. *(470)*

MAKOTO KOMATSU was born in 1943 in Tokyo. He graduated from art school in Tokyo, then went to work for the Swedish glassmaker Gustavsberg. After returning to Japan he began working as an independent designer. His work is in the permanent collections of the Museum of Ceramics, Faenza, the New York Museum of Modern Art and the Victoria and Albert Museum, London. *(267, 311–315)*

YRJO KUKKAPURO was born in Ywipuri, Finland in 1933. He is the furniture designer for Avarte Oy, and from 1974 to 1980 was a professor at the University of Industrial Arts, Helsinki. From 1978 to 1980 he was rector of the university. Examples of his work are in the permanent collection of the Victoria and Albert Museum, London and the Museum of Modern Art, New York. His awards include the Design Award of the Republic of Finland, 1970; the Artek Prize, 1982; and the Pro Finlandia Award, 1983. In 1984, the Institute of Business Designers in the USA awarded him the IBD Award for his design of the *Experiment* chair. *(12, 13)*

SHIRO KURAMATA was born in Tokyo in 1934. He started an independent practice as a furniture designer in 1965, having served an apprenticeship in cabinet-making. Apart from his celebrated glass armchair of 1976, and a number of other equally elegant but quirky pieces of furniture, Kuramata has designed interiors for the fashion designer Issey Miyake and for the Siebu stores. (168–171)

MASAYUKI KUROKAWA was born in Nagoya, Japan, in 1937. He graduated from the Department of Architecture at the Nagoya Institute of Technology in 1961 and completed his training in the Graduate School of Architecture at Waseda University in 1967. That same year he established Masayuki Kurokawa Architect and Associates. He has been accorded numerous prizes for his work. In 1970 he won first prize in the International Design Competition for a mass-production house, in 1973 he won first prize in the Competition for Interior Vertical Element of House, and in 1976 he won the annual prize of the Japan Interior Designers' Association for a series of interior elements. He has won six IF prizes for his designs of tables and lighting fixtures. (67, 427, 478)

L

JURGEN LANGE was born in 1940 in Ratzeburg, West Germany. He was apprenticed as a cabinetmaker, then studied art and design at the state art college, Braunschweig. In 1968 he established his own studio, and he has been Professor of Furniture Design at Offenbach, West Germany, since 1982. (100)

ANN LARSSON-KJELIN was born in Sweden in 1953. In 1974 she received a degree from the Textile Institute, and since 1977 has been associated with the Swedish firm of Marks Pelle Vävare AB. She has designed upholstery fabrics, bedspreads and cotton fabrics, and has worked in conjunction with interior architects on such projects as the Swedish Parliament, the Government Building in Stockholm, the City Express (the Swedish public railway) and the jet-cat ferries in Hong Kong. (357)

DAVID LAW was born in Pittsburgh, Pennsylvania in 1937, and studied at the Art Center College of Design, Los Angeles. In 1967 he joined Unimark International as an executive designer for the Detroit and Chicago offices. He became a co-founder of Design Planning Group, Chicago in 1972, then manager of packaging design at J.C. Penney, New York in 1975. He joined Vignelli Associates in 1978. He has designed graphics, packaging, exhibitions, products and furniture, as well as undertaking environmental and interior design. His work is represented in the permanent collection of the Cooper-Hewitt Museum. See also **LELLA AND MASSIMO VIGNELLI**. (21, 82–84, 284)

BORGE LINDAU was born in Ahus, Sweden, in 1932. He was educated at the Gothenburg School of Arts and Crafts from 1957 to 1961, and worked as an interior designer in Helsingborg until 1964, when he formed a partnership with **BO LINDEKRANTZ** (born in 1932 in Gothenburg). Together they have collaborated on a series of pieces of furniture. In 1969 they were awarded the Linning prize. Their other awards include the Association of Swedish Industrial Designers prize in 1975, for their 75 tubular steel folding chair, and the National Swedish Association of Interior Architects'

award for the best piece of contract furniture of 1983. (62, 63)

BO LINDEKRANTZ, Swedish furniture designer, was born in 1932 in Gothenburg. He graduated from the Gothenburg School of Arts and Crafts in 1961, and worked as an interior designer until 1964, when he formed a partnership with **BORGE LINDAU**, producing many pieces of furniture including the *Planaka* chair in 1985. (62, 63)

DAVID LINLEY was born in Britain in 1961. He trained as a furniture designer and cabinetmaker at Parnham House, Dorset, under the direction of John Makepeace. In 1985 he established David Linley Furniture Ltd, with the painter **MATTHEW RICE**. (186)

MARY LITTLE, British furniture designer, graduated from the Royal College of Art, London, in 1985. (54, 55)

PAOLO LOMAZZI was born in Italy in the 1930s. See also **JONATHAN DE PAS** and **DONATO D'URBINO**. (141, 142, 231–236, 495)

PAUL LUDICK is an American designer who graduated in fine arts. He has been showing his designs in New York since 1980, and has exhibited from Poland to Atlanta Georgia. He has worked with Art et Industrie since 1983. (173, 175)

M

NANNY STILL McKINNEY was born in Finland in 1925 and graduated from Helsinki School of Art in 1949. She has worked designing glassware, light fittings and stainless steel cutlery. Her work has been exhibited at numerous exhibitions, including the Milan Triennale. She is represented in the collections of the Victoria and Albert Museum, London, the Museum of Modern Art, New York, the Metropolitan Museum of Art, New York, the Corning Museum of Glass and the Nordenfjelske Museum, Trondheim. (316)

VICO MAGISTRETTI was born in Milan, Italy, in 1920. He took a degree in architecture in 1945 and subsequently joined his father's studio. Until 1960 he was mainly concerned with architecture, town planning and the interior layout of buildings. He started designing furniture and household articles for his buildings in about 1960, and from then on began collaborating with the companies who realized his designs. He has participated in nearly all the Triennali since 1948, and in 1960 joined the National Academy of S. Luca. He was awarded the Medaglia d'Oro at the 9th Triennale in 1951, the Gran Premio at the 15th in 1954 and the Compasso d'Oro in 1967 and 1979. He has designed furniture, lamps and other household objects for Artemide, Cassina, B & B Italia, Conran, Knoll International and many other firms. Twelve of his pieces are in the permanent collection of the Museum of Modern Art, New York. (38, 39, 40–42, 485)

PETER MALY is a German designer and was born in 1936 in Trautenau, Czechoslovakia. He studied interior design in Germany, and since 1970 has worked as an independent designer in Hamburg, specializing in furniture and fabrics. (64)

ANGELO MANGIAROTTI was born in 1921 in Milan, Italy and educated there, graduating from the Politecnico in 1948. He has worked as a designer in America and in Italy, as well as teaching at the Illinois Institute of Technology's design school. He has specialized in small, highly-finished sculptural objects, often intended for the table-top, including a stainless-steel clock for Portescap, and other pieces for Knoll and Munari. (73, 217)

MARIO MARENCO was born in Foggia, Italy, in 1933, and graduated in architecture from the University of Naples in 1957. He has worked as an industrial designer, since 1962 designing small family houses, exhibition stands and furniture, for B & B Italia among others. (81)

ENZO MARI is an Italian designer, born in 1932. He studied at the Brera Academy of Fine Art in Milan, and taught design methods at the Milan Politecnico. He participated in the 1972 exhibition at the Museum of Modern Art, New York, 'Italy: The New Domestic Landscape'. Since the 1950s he has worked on the design of glass for Danese as well as on furniture for Driade and Gabbianelli. He has twice been awarded a Compasso d'Oro, in 1967 for his research, in 1979 for his *Delfina* chair, manufactured by Driade. (26, 27, 428–438)

JAVIER MARISCAL, a Spanish designer, was born in 1950. He trained as an artist and graphic designer and collaborated on the Memphis collection of 1981. His lights, designed in collaboration with **PEPE CORTÉS**, have been in production with the Barcelona firm BD. (268–276)

MITCHELL MAUK was born in America in 1957 and educated at the Art Center College of Design, Pasadena, graduating in graphics and packaging design in 1979. He has worked as a graphic designer on corporate identity projects and packaging in the California design consultancy Mark Anderson Design, and has developed a quartz halogen lighting system for Artemide. (206)

INGO MAURER was born in West Germany in 1932. After training as a typographer and graphic artist in Germany and Switzerland, he emigrated to the USA in 1960. He moved back to Europe in 1963 and started his own lighting design firm, Ingo Maurer GmbH, in 1966. His work has been collected by museums in Israel and Japan, by the Museum of Modern Art, New York, and by the Neue Sammlung, Munich. (254, 255)

MARGARET McCURRY is a principal in Tigerman, Fugman, McCurry, in Chicago. She often collaborates with **STANLEY TIGERMAN**. (347)

ALBERTO MEDA was born in 1945 in Como, Italy. He graduated in mechanical engineering from the Milan Politecnico. Between 1973 and 1979, he worked as the technical manager of Kartell, the leading plastics furniture company. In 1979, he established his own consultancy in product design and engineering work, with commissions from, among others, Fontana Arte, Vistorsi, Centrokappa and Gaggia. Since 1981 he has had a consultancy role with Alfa Romeo. He is Professor of Industrial Technology at the Domus Academy in Milan. (215, 218)

RICHARD MEIER was born in the USA in 1934. He worked in various architectural partnerships, including Owings and Merrill, and Marcel Breuer and Associates, before founding Richard Meier and Partners Architects in New York in 1963. He has taught at the Cooper Union, New York, Yale and Harvard Universities, and has designed housing, hospitals, museums, schools and university buildings. *(349, 350)*

ALESSANDRO MENDINI was born in Milan, Italy, in 1931. He was a partner of Nizzoli Associates until 1970, and a founder member of Global Tools. He then edited *Casabella* and *Modo* and, until 1985, *Domus*. He has collaborated with a number of companies, has written widely, and received the Compasso d'Oro prize in 1979. *(140)*

DAVIDE MERCATALI was born in Milan, Italy, in 1948. After receiving a degree in architecture in 1973, he worked as an illustrator and graphic designer for advertising agencies, publishing houses and his own clientèle. His first forays into industrial design were decorations for materials and tiles. Then in 1978 he and **PAOLO PEDRIZZETTI** designed *I Balocchi*, a collection of coloured taps and bathroom accessories produced by Fantini. Since then he and Pedrizzetti, with whom he formed a design partnership, Associated Studio, in 1982, have branched out into a number of different areas, designing household goods, electrical appliances, interior decoration, lighting fixtures, accessories and building components and tools. They have twice won the Compasso d'Oro. *(491–493)*

ARNOLD MERCKX is a Dutch furniture designer whose work includes pieces for the Metaform company. *(70)*

MINALE, TATTERSFIELD AND PARTNERS is a firm of international design consultants working in the field of graphic design, corporate identity, packaging, architectural graphics, interior design, and furniture and product design. It is the consultant for Cubic Metre Furniture Ltd, and has also undertaken major product/furniture projects for such companies as Zanotta and Aqualisa Showers. *(122)*

SANTIAGO MIRANDA was born in Seville, Spain, in 1947 and studied at the School of Applied Arts, Seville. He then moved to Italy. *See also* **PERRY A. KING**. *(241–244)*

BILL MOGGRIDGE is a British industrial designer who was born in 1943. He was educated at the Central School of Art and Design, graduating in 1965. He established his own office in London in 1969, opening ID Two, a Californian off-shoot, in 1979. Moggridge has specialized in computer design, and scientific and consumer products for such firms as Hoover and Pitney Bowes. *(441; 442)*

CHARLES MOORE is partner in the Connecticut architectural firm of Moore, Grover, Harper, and in the Californian firm of Moore, Ruble, Yudell. He is principal architect of the Urban Innovations Group and head of the architecture programme of the University of California, Los Angeles. He has won more than 40 architectural awards. His work spans three decades and has been seminal in the growth of Post-Modernism. *(194, 195)*

MARCELLO MORANDINI, an artist and designer, was born in 1940 in Varese, Italy. He has worked with Rosenthal since 1979. *(79)*

MASAHIRO MORI was born in 1927 in Saga-Ken, Japan. He is a ceramics and industrial designer whose awards include the gold medal of the International Competition of Contemporary Art Ceramics, Faenza, Italy in 1975, and the Grand Prix of the 13th Annual Industrial Design Competition, Valencia. *(297, 298)*

HIROSHI MORISHIMA is a Japanese designer/craftsman. He was born in 1944 and graduated from the Tama Design Art School in 1965. He went on to study at the Art Center School, Los Angeles in 1967. He works chiefly in paper. His awards include the Art Directors' Club Prize, the Silver Prize of the Japan Design Forum and the Kokui Kitaro Industrial Craft Award. *(185, 202, 371)*

MASAKI MORITA, a Japanese interior and furniture designer, was born in 1950. He graduated from the Kuwasawa Design Institute in 1975. He has been at pains to distance himself from a specifically Japanese approach, and has created a number of pieces of furniture as part of his interior design work for shops and bars. His work includes the *Amoeba* chair of 1980 and his Bag Shop in Tokyo, 1982. Recently he has worked for the French Company Tribu. *(110)*

MASSIMO MOROZZI was born in Florence, Italy, in 1941. Trained as an architect, until 1972 he was a member of Archizoom Associates, the leading avant-garde architectural group of the day in Italy. During this period Morozzi collaborated on the design of the *Aeo* chair for Cassina. For five years he ran Montedison's textile design research centre. After 1977 he worked with the CDM group on a corporate identity programme for Rome airport. In 1982 he opened his own studio specializing in consumer goods. *(8, 9, 474, 476)*

N

PAOLO NAVA was born in Italy in 1943 and studied at the Milan Politecnico and in Florence. He worked for various design studios in England. *(1–4)*

HIDETOSHI NOZAWA is a Japanese glass designer and glassmaker. Based in Tokyo, he has produced numerous designs for the Nigara glass company, experimenting with tinting and sandblasting techniques. *(289–292)*

ANTTI NURMESNIEMI is a Finnish designer who trained in interior design and began work in the 1950s. After five years in an architectural office he started Studio Nurmesniemi in 1956. He has taught and been exhibited widely and has received many awards. He collaborates with his wife, Vuokko Eskolin-Nurmesniemi, and is responsible for the furniture and lighting design of Vuokko Oy. *(16, 447, 448)*

O

GIOVANNI OFFREDI was born in Milan in 1927. He has designed for Bazzani, Ultravox, GM Arredamenti, Bando Line, ITT and Saporiti Proposals, among others. He took part in the 1959 Formica-*Domus* competition in Milan, the 1964 to 1968 Marionao Biennal Exhibitions and the 1968 exhibition in Trieste. His work has been shown in the Museum of Modern Art, New York, and the Victoria and Albert Museum, London, and was selected for the 1981 Compasso d'Oro. *(94)*

FREI OTTO is a German architect and engineer, born in 1925 in Seigmar. After serving his military service as a pilot, Otto studied architecture before travelling in the United States to study the work of Saarinen and others. Otto's concern has been to develop a socially responsible, rational engineering which despite its strikingly sculptural forms, often derived from naturally occurring shapes, provides the maximum amount of coverage in return for the minimum use of materials. Otto's best-known project was the canopy for the Munich Olympic Stadium of 1972. Since then he has worked extensively in the Middle East. In 1985, he became involved with the Golden Eye project, designing utensils intended to be made by Indian craftsmen. *(301, 480–482)*

P

PDD LTD is a design company run by **BRIAN SMITH**. He was born in Scotland in 1957 and studied at Napier College, Edinburgh, qualifying in 1979 with the college medal. Starting work as UK industrial designer for an American process control company, he moved to PDD in 1980 as design director. *(444)*.

PAOLO PEDRIZZETTI studied architecture at the Milan Politecnico, graduating in 1973. He worked in building design and building-site management until 1978, when he turned to product design. Pedrizzetti is also a journalist and collaborates with various Italian and foreign newspapers and magazines. *See also* **DAVIDE MERCATALI**. *(491–493)*

PELIKAN DESIGN is a Danish design consultancy established in 1975 by **LARS MATHIESEN** and **NIELS GAMMELGAARD**. They have produced a number of pieces of innovative furniture design together, working mostly in metal, as well as children's toys and bathroom fittings. Their designs include a sofa for IKEA, the Swedish manufacturer and retailer. In 1983 they designed the *Café* chair for Fritz Hansen, in rubber and steel. *(45–47)*

MAURIZIO PEREGALLI, an Italian interior and furniture designer, is a founder member of the Zeus organization, a gallery, shop and manufacturing label which mixes design with art and fashion. He has also been responsible for the design of a number of shop interiors, notably for Giorgio Armani. *(113, 114)*

ROBERTO PEZZETTA was born in Treviso, Italy, in 1946. An industrial designer with experience of a number of large Italian companies, he has been head of industrial design for Zanussi Elettrodomestici since 1982. *(445, 446)*

RENZO PIANO was born in Genoa, Italy, in 1937 and graduated in architecture from the Milan Politecnico in 1964. He has worked with the British architect Richard Rogers on a number of projects, including most notably the Centre Georges Pompidou in Paris, completed in 1977. Since 1977 he has worked in partnership with the engineer Peter Rice on architectural and design projects including a prototype car for Fiat. *(32)*

PAOLO PIVA was born in Italy in 1950. He attended the International University of the Arts, Venice and studied at the Faculty of Architecture, Venice under Carlo Scarpa. In 1975, while working for the Institute of History and Architecture, Venice, he organized a major exhibition on Vienna during the socialist period. This exhibition gave birth to a similar one in Rome in 1980 called 'Red Vienna'. In 1980 he was invited to design the Kuwait Embassy in Qatar. He has worked for a wide variety of companies in Europe and the USA and has designed the interior displays of several clothing-shop chains. *(56)*

FERDINAND ALEXANDER PORSCHE was born in West Germany in 1935. He was educated at the Ulm Design School then worked briefly in an engineering company before joining the family car-making business. He was responsible for the design of two sports models including the classic *911*. In 1972 he established his own product design consultancy, **PORSCHE DESIGN**, in Zell-am-Zee in Austria, working on a range of goods that includes wrist watches and sunglasses, marketed under the Porsche Design label, as well as furniture, lighting and electrical equipment for other companies. *(207–212, 460)*

JULIAN POWELL-TUCK, interior designer and architect, born in Britain in 1954, works in the London consultancy Powell-Tuck-Connor, architects and designers. *(219–221, 228)*

BRUNO POZZI was born in Varese, Italy in 1931. He started work in 1951, designing ceramics for Rosenthal in West Germany, lighting for Guzzini and cutlery for Alitalia; he has worked too for Pierre Cardin, among many other clients. He is a member of the Italian Association for Industrial Design and in 1984 won the Hanover Die Gute Industrieform Award. *(57)*

R

FRANCO RAGGI was born in Milan, Italy, in 1945 and graduated in architecture from the Milan Politecnico in 1969. He has edited a number of journals and organized several major design exhibitions. He has written extensively and his work has been widely published. He has collaborated with a number of major companies. *(95)*

HANS-PETER RAINER is an Austrian industrial and furniture designer. *(85, 86, 89)*

MATTHEW RICE is a British artist and designer, co-founder (with **DAVID LINLEY**) of David Linley Furniture Ltd. He trained as a painter at the Chelsea Art School, and at the Central School of Art, London, in theatre design. *(186)*

MARK ROCHESTER was born in Britain in 1958. From 1977 to 1980 he studied at the Central School of Art and Design, London. He subsequently worked for the textile company Warners for five years, designing and colouring fabrics, and has also designed, printed and made limited-edition shirts for Scott Crolla. *(354)*

CHRIS ROSE was born in Britain in 1950. He studied industrial design at the Central School of Art and Design, London, and furniture and environmental design at the Royal College of Art, London, where he met **FRED BAIER**. He has undertaken special furniture commissions,

consultancy and art direction. He is at present a second-year course tutor at the School for Craftsmen in Wood, Parnham, Dorset. He has exhibited in London, Philadelphia and Brisbane. *(187)*

BRUNO ROTA was born in Agen, France, in 1941. He works as a furniture designer and industrial designer, and was awarded the Compasso d'Oro in 1979 and the Dunlopillo Design Award in 1981 for a project for an electronically-controlled adjustable seat. He is a lecturer at Parsons School of Design and the European Institute of Design, Milan. *(6, 7, 20)*

S

ELIEL SAARINEN was born in Finland in 1873 and died in 1950, a naturalized American citizen. Saarinen trained simultaneously as an architect and a painter in Helsinki. After a distinguished career in Finland, working in a romantic, nationalistic interpretation of Classicism, Saarinen moved to America in 1923, on the strength of a well-received submission in the Chicago Tribune Competition. There he became the leading light of the Cranbrook Academy of Art, while also pursuing an independent architectural practice, in the years after 1945, in partnership with his son Eero. *(197)*

MARIA SANCHEZ is an Argentinian designer now based in Italy. She works for **ETTORE SOTTSASS JR** in his Milan consultancy, Sottsass Associati. She contributed a piece to the 1985 Memphis collection. *(328)*

DENIS SANTACHIARA was born in Italy in 1951. He is self-taught, and began working in the car industry designing car bodies in Modena. He participated in the 1983 Milan Triennale with his *Dream House* project. Since then he has produced numerous designs that blur the distinctions between art and design. *(256, 258)*

FUMIO SASA was born in Japan in 1924 and graduated from the Institute of Industrial Art and Technics, Tokyo. He is senior executive managing director of the Hoya Corporation and Chairman of the Japan Craft Design Association. He designs glassware, and his works have been chosen for the permanent collection of the Corning Museum of Glass, New York. *(287)*

RICHARD SATHERLEY was born in New Zealand in 1946. He studied at art schools in Auckland and in Cape Town before completing a Master's degree in design at the Royal College of Art, London. In 1975 he established a design consultancy specializing in industrial design. His work for Logica UK's data terminal helped the company win a Queen's Award for Industry. His designs have also been selected by the Design Council, London, and are included in the permanent collection of Die Neue Sammlung, Munich. *(462)*

FELIX SCARLETT is a British designer who trained at the Royal College of Art, London in product design. After graduating he worked with the Munich consultancy **SCHLAGHECK & SCHULTES DESIGN** on a range of lights. In 1985 he established Atlantic Design in London with Richard Appleby. Their clients include Excel, Wharfedale and Sony. *(223)*

AFRA SCARPA was born in Montebelluna, Italy, in 1937, and graduated from the Architectural Institute, Venice.

She and her husband **TOBIA SCARPA** have worked together for more than 25 years. In 1958 they began working in glass with Venini at Murano. They created the *Bastiano* divan and *Vanessa* metal bed for Gavina, and for Cassina they designed the *Soriana* armchair, which won the Compasso d'Oro award in 1970, and the *925* armchair, which is on permanent display at the Museum of Modern Art, New York. The *Torcello* system, designed for Stildomus, and the *Morna* bed are among their other famous creations. They are responsible for the image of the Benetton shops in Europe and America, and they occasionally work as architects as well as designers. Examples of their architectural work include the restoration of the Fragiacomo family house in Trieste, the Lorenzin family house at Abano Terme, and the Benetton woollen factory and house at Ponsano. Their pieces can be seen in major museums all over the world, and many have been chosen for various international design exhibitions. *(78)*

TOBIA SCARPA was born in 1935 in Venice, Italy. After a brief time working in the glass industry, he launched a highly successful design collaboration. *See also* **AFRA SCARPA**. *(78, 249, 250)*

SCHLAGHECK & SCHULTES DESIGN is based in Munich and is responsible for, among other things, a number of lights for Vereinigte Werkstätten. Its president is **HERBERT SCHULTES**, a German industrial designer who was born in Freiburg in 1938. He studied in Munich and went on to lecture at the Cologne Technical College and the Fachhochschule, Munich. He has been the chief designer at Siemens since 1985. *(223)*

OLE SCHJOLL is a Danish furniture designer. He trained as a cabinetmaker but now designs for mass production as well as making his own pieces. He has exhibited at shows including the Copenhagen Cabinetmakers' Exhibition in 1985. *(48)*

WULF SCHNEIDER, German furniture designer and interior architect, was born in 1943. He studied at the School of Applied Arts, Stuttgart, then worked as an independent designer and interior architect before starting his association with **ULRICH BOEHME**, working for Gebrüder Thonet. *(30, 31)*

AKIRA SHIRAHATA was born in Tokyo, Japan, in 1944, and is employed at the Musashi crystal factory as an art sculptor. *(294)*

PETER SHIRE was born in Los Angeles in 1947, and was educated at the Chovinard Institute of Art. His sculptural furniture designs attracted the attention of **ETTORE SOTTSASS**, and from 1981 onward he has been involved in producing furniture with the Memphis group. *(151)*

PIOTR SIERAKOWSKI was born in Warsaw, Poland, in 1957. He studied industrial design at the Brussels La Cambra National School of Architecture and the Visual Arts. *(75)*

ASAHARA SIGHEAKI was born in Tokyo in 1948. He lived in Italy between 1967 and 1971, and opened a design and furnishing studio in Tokyo in 1973. He now divides his time between Japan and Italy. He has worked for a number of companies in each country, and is also interested in conceptual sculpture. *(203, 204)*

BOREK SIPEK was born in Prague, Czechoslovakia, in 1949 and studied furniture design at the Prague School of Arts until 1968. In 1969 he started an architecture course at the Hamburg Academy of Art. From 1979 to 1983, he was a lecturer in industrial design at the University of Essen. Since 1983 he has worked as an independent designer and architect in Amsterdam. *(285, 286, 288)*

ALVARO SIZA was born in Matosinhos, Portugal, in 1933. He trained as an architect at the University of Oporto and is one of Portugal's best known architects internationally. He is responsible for a number of social housing schemes. Recently he has begun to design furniture in addition to his architectural work, and teaching at Oporto where he is now Professor of Architecture. *(107)*

SMART DESIGN INC. is run by an American, **DAVID STOWELL**, born in 1953. He graduated from Syracuse University, New York State, in industrial design and has been in practice as an industrial designer since 1979, since 1986 under the name of Smart Design. His projects include corporate-identity schemes, packaging, consumer products and industrial equipment. *(295, 455, 456)*

ETTORE SOTTSASS JR was born in Austria in 1917. He studied at the Milan Politecnico, and opened an office there in 1947. Since 1957 he has worked for Olivetti SpA, but is also active in fields as various as ceramics, jewellery, decorations, lithographs and drawings. He has taught and exhibited widely. In 1980 he established Sottsass Associati with some other architects, and has designed many pieces of furniture that are part of the Memphis collection. *(152–154, 322–324, 479, 484)*

GEORGE SOWDEN was born in England in 1942. He studied architecture at Cheltenham College of Art from 1960 to 1968, and in 1970 moved to Milan to work in the Olivetti design studio with **ETTORE SOTTSASS**, particularly in the area of information technology. He is a founder member of the Memphis group, and has produced furniture for each of its collections, as well as continuing in a consultancy role and collaborating independently with **NATHALIE DU PASQUIER**. *(150, 156–159, 335, 379–385)*

PHILIPPE STARCK was born in Paris in 1949 and works as a product, furniture and interior designer. His interiors include private apartments for President Mitterrand at the Elysée Palace, and the Café Costes restaurant in Paris. His furniture is made in Italy and Spain by a number of companies including Driade (Aleph) and Disform. *(124–139)*

ROBERT A. M. STERN was born in New York in 1939. He studied at Columbia and Yale Universities, and became a partner in the firm John S. Hagmann, architects and planners, in 1969. He also worked as a designer in **RICHARD MEIER'S** New York office, and as a consultant to Philip Johnson for a television documentary on New York. He teaches at Columbia, has held office in a number of professional bodies, and has been a member of several architectural and pedagogical committees. *(308, 309)*

GIOTTO STOPPINO was born in Vigerano, Italy, in 1926, and studied architecture in Milan. From 1953 until 1968, when he opened his own office, he worked with Vittorio Gregotti in the partnership of Architetti Associati. Stoppino has designed furniture for Bernini, Kartell and Acerbis, lights for Arteluce, and took part in the New York Museum of Modern Art exhibition, 'Italy: The New Domestic Landscape'. *(49, 50, 310)*

MARTIN SZEKELY, a French artist and furniture designer, was born in 1956. He is one of the group of young designers loosely grouped under the umbrella of Via, the government-sponsored Paris showroom set up by Mitterrand's government to promote design. He was the winner of a Castelli bursary in 1984. His furniture is in the permanent collection of the Musée des Arts Decoratifs de Paris and the French National Collection of Contemporary Art. *(109)*

KAZUNA TANAKA, born in Tokyo, is now resident in America. He graduated in graphic design from the Boston Museum School of Fine Arts, and in industrial design from the Pratt Institute in 1974. In 1980 he established his own design consultancy in New York with **JEFFREY KAPEC**, called the Tanaka Kapec Design Group. *(457, 458, 490)*

RITA TASKINEN was born in Helsinki, Finland, in 1949. She attended the University of Applied Arts, Helsinki, from 1977 to 1982. Since 1979 she has been a freelance designer, working in furniture, interior, exhibition and graphic design. In addition Taskinen has worked as a journalist and has written extensively about the design field. *(90, 91)*

GERARD TAYLOR, born in Britain in 1954, worked in Milan with Sottsass Associati in connection with Memphis, producing furniture and interior designs. He was a winner of the Gordon Russell office furniture design prize. In 1985 he established a partnership in London with Daniel Weil. *(76)*

CHRISTIAN THEILL was born in Remscheid, West Germany in 1954. He moved to Italy in 1975 and studied in Florence at the Italian State Design University, graduating in 1980. He worked with various design consultancies, including **ANTONIO CITTERIO**. In 1981 he established an independent industrial and interior design consultancy, producing furniture for, among others, Poltrovova, and lights for Eleusi. *(147)*

GRAHAM THOMSON is a Scottish designer, who graduated in industrial design from Napier College, Edinburgh. He spent two years with the design consultancy Ogle before moving for two years to Loewy. He joined Brand New in 1983, where he was responsible for setting up their activities in industrial design. *(401–403)*

MATTEO THUN was born in Austria in 1952 and graduated from Florence University. He was a founding member of the Memphis design group and established his own design company in Milan in 1984. His work has been shown in Berlin, Hanover, Düsseldorf, Vienna, Los Angeles and at the 1983 Milan Triennale. He is a Professor of Product Design and Ceramics at the Academy of Arts, Vienna. *(61, 266)*

STANLEY TIGERMAN was born in 1930. He is a controversial American architect who studied at the Yale School of Architecture, and is now a principal in Tigerman, Fugman, McCurry, in Chicago. He organized the 'Chicago Seven' and curated their shows. His designs have been exhibited internationally, including at the Museum of Modern Art, New York. He has published widely and has been awarded numerous prizes. He often collaborates with **MARGARET McCURRY**. *(346, 347)*

MAISA TIKKANEN was born in 1952 in Oulujoki, Finland. She studied textile design at the University of Industrial Arts and has, since 1973, participated in several exhibitions in Finland and abroad. She won a bronze medal at the 5th International Textile Triennial at Lodz, Poland in 1985. *(392, 393)*

OSCAR TUSQUETS was born in Barcelona, Spain, in 1941. He attended the Higher Technical School of Architecture, Barcelona and in 1964 he established the Studio PER with Lluis Clotet, with whom he collaborated on nearly all of his projects until 1984. He has been a guest professor and lecturer at universities in Germany, France and the USA, and his work has been exhibited in many parts of Europe and the USA. He has received many awards, for his work both as an architect and as a designer. *(33, 43, 44)*

ALAN TYE DESIGN is run by **ALAN TYE**, who studied as an architect but has practised product design for 20 years. His firm is one of Britain's leading design practices and has received 23 design awards. Over 10 million Alan Tye Design products have been sold worldwide. *(486)*

MASANORI UMEDA was born in Kanagawa, Japan, in 1941. He graduated from the Kuwazawa Design Institute in 1962 and won the Braun Prize in 1968. Since 1970 he has been consultant to Olivetti. He established the Umeda design studio in 1979, and has been associated with the Memphis group since 1981. *(263, 264)*

CARLO A. URBINATI-RICCI was born in Italy in 1955. He studied architecture at Rome University and now works in collaboration with **ALESSANDRO VECCHIATO** designing lamps for Foscarini. *(259, 262)*

JAAK FLORIS VAN DEN BROECKE was born in 1945 in Harlingen, the Netherlands. He was educated in the Department of Painting, Arnhem Academy and the School of Furniture Design, Royal College of Art, London. He has been Professor of Furniture Design at the Royal College of Art since 1985, and is a furniture maker and designer. *(96–99)*

CHARLES VANDENHOVE, Belgian architect and furniture designer, was born in 1927. He graduated in architecture at Brussels in 1951. He has been Dean of Studies at Mons Polytechnic since 1970. *(181–184)*

PETER VAN DER HAM was born in the Netherlands in 1950. He studied product design at the Academy for Industrial Design, Eindhoven, and worked for 10 years as a staff designer for a variety of Dutch furniture firms. Since

1984 he has worked as an independent designer in the fields of ergonomics, exhibition design and graphics. *(80)*

MARC VAN HOE was born in Zulte, Belgium, in 1945, and studied at the Royal Academy of Fine Arts, Kortrijk. Since 1975 he has been a freelance designer and technical researcher in the field of industrial textiles and tapestry. He is a teacher at the Royal Academy of Fine Arts, Kortrijk, and a Docent at the Academie voor Beeldende Vorming in Tilburg, the Netherlands. He has had exhibitions of his work in Belgium, France, Switzerland, Poland, Hungary and England. *(366, 367)*

ANDRIES VAN ONCK was born in Amsterdam in 1928, and is now a resident of Milan. He studied with Rietveld in Holland and at the Ulm Hochschule für Gestaltung under Max Bill and Thomas Maldonado, and collaborated with **ETTORE SOTTSASS** on the design of Olivetti's first main frame computers. In 1965 he opened his own studio in Milan and now, with his wife **HIROKO VAN ONCK**, works for many companies, including Zanussi, Philips and La Rinascente. His work won a Compasso d'Oro in 1979. *(487–489)*

MART VAN SCHIJNDEL was born in 1943 in Hengelo, the Netherlands. He is a lecturer at the Dutch Academy of Architecture, and at the University of Düsseldorf. He has been in practice as an architect in Utrecht since 1969; his principal works include stations for the Netherlands Railways and the Utrecht Chamber of Commerce, as well as interior and product design. *(300)*

ALESSANDRO VECCHIATO was born in Italy in 1959. He studied architecture in Venice. *See also* **CARLO A. URBINATI-RICCI.** *(259, 262)*

JORMA VENNOLA was born in Helsinki, Finland, in 1943. He studied in the department of Industrial Design at Helsinki University. He has worked as a toy designer in the USA, and for the Corning glassworks on household utensils. Since 1975 he has been working as a glass designer for littala. *(319–321)*

ROBERT VENTURI, born in 1925, is an American architect whose works have won international recognition. He has been the subject of innumerable exhibitions, awards and special publications. He was educated at Princeton University, where he received both his AB and MFA, and at the American Academy, Rome. He was a Rome Prize Fellow from 1954 to 1956. He holds several honorary doctorates from American universities, and in 1983 was the recipient of the Louis Sullivan Award and Prize of the International Union of Bricklayers and Allied Craftsmen. That same year Virginia University honoured him with the Thomas Jefferson Memorial Foundation Medal. He is a partner in the architectural firm Venturi, Rauch and Scott Brown, and is the author of several books on architecture, notably *Complexity and Contradiction*. He was recently commissioned by the National Gallery, London, to design a new extension, and has designed furniture for Knoll International, and products for Alessi. *(471–473)*

LELLA AND MASSIMO VIGNELLI are a husband-and-wife-team. They studied in Venice, Italy, and in 1960 established the Massimo and Lella Vignelli Office of Design and Architecture in Milan, working with graphics, products, furniture and interiors. In 1965 they founded Unimark International Corporation, and, in 1971, Vignelli Associates, with an office in New York and liaison offices in Paris and Milan. They provide designs for a wide range of major companies, and have received awards and honorary doctorates for their work. *(21, 82–84, 284)*

GIANPIER VITELLI is an Italian furniture designer. He began his careeer as an independent designer in 1954 with an armchair for Rossi di Albizzate. From 1964 he began a partnership with **TITINA AMMANNATI**, producing furniture for Rossi, Brunati and Pozzi & Verga. *(5)*

HANS VON KLIER was born in Teschen, Czechoslovakia, in 1934. He graduated in industrial design at the Hochschule für Gestaltung, Ulm, in 1959, then worked in the office of **ETTORE SOTTSASS** until 1968. Since 1969 he has been head of Olivetti's corporate identity department. His furniture designs include the *Ponte* conference table for Skipper, 1972, and the *Sit* system for Rossi Arredementi. At Olivetti he has collaborated on the design of electric typewriters and calculators. *(222)*

W

STEFAN WEWERKA was born in 1928 in Magdeburg, Germany, and lives in Cologne and Berlin. Wewerka is a polymath who worked initially as an architect then moved into sculpture and painting during the course of the 1960s. In 1974 he designed his first chair for Tecta, and since then has produced a number of increasingly elaborate pieces of environmental furniture for them, in addition to designing clothes and jewellery. *(34, 35)*

TAPIO WIRKKALA was born in Hanko, Finland, in 1915 and died in 1985. He graduated from the Academy of Arts in Helsinki, where he was later artistic director. Originally a sculptor and graphic designer, he gained world-wide recognition as a designer of tableware, and in particular for the glass which he made for littala. He won seven Grand Prix awards from the Milan Triennale. He was a member of the Finnish Academy, the Royal Society of Arts, London, and the holder of an honorary doctorate from the Royal College of Art, London. *(317)*

DIETER WITTE was born in Germany in 1937. He studied in Hanover from 1957 to 1961, and worked in a design group until he opened his own office in 1966 together with his designer wife, Heidi Witte. In 1977 he began to work permanently with Osram. *(213, 214)*

RICK WRIGLEY is an American craftsman designer. He trained at the School for American Craftsmen at Rochester Institute of Technology, and is based in Holyoke, Massachusetts. His work has been featured in exhibitions at such museums and galleries as the Renwick Gallery of the National Museum of American Art, the Cooper-Hewitt Museum, New York and the Musée des Arts Decoratifs, Montreal. (The Publishers wish to apologize for their transposition of the details of a piece of furniture by Mitch Ryerson, no. 167, with those of a piece by Rick Wrigley, no. 168, in the 1985/86 *International Design Yearbook*. Rick Wrigley's piece was in fact not manufactured by the Formica Corporation, USA but by himself.) *(189, 190)*

Z

MARCO ZANINI was born in Italy in 1954. He studied architecture at the University of Florence, graduating in 1978. Since then he has been a designer with Sottsass Associati in Milan. *(162, 327)*

MARCO ZANUSO JNR was born in Milan, Italy, in 1954, the son of the distinguished Italian designer Marco Zanuso. He graduated in architecture from the University of Florence and established his own office in 1980, working on exhibition design, architecture and industrial design. In 1981 he established Oceano Oltreluce, a lighting company, with Bepi Maggiori and Luigi and Pietro Greppi. *(265)*

SUPPLIERS

Fullest possible details are given of suppliers of the designs featured here; the activities of some outlets and manufacturers however are limited solely to the place of origin of their work.

A

ACERBIS INTERNATIONAL Via Brusaporto 31, 24068 Seriate, Bergamo, Italy.
Outlets France: Roger van Barry, 18 Rue Laffitte, 75009 Paris. UK: Artemide GB Ltd, 17/19 Neal Street, London WC2H 9PU. USA: Memphis Milano, 150 E. 58 Street, New York, NY 10155.

ADELTA OY Tunturikatu 9 A 1, 00100 Helsinki, Finland.

ALEPH Driade, Via Felice Casati 20, 20124 Milan, Italy.

ALESSI SPA Via Privata Alessi, 28023 Crusinallo (No), Italy.
Outlets France: DBM Associés sarl, 12 Rue Martel, 75010 Paris. The Netherlands: Interhal Bv, Lindtsedijk 74, 3336 Le Zwijndrecht. UK: Penhallow Marketing Ltd, 3 Vicarage Road, Sheffield S9 3RH. USA: The Schawbel Corporation, 281 Albany Street, Cambridge, Massachusetts 02139. West Germany: Fulvio Folci, Dahlenweg 14, 4000 Düsseldorf 30.

ALIAS SRL Via Respighi 2, 20122 Milan, Italy.
Outlets UK: Alias UK Ltd, 17/19 Neal Street, London WC2H 9PU.

G & S ALLGOOD LTD 297 Euston Road, London NW1 3AQ, UK.
Outlets Hong Kong: McLaren Coghill, 13/F Guardian House, OI Kwan Road. Japan: Sun Trading Co. Ltd, PO Box 77, OMM building, Osaka 540. USA: The Ironmonger, 1822 North Sheffield Avenue, Chicago, Illinois 60614.

ALTAFORM Gladzaxevej 311, 2860 Soborg, Denmark.

AMADEO LTD 2–4 Camden High Street, London NW1, UK.

JUNICHI ARAI, Antoroji KK, Sakai-no-cho 1-1228, Kiryu-shi, Gunma-ken, Japan.

ARAM DESIGNS LTD 3 Kean Street, London WC2 4AT, UK.

ARFLEX SPA Via Monte Rosa 27, Limbiate, Milan, Italy.
Outlets France: Altras, 18 Rue Lafitte, 75009 Paris. Japan: Arflex Japan Ltd, Axis Building, B1-5-171 Rappongi Minato-ku, Tokyo. The Netherlands: Andrea Kok, Bilderdijkkade 5HS 1052 RS, Amsterdam. UK: Neil Rogers, 22 Englewood Road, London SW12 9NA. USA: Beylerian Ltd, 305 E. 63 Street, New York, NY 10021.

ARTELUCE Via Moretto 58, Brescia, Italy.
Outlets France: Flos Sarl, 23 Rue de Bourgogne, Paris 73007. Switzerland: Flos SA, 36 Place de Bourg de Feur, Geneva 1204. UK: Flos Ltd, Heath Hall, Heath, Wakefield, W. Yorks. WF1 5SL. USA: Atelier International, 595 Madison Avenue, New York.

ARTEMIDE SPA Via Brughiera, 20010 Pregnana Milanese, Milan, Italy.
Outlets France: Artemide SA, Rue du Faubourg St Honoré, 75008 Paris. Japan: Artemide Inc., 3-12-4 Sotokanda Chiyodaku, Tokyo 101. UK: Artemide GB Ltd, 17/19 Neal Street, London WC2H 9PU. USA: Artemide Inc., 150 E. 58 Street, New York, NY 10155. West Germany: Artemide GmbH, 60 Koenigsallee, 4000 Düsseldorf.

ART ET INDUSTRIE LTD 594 Broadway, New York, NY 10012, USA.

ARTIFORT St Annalaan 23, 6214 AA Maastricht, The Netherlands.
Outlets France: Artifort France, 221 Rue Benoit Frachon, 78500 Sartrouville. Italy: FAI, Via Garibaldi 6, Cas. Post. 129, 2033 Desio Milan. Japan: Houtoku Company Ltd, Kyogin Building, 22-chome, 15-2 Nishiki, Nakaku, Nagoya. UK: Interspace, 22 Rosemont Road, London NW3 6NE. USA: Castelli Furniture Inc., 116 Wilbur Place, Bohemia, NY 11716. West Germany: Artifort Möbel GmbH, 256 Kölnerstrasse, 5000 Cologne 90.

ATERIA 6-3-11-802 Minami-Aoyama, Minato-ku, Tokyo 107, Japan.

AUTHENTICS (COVENT GARDEN) LTD, 42 Shelton Street, London WC2H 9HZ, UK.

AVARTE OY Kalevankatu 16, SF–00100 Helsinki, Finland.
Outlets UK: Bristol International, Euroway Industrial Park, Swindon SN5 8YW. US: Beylerian Ltd, 305 E. 63 Street, New York, NY 10021.

AXIL Via Gáldini 205, 20036 Meda (Mi), Italy.

B

B&B ITALIA Strada Provinciale, 72060 Novedrate (Como), Italy.

BALERI ITALIA 24035 Curno, Bergamo, Italy.
Outlets Belgium: Kreymborg, Avenue Molière 66, 1180 Brussels. France: Sarah Nathan, 27 bis Boulevard Raspail, 75007 Paris. Japan: Casatec Ltd, 0906 Higashi 2, Chome-Shibuya-ku, Tokyo 150. The Netherlands: Kreymborg, Minervalaan 63, 1077 Nr Amsterdam. Sweden: Design Distribution, Dobelnsgatan 38/A1, 11352 Stockholm. UK: SCL Ltd, 135–139 Curtain Road, London EC2A 3BY. USA: ICF Inc., 305 E. 63 Street, New York, NY 10021. West Germany: Ital Import GmbH, Sofienhohe 6, D8501 Heroldsberg.

BANG & OLUFSEN AS 7600 Struer, Denmark.
Outlets Australia: Bang & Olufsen (Aus) Pty Ltd, 136 Camberwell Road, East Hawthorn, Victoria 3123. Canada: Lenbrook Industries Ltd, 1145 Bellamy Road, Scarborough, Ontario M1H 1H5. Finland: OY Bang & Olufsen AB, Kuortanegatan 1, 00520 Helsingfors 52. France: Bang & Olufsen France SA, 4 Rue du Port,

92110 Clichy. Israel: Danish Elecironichs Ltd, Salesian Str, 3 Haifa 33032. Italy: Dodi SpA, Via Enrico Fermi 1, 20090 Noverasco D'Opera (Mi). Japan: Bang & Olufsen of Japan Ltd, Bancho Matsufuji Building 211, Rokubancho 1, Chiyoda-ku, Tokyo. The Netherlands: Bang & Olufsen Nederland BV, Koninginneweg 54, 1241 CV Kortenhoef. Spain: Gaplasa SA, C/Sandalo, 5 Madrid 22. Sweden: Bang & Olufsen Svenska AB, Albygatan 113, Solna. Switzerland: Bang & Olufsen AG, Grindelstrasse 15, 8303 Bassersdorf. UK: Bang & Olufsen United Kingdom Ltd, Eastbrook Road, Gloucester GL4 7DE. USA: Bang & Olufsen of America Inc., 1150 Feehanville Drive, Mt Prospect, Illinois 60056. West Germany: Bang & Olufsen (Deutschland) GmbH, Wandalenweg 20, 2000 Hamburg 1.

BD MUEBLAS, Mallorca 293, Barcelona, Spain.

BEHR MÖBELFABRIK GMBH & CO. KG, PO Box 1254, D-7317 Wendlingen, West Germany.

BENT KROGHS STALMÖBELFABRIK AS 8660 Skanderbord, Denmark.

BIANCHI Via Como 15, 22060 Figino Serenza (10), Italy.

BIEFFEPLAST SPA PO Box 406, 1-35100 Padova, Italy.

BLACK & DECKER (US) INC. 701 East Joppa Road, Towson, Maryland 21204, USA.
Outlets Australia: Black & Decker Australasia Pty, Maroondah Highway, Croydon, Victoria 3136. Canada: Black & Decker (Canada) Inc., 100 Central Avenue, Brockville, Ontario, Canada K6Y 5W6. France: Black & Decker (France), PO Box 0633 Lyon RP, 69239 Lyon Cedex 02. Israel: Black & Decker (Israel), PO Box 116 Area Code 58815, 26 Hasadna Street, Industrial Area, Holon. Italy: Black & Decker Italia SpA, Via Broggi 16, 22040 Civate (Como). The Netherlands: Black & Decker (Nederland) BV, Postbus 11070, Industrieweg 167, 3044 As Rotterdam. Norway: Black & Decker (Norge) AS, PO Box 93, Rislokka, 0516 Oslo 5. Portugal: Black & Decker (Portugal) Lida, Apartado 19, S Joao do Estoril, 2768 Estoril Codex. Singapore: Black & Decker South East Asia Pty, 33 Gul Avenue, PO Box 114, Jurong Town, Singapore 22. Spain: Black & Decker de España SA, Crta acceso a Roda de Bara, KM 0.7, Roda de Bara, Tarragona. Sweden: Black & Decker AB, Box 603, 421 26 Vastra Frolunda. Switzerland: Black & Decker Schweiz AG, Huettenwiesenstrasse 8, 180A Daellikon, Zurich. UK: Black & Decker, Westpoint, The Grove, Slough, Berkshire SL1 1QQ. West Germany: Black & Decker (Deutschland) GmbH, Postfach 1202, Black & Decker Strasse 40, 6270 Idstein/Taunus.

CANON INC. PO Box 5050, Shinjuku Dai–Ichi Seimei Building, Tokyo 160, Japan.
Outlets Austria: Canon Gesellschaft mbh, Modecenterstrasse 22 A-2, 1030 Wien. Belgium: Canon Copiers Belgium nVISA, Luidlaam 33-Bus 6, 100 Brussels. Canada: Canon Canada Inc., 3245 American Drive, Mississauga, Ontario L4V 1N4. Denmark: Christian Bruhn AS, Vasekaer 12, 2739 Herlev. France: Canon

France SA, PO Box 40, 93151 Le Blanc Mesnil. Italy: Canon Italia SpA, Centro Direzionale, Palazzo Verrocchio, 20090 Milano 2 - Segrate (Mi). The Netherlands: Canon Verkooporganisatie Nederland BV, Cruquiusweg 29, 2102 LS Heemstede, Amsterdam. Norway: Noiseless AS, Tvetenveien 30B, Oslo 6. Spain: Canon Copiadoras de España SA, Avd. Menendez Pelayo, 67, Torre Del Retiro, Madrid. Sweden: Canon Svenska AB, Box 2084, Stensätravä gen 13, 127 02 Skärholmen. Switzerland: Canon SA, Genève, 1 Rue de Hesse, 1204 Geneva. UK: Canon (UK) Ltd, Canon House, Manor Road, Wallington, Surrey SM6 0AJ. USA: Canon USA Inc., One Canon Plaza, Lake Success, New York 11042–9979. West Germany: Canon Copylux GmbH, Luerriper Strasse 1–13, 4050 Moenchen-gladbach.

CAPPELLINI INTERNATIONAL INTERIORS SNC 2060 Carugo, Italy.

CASAS Milagro 40, 08028 Barcelona, Spain.
Outlets France: Signature, 146 Boulevard Camelinat, 92240 Malakoff, Paris. Portugal: SPI International, Lisbon. USA: ICF, 305 E. 63 Street, New York, NY 10021.

CASIGLIANI SRL Via P. Barsanti 4, 56014 Ospedaletto, Pisa, Italy.
Outlets Belgium: Interdiff, 21 Rue de la Sablonnière, 1000 Brussels. France: Stephen Simon, 40 Rue de Châteaudun, 94200 Ivry, Paris. Japan: Harada Sangyo Kaisha Ltd, 3-3 Chiba, 2-chome, Minateo-ku, Tokyo. UK: Bomain, 10 Jeffries Passage, Guildford, Surrey. USA: ICF International Contract F, 145 E. 57 Street, New York, NY 10022.

CASSINA SPA 1 Via Busnelli, 20036 Meda, Milan, Italy.
Outlets France: Cassina, 168 Rue du Faubourg St Honoré, Paris. The Netherlands: Mobica, Middenweg 31, MB Ijsselstein. Spain: Mobil Plast SL, Corso Milagro 40, Barcelona 28. UK: Environment, Heath Hall, Heath, Wakefield, W. Yorks WF1 5SL. USA: Atelier International, 595 Madison Avenue, New York.

CAST DESIGN SRL Via delle Nazioni 97, 41100 Modena, Italy.
Outlets France: J.E. Lehoux, Pontmort, 63200 Riom. The Netherlands: GIMKO International BV, Smidswater 11, 2514 BW den Haag. USA: Dennis Lamothe, 515 Magellan Road, Arcadia, California 91006. West Germany: Intraform String, Ebersberger Strasse 11, 8000 Munchen 86.

CASTELIJN COLLECTION BV Vrouwenweg LC, 3864 DX N Nijkerkerveen, The Netherlands.
Outlets Belgium: Hadex, Brussel Int. Trade Mart, Atomium Square, Brussels. Switzerland: LCM Promotions, 30c Route du Prieur, 1257 Croix de Rozen. UK: John Summerhill Design, Hill House, Frances Road, Middle Barton OX5 4ET. West Germany: Herr H. G. Wulf, Düsterstrasse 29, 4630 Bochum.

CERAMIC JAPAN CO LTD 118 Hironota-cho, Seto-chi, Aichi-Ken, 480-12, Japan.

CIATTI SPA 500100 Badia A, Settimo, Florence, Italy.
Outlets UK: Idea for Living, 5 Kensington High Street, London W8.

CITIZEN PO Box 238, Shinjuku Mitsui Building, 1-1 2-chome, Nishi Shinjuku, Shinjuku-ku, Tokyo 160, Japan.
Outlets Australia: Citizen Watches Australia Ltd, 122 Old Pittwater Road, Brookvale, New South Wales 2100. Austria: Hantor-Warenhandel, GmbH & Co. KG, Kirchengasse 3, Postfach 119, A-1071 Vienna 7. France: Japan Time SA, 24 Rue de Montmorency, 75003 Paris. Italy: Citizen Italia SPA, Viale Restelli 5/A, 20124 Milan. The Netherlands: Borsumij Time BV, Hoevenseweg 43, 4877 La Etten-Leur, PO Box 345, 4870 Ah Etten-Leur. Spain: Prenisa Iberica SA, Torre de Madrid, P13-7, Calle Princesa 1, PO Box 50105, Madrid 13. Sweden: Kauko Time AB, PO Box 1385, S 17127 Solna. Switzerland: Toki Time SA, 2 Rue Grenus, 1201 Geneva. UK: Citizen Watch (UK) Ltd, CP House, 97/107 Uxbridge Road, Ealing, London W5 5TP. USA: Citizen Service Headquarters, 8506 Osage Avenue, Los Angeles, CA 90045. West Germany: Citizen Europe Uhrenhandelsgesellschaft mbH, Horner Landstrasse 302–304, 2000 Hamburg 74.

CONCORD LIGHTING LTD Concord House, 241 City Road, London EC1V 1JD, UK.
Outlets France: Jumo Concord SA, 2 Rue Sadi-Carnot, 93170 Bagnolet, Paris. Italy: Tecnolyte Spa, Via Nazional 193, 00184 Rome. The Netherlands: Indoor BV, Paulus Potterstraat 22–24, Amsterdam 1071. Norway: Hoevik Lys, PO Box 100, 1751 Halden. Switzerland: Regent Beleuchtungskorper, Dornacherstrasse 390, 4018 Basel. USA: Lightolier Incorporated, 346 Claremont Avenue, Jersey City, New Jersey 07350. West Germany: Interlumen Lichtarchitektur GmbH, Zeiss Strasse 2, 5000 Köln 40.

COPCO Wilton Enterprises, 41 Madison Avenue, New York, NY 10010, USA.

COR–SITZKIMFORT Postfach 1229, 4840 Rheda-Wiedenbruck, West Germany.
Outlets Italy: Fai sas Internazionale, Via Garibaldi 6, 20033 Desio, Milan. The Netherlands: Hans Born BV, Hoofdstraat 170, 2070 BA Santpoort Noord. UK: Interlubke Ltd, 239 Greenwich High Road, London SE10 8NB.

CUBIC METRE FURNITURE 17–18 Great Sutton Street, London EC1, UK.
Outlets Sweden: Widen Sales Promotion, PO Box 39020, 40075 Gothenberg. UK: Cubic Metre Furniture, 6–10 Clerkenwell Road, London EC1.

DAICHI CO LTD 3-24-14 Toyo, Koto-ku, Tokyo, Japan.

DAIKO ELECTRIC CO. LTD 15–16 Nakamichi 3-chome, Higashinari-ku, Osaka 537, Japan.

DANBER Via la Repubblica 67, 20035 Lissone (Mi), Italy.

BRUNO DANESE SNC Piazza San Fedele 2, 20120 Milan, Italy.
Outlets Denmark: Interstudio, Esplanaden 6, 1263 Copenhagen. France: Danese France sarl, Boulevard Voltaire, 75011 Paris. Japan: Apex, Chez Azabut 101, 4-14-12 Nishiazabu, Minato-ku, Tokyo 106. The

Netherlands: Kreymborg, Minervalaan 63, 1077 Amsterdam. UK: The Architectural Trading Co, 219–229 Shaftesbury Avenue, London WC2H 8AR. West Germany: Designfocus GmbH, AM Schiessendahl 11 A, 5042 Erfstadt.

DAWN SYSTEMS LTD 25 Highcroft Industrial Estate, Down Road, Hurndean, Hants, UK.

DEAN LUSE COMPANY Suite E, 909 W. 22 Street, Houston, Texas 77008, USA.
Outlets USA: Grace Designs, World Trade Center, PO Box 58108, Dallas, Texas 75258.

DEGRAAFF FURNITURE 162/164 Abbey Street, London SE1, UK.

DESIGNERS GUILD 277 King's Road, London SW3 5EN, UK.
Outlets France: Etamine Distribution, BP 239 Le Coudray, 28001 Chartres Cedex. Italy: Augusto Giuliani, Via Capo Le Case 28, 00187 Roma. Japan: N. Nomura & Co Ltd, 33-2, Minai-Honmachi Higashi-ku, Osaka. The Netherlands: Wilhelmine van Aerssen, De Lairessestraat 60, 1071 PD Amsterdam. Norway: Designers Guild AS, Arbosgt. 2 (Inng Kirkeven), Oslo 3. West Germany: Nobilis Fontan GmbH, Postfach 165, Wendle Dietrich Strasse 4, 8000 Munich 19.

DESIGN M INGO MAURER GMBH, Kaiserstrasse 47, 8000 Munich 40, West Germany.
Outlets Denmark: Finn Sloth, Heilsmindeven 1, 2920 Charlottenlund. France: Altras, 18 Rue Lafitte, 75009 Paris. The Netherlands: PA Hesselmans & Zn, Korfgraaf 24, 4174 GM Hellouw. Sweden: Sandklef AB, Box 94, 29401 Sölvesborg.

DESIRON & LIZEN 42 Rue des Clarisses, B 4000 Liège, Belgium.

DISFORM Ronda General Mitre 63, 08017 Barcelona, Spain.
Outlets France: Edifice, 27 bis Boulevard Raspail, 75007 Paris. Italy: High Tech, Corso Porta Ticinese 12, 20123 Milan. Japan: Eishin Trading 6–5 Morishita 3-chome, Koto-ku, Tokyo 135. UK: Maison Designs, 917–919 Fulham Road, London SW6 5HU. USA: Vivere Corporation, 250 W. 57 Street, New York, NY 10019. West Germany: Kleine Friedrichstrasse 128, Siegen 1.

DYMENSION MODELS LTD 8–16 Cromer Street, London WC1H 8LL, UK.

E

EDILKAMIN SPA 20020 Lainate, Milan, Italy.

THOMAS EISL 39 Earlsfield Road, London SW18, UK.

MISURA EMME Via IV Novembre 72, 22066 Mariano Comense (Co), Italy.

ESPRIT 900 Minnesota Street, San Francisco 94107 CA, USA.

F

FLLI FANTINI SPA Via Buonarroti 4, 28010 Pella (No), Italy.

FIRMA FRANZ FERTIG 6900 Buchen Odenwald, West Germany.

FLOS SPA Via Moretto 58, Brescia, Italy.
Outlets France: Flos Sarl, 23 Rue de Bourgogne, Paris 75007. UK: Flos Ltd, Heath Hall, Heath, Wakefield, W. Yorks. WF1 5SL.

FONTANA ARTE SPA Via Alzaia Trieste 49, 20094 Corsico, Milan, Italy.
Outlets The Netherlands: Silvera BV, Postbus 163, 1250 Ad Laren. USA: Interna Design Ltd, The Merchandise Mart, Suite 6–168, Chicago, Illinois 60654.

FORGES SPA Via XXV Aprile, 12-24040 Bonate Sotta, Italy.
Outlets Australia: Panacon Australia Pty Ltd, 1/256 Stirling Highway, Claremount 6010, Western Australia. Belgium: Valli E Colombo Benelux NV, Koningin Astridlaan 2, 2550 Kontich. France: Valli E Colombo France sarl, 1 Avenue de L'Escouvier, Parc Industriel, 95200 Sarcelles. Japan: Ohta Kogyo Co. Ltd, 41 Konya-cho Kanda, Chiyoda-ku, Tokyo 101. Norway: Nibu AS, Postboks 34, 1321 Stabekk, Oslo. UK: Valli E Colombo Ltd, 8 Gerrard, Lichfield Road Industrial Estate, Tamworth, Staffs B79 7UW. USA: Valli E Colombo (USA) Ltd, PO Box 245, 1540 Highland Avenue, Duarte, CA 91010. West Germany: Valli E Colombo GmbH & Co., Industriestrasse 1, Postfach 208, 7107 Bad Wimpfen/Neckar.

FOSCARINI SPA, Fondamenta Manin 1, 30120 Murano Venezia, Italy.
Outlets Canada: Les Importations Volt, 281 Laurier Ouest, Montreal, Quebec. The Netherlands: Koos Rijske Agency, PR Chrisinalaan 1, 7437 XZ Bathmen. West Germany: Alta Lines, Sandhof 6, 4040 Neuss 21 Nord.

KAZUKO FUJIE 29-8 Sarugaku-cho, Shibuya-ku, Tokyo, Japan.

FUJITSU LTD GK Industrial Design Associates, 2-19-16 Shimo-Ochiai, Shinjuku-ku, Tokyo 161, Japan.
Outlets Finland: Oy Heltel, Huovitie 3, 00400 Helsinki.

FURNITURE DESIGNERS Telescope House, 63 Farringdon Road, London EC1M 3JB, UK.

FUSITAL SPA Via Gavazzi 16, 22035 Canzo (Co) Italy.
Outlets Australia: Panacon Australia Pty Ltd, 1/256 Stirling Highway, Claremount 6010, Western Australia. Belgium: Valli E Colombo Benelux NV, Koningin Astridlaan 2, 2550 Kontich. France: Valli E Colombo France sarl, 1 Avenue de L'Escouvier, Parc Industriel, 95200 Sarcelles. Japan: Everfast Ltd, Azabu Heights 302-5-10, 1-chome Roppoggi, Minato-ju, Tokyo 106. Norway: Nibu AS, Postboks 34, 1321 Stabekk, Oslo. UK: Valli E Colombo Ltd, 8 Gerrard, Lichfield Road Industrial Estate, Tamworth, Staffs B79 7UW. USA: Valli E Colombo (USA) Ltd, PO Box 245, 1540 Highland Avenue, Duarte, CA 91010. West Germany: Valli E

Colombo GmbH & Co., Industriestrasse 1, Postfach 208, 7107 Bag Wimpfen/Neckar.

G

PIER-LUIGI GHIANDA Via Desio 55, Bovisio Masciago, Italy.
Outlets France: Perkal, 8 Rue des Quatre Fils, 75003 Paris.

GLASHÜTTE SÜSSMUTH GMBH, D-3524 Immenhausen, West Germany.

MATTEO GRASSI SPA Via S, Caterina da Siena 26, 22066 Mariano (Co), Italy.
Outlets UK: Oscar Woollens Interiors International, 421 Finchley Road, London NW3 6HL.

H

HAKUSAN PORCELAIN CO. LTD Uchinomi Hasami-machi, Nagasaki-Ken, 859-37, Japan.

FRITZ HANSENS EFT. Depotvej 1, DK–3450 Allerod, Denmark.

HOYA CORPORATION 2-7-5 Nakaochiai, Shinjuku-ku, Tokyo 161, Japan.

I

IITTALA GLASSWORKS/A. AHLSTRÖM OSAKEYHTIÖ SF-14500 Iittala, Finland.
Outlets France: AG Distribution sarl, 56 Rue de Paradis, 75010 Paris. Iceland: Kristján Siggeirsson Ltd, PO Box 193, Reykjavik. Italy: Seambe srl, Via Marchesi de Taddei 10, 20146 Milan. Japan: Actus Corporation, 2-1-13 Shibuya, Shibuya-ku, Tokyo 150. The Netherlands: Max Sittkoff Marketing, Paulus Potterlaan 7, 3941 CP Doorn. Norway: Carl F. Myklestad, Postboks 153, Strömsvn 91 C, 1473 Skårer. UK: Storrington Trading Company Ltd, Eastmead Industrial Estate, Midhurst Road, Lavant, Chichester, West Sussex PO18 0DE. USA: Ahlström-Iittala Inc., 176 Clearbook Road, Elmsford, NY 10523. West Germany: Günter Lindenau, Riedener Strasse 12, 8000 München 71.

INNO TUOTE OY Merikatu, 1, 00140 Helsinki 14, Finland.
Outlets France: Jean Marc Lelouch, Passage Verdeau 22, 75009, Paris. Italy: Fin Form, Viale Montesanto 4, 20124 Milan. Norway: Scandinavia Martens Interior, Nobels Gate, 0268 Oslo. UK: Auvinen, 5 Belgrave Mews South, London SW1. USA: Polardesign, 2112 N. Halsted, Chicago, Illinois 60614. West Germany: Aami, Postfach 1128, D-Oelde 4, Stromberg.

ISHIMARU CO. LTD 1st Floor, Maison Akashi, Roppongi 7-3-24, Minato-ku, Tokyo, Japan.

K

KIMURA GLASS CO. LTD 3-10-7 Yushima, Bunkyo-ku, Tokyo 113, Japan.

KNOLL INTERNATIONAL LTD The Knoll Building, 655 Madison Avenue, New York, NY 10021, USA.
Outlets UK: 20 Savile Row, London W1.

KOCH + LOWY INC., 21–24 39th Avenue, Long Island City, NY 11101, USA.

MAKOTO KOMATSU 500-2 No, Gyôda-shi, Saitama-Ken 361, Japan.

L

LAMMHULTS MEKANISKA AB PO Box 26, 36030, Lammhult, Sweden.
Outlets France: Jacques Cabantous, 10 Rue Renault, 94160 Saint Mande. Italy: Rapsel SpA, Piazza de Angeli 7, 20146 Milan. The Netherlands: Frans Luten, Couwenhoven 63-17, 3703 HR Zeist. UK: The House of Sweden, 44–52 Hampstead Road, London NW2 2PD. West Germany: Werner Schmitz Collectionen GmbH, Düsseldorfer Strasse 151, 4000 Düsseldorf.

LIGHTOLIER INC., 346 Claremont Avenue, Jersey City, NJ 07305, USA.

DAVID LINLEY FURNITURE LTD 1 New King's Road, London SW6 4SB, UK.

MARY LITTLE 37 Henty Close, Ethelburga Street, London SW11, UK.

LOEWE OPTA GMBH Industriestrasse 1, 8640 Kronach, West Germany.
Outlets Austria: Loewe Opta Austria GmbH, Dierzerstrasse 20, 4020 Linz. UK: Loewe Opta UK Ltd, Farnell House, Church Street, Old Isleworth, Middlesex.

LONDON LIGHTING CO. 133–135 Fulham Road, London SW3 6RT, UK.

LUCEPLAN 48 Via Bellinzona, 20155 Milan, Italy.

LUCI SPA Via Pelizza da Volpedo 50, 20092 Cinisello Balsamo, Milan, Italy.

M

MARGO INTERNATIONAL FABRICS LTD 108 Shakespeare Road, London SE24 0QQ, UK.
Outlets Australia: Richard Clough, PO Box 452, Pymble, New South Wales. Belgium: Ets Bogaert, 31 Rue Ernest Allard, 1000 Bruxelles. France: Parimètre, 28 Rue des Bernadins, 75005 Paris. Italy: Vitorrio De Benedetti, Via GB Gisleni, Rome 00163. Norway: Bjorn Brandvold, Sofiesgate 66, 0168 Oslo 1. Portugal: David Israel, Rua General Taborda 74-1, 1000 Lisbon. Singapore: Anglo Swiss Trading Co. Pte Ltd, 66 Tannery Lane, Sindo Building, Singapore 1334. Sweden: Y. Berger & Co., PO Box 2025, S-42102 Vastra Frolunda. USA: Almondbury Ltd, The Ian Wall Studio, 979 3rd Avenue, New York, NY 10022.

MARIMEKKO OY Vanha Talvitie 3, 00500 Helsinki 50, Finland.

MARKS-PELLE VÄVARE AB S-51104 Kinna 4, Sweden.
Outlets Denmark: Bella Center, STM B4-238, Center Boulevard, 2300 Copenhagen. Finland: OY Lateco-Botim AB, PB 42, Spiselvägen 6, 00371 Helsinki. France: Tisca France SA, 46 Rue de Grenelle, 75007 Paris. Hong Kong: Design International Resources, 1002 A, Wanchai Commercial Centre, 194–204 Johnston Road, Hong Kong. The Netherlands: Han Hazevoet Interieurstoffen, Vondelstraat 25, 1054 GH Amsterdam. Singapore: Mohil Consultants Pte Ltd, 63 Robinson Road, 04–07 Afro-Asia Building, Singapore 0106. UK: The House of Sweden Associated Aims Ltd, 44–52 Hampstead Road, London NW1 2PD. West Germany: Werner Schmitz, Düsseldorfer Strasse 151, 4000 Düsseldorf 11.

MARTECH Geertestraat 2b, 3511 xe Utrecht, The Netherlands.

MARUICHI SELLING CO. LTD Awatabe, Imadate-cho, Fukuo-ken, 910-02 Japan.

MATSUSHITA ELECTRIC TRADING CO. LTD 2 Matsushita-cho Moriguchi, Osaka, Japan.
Outlets Australia: National Panasonic (Australia) Pty Ltd, 95–99 Epping Road, North Ryde, NSW 2113. Canada: Matsushita Electric of Canada Ltd, 5770 Ambler Drive, Mississauga, Ontario L4W 2T3. Hong Kong: MET (Hong Kong) Ltd, 9/F Peninsula Centre, 67 Mody Road, Tsimshatsui East, Kowloon. Italy: Panasonic Italia Spa, Via Lucini 19, 20125 Milan. Malaysia: Matsushita Sales & Service SDN. BHD, Bangunan Masco, Lot 10, Jalan, 13/2 Petaling Jaya, Selangor. The Netherlands: Haagtechno bv, Rietveldenweg 60, 5222AS S'-Hertogenbosch. Sweden: Panasonic Svenska AB, Instrumentvagen 30, Hagersten, Box 43047, S-100 72 Stockholm. UK: Panasonic UK Ltd, 300 Bath Road, Slough, Berkshire SL1 6JB. USA: Matsushita Electric Corporation of America, One Panasonic Way, Secaucus, New Jersey, 07094. West Germany: Panasonic Deutschland GmbH, Winsbergring 15, 2000 Hamburg 554.

MCLANDIA SRL Via Castello, 3-36015 Schio, Vicenza, Italy.

MAXALTO Strada Provinciale, 22060 Novedrate (Co), Italy.

MELNOR INDUSTRIES One Carol Place, Moonachie, New Jersey 07074, USA.

MEMPHIS SRL Via Breda, 1-20010 Pregnana, Milan, Italy.
Outlets France: Artemide, 157–9 Rue du Faubourg St Honoré, Paris 75008. UK: Artemide GB, 17–19 Neal Street, London WC1 2HG. West Germany: Agentur Brombauer, Eckstrasse 51, 2800 Bremen 33.

TER MOLST INT. Molstenstraat 42, 8780 Oostrozebeke, Belgium.

NASON & MORETTI Via Serenella 12, 30121 Murano, Venezia, Italy.

NIGARA INC. 2–6 Nihon Bashi, Honcho, Chuo-ku, Tokyo 103, Japan.

NIPPON LIGHT METAL COMPANY LTD Nikkei Building 11F, 3-13-2 Mita Minato-ku, Tokyo.

O

OLIVARI BSRL Via G. Matteotti 140, 28021 Borgomanero (No), Italy.
Outlets UK: Sigmaward Ltd, 7 Green Avenue, Mill Hill, London NW7 4PX.

OLUCE Via Conservatorio 22, 20122 Milan, Italy.

OMK DESIGN LTD Stephen Building, Stephen Street, London W1P 1BN, UK.
Outlets France: Protis, 67-101 Avenue Vieux Chemin, Saint Denis 92230 Gennevilliers. Italy: Bieffeplast Spa, PO Box 406, 1-35100 Padova. The Netherlands: Horas, Beemdstraat 25, 1610 Raisbroex. USA: Bieffeplast USA, 227 W. 17 Street, New York, NY 1001.

ONE-OFF LTD, 56 Neal Street, London WC2, UK.

OSBORNE & LITTLE PLC 49 Temperley Road, London SW12 8QE, UK.

OSRAM GMBH Hellabrunner Strasse 1, Berlin, West Germany.

OTAKI PAPER LAND 11-11 Otaki, Imadate-cho, Fukui-pref 915, Japan.

P

PALOMA INDUSTRIES 24 Banchi Momozono-cho, Mizuho-ku, Nagoya-shi, Aichi-ken, Japan.

ELIO PALMISANO EDIZIONI TESSILI Via Roma 10, 22070 Guanzate (Co), Italy.

PANASONIC 300–318 Bath Road, Slough, Berkshire SL1 6JB, UK.
Outlets Australia: National Panasonic (Australia) Pty Ltd, 95-99 Epping Road, North Ryde, NSW 2113. Canada: Matsushita Electric of Canada Ltd, 5770 Ambler Drive, Mississauga, Ontario L4W 2T3. Italy: Panasonic Italia Spa, Via Lucini 19, 20125 Milano. Hong Kong: MET (Hong Kong) Ltd, 9/F Peninsula Centre, 67 Mody Road, Tsimashatsui East, Kowloon. Japan: Matsushita Electric Trading Co Ltd, CPO Box 288, Osaka 530-91. Malaysia: Matsushita Sales & Service SDN BHD, Bangunan Masco, Lot 10, Jalan, 13/2 Petaling Jaya, Selangor. The Netherlands: Haagtechno BV, Rietveldenweg 60, 5222AS S'-Hertogenbosch. Sweden: Panasonic Svenska AB, Instrumentvagen 30, Hagersten, Box 43047, S-100 72 Stockholm. USA: Matsushita Electric Corporation of America, One Panasonic Way, Secaucus, New Jersey, 07094. West Germany: Panasonic Deutschland GmbH, Winsbergring 15, 2000 Hamburg 554.

PAPYRUS 31 Boulevard Raspail, 75007 Paris, France.

PASTOE Member of the Dutch Design Centre, Rotsoord 3, PO Box 2152, 3500 GD Utrecht, The Netherlands. *Outlets* UK: Equinox Interiors Ltd, 64–72 New Oxford Street, London WC1A 1EU.

PLUS CO. LTD, 1-20-11 Otowa, Bunkyo-ku, Tokyo, Japan.

POLTRONOVA SPA 51031 Agliana, Pistoia, Italy.

PORSCHE DESIGN GMBH Ferdinand Alexander Porsche, Flugplatzstrasse 29, A-5700 Zellamsee, Austria.

PROFESSIONAL WOODWORKERS LTD 1 Church Street, Pewsey, Wiltshire, UK.

PROFORMA Hietalahdenkatu 4, 00180 Helsinki, Finland.

Q

QUATTRIFOLIO Via Vigevano 33, 20144 Milan, Italy.

R

RAINSFORDS METAL PRODUCTS P/L Sherriffs Road, Lonsdale, South Australia 5160.

RASTAL GMBH & CO. Lindenstrasse, 5410 Hohr, Genzhausen, West Germany.

MICHAEL REED CABINETMAKERS Arch 12, Kingsdown Close, London W10 6RL. *Outlets* France: Denis Beauge, Secretaire Général, La Maison des Metiers d'Art Français, 27 Rue de l'Université, 75007 Paris. The Netherlands: Eric Wijntjes, Quarntaine, Weg 1, 3089 KP Rotterdam. UK: IDF, Studio All, The Met., Enfield Road, London N1 5A2. USA: Gabrielle Hayden, Manager, Workbench Gallery, 470 Park Avenue South, New York, NY 10016.

LILY RIVER 25460 Toija, Finland.

ROSENTHAL EINRICHTUNG Wittelsbacherstrasse 43, 8672 Selb, West Germany. *Outlets* France: Nova Distribution sarl, Bureau 1002 BP 258, Cit, Tour de Montparnasse, 75749 Paris. Italy: Contemporary Interior, Jürgen P. Ulrich, 25 Via Pinturicchio, 20133 Milan. Japan: Rosenthal, Axel Braun, O.A.G. Haus, Room 405, 5-56 Akasaka, 7-chome, Minato-ku, Tokyo. The Netherlands: Noteborn BV, Bochholtzerweg 12, 6369 TG Simpelveld. Sweden: Rosenthal Skandinavien Försäljnings AB, Karlävagen 51, 10246 Stockholm. UK: Aram Designs Ltd, 3 Kean Street, London WC2 4AT. USA: Rosenthal USA Ltd, 66–26 Metropolitan Avenue, Middle Village New York, NY 11379.

ROSS ELECTRONICS 49–53 Pancras Road, London NW1 2QB. *Outlets* France: ATL, 35 Boulevard Roch, 93800 Epinay-Sur-Seine. Italy: Hi Fi United, Via Nono Bixio 88, 43110 Parma. The Netherlands: Artec Nederland BV, Deccaweg 20-20-24 1042 AD, Amsterdam. Norway: Ross Norge, Box 699, Krossen, 4301 Sandnes. Sweden: TTC AB, PO Box 7261, S-402 35,

Gothenburg. USA: International Music Company, PO Box 2344, Fort Worth, Texas 76113. West Germany: Worlein GmbH, Hindenburgstrabe 37, D-8501 Cadolzburg.

GORDON RUSSELL LTD Broadway, Worcestershire WR12 7AD, UK.

T.I. RUSSELL HOBBS LTD PO Box 1, Blythe Bridge, Stoke-on-Trent, ST11 9LN, UK. *Outlets* Canada: Russell Housewares Ltd, 190 Britannia Road East, Unit 18, Mississauga, Ontario, L4Z 1W6. Eire: Beaumark Ltd, Unit L5, Ballymount Trading Estate, Ballymount Drive, Walkingtown, Dublin 12.

S

SANYEI AMERICA CORP. 2 Executive Drive, Fort Lee, New Jersey 07024, USA.

SAPORITI ITALIA Via Gallarate 23, 21010 Besnate, Italy. *Outlets* Germany: Magade, 9 Rue de l'Eglise, 067 Strasbourg. UK: Contract Interiors, 23 Ridgmount Street, London WC1. USA: Campaniello Imports, 225 E. 57 Street, New York, NY 200122.

SASAKI CRYSTAL 41 Madison Avenue, New York, NY 10010, USA.

SECCOSE Industrie Secco SpA, PO Box 101, 31100 Treviso, Italy.

HATTORI SEIKO CO LTD 2-6-21 Kyobashi, Chuo-ku, Tokyo, Japan.

HARRIET SELLING 23 Corso Monforte, 20122 Milan, Italy.

SHARP CORP. 22–22 Nagaike-cho, Abeno-ku, Osaka 545, Japan.

SIRRAH SPA Via Molio Rosso 8, 40026 Imola, Italy.

ALVARO SIZA Rua da Allegria 399A-1°A, 4000 Oporto, Portugal.

SKIPPER Via S. Spirito 14, Milan, Italy.

SONY 6-7-35 Kita-Shinagawa, Shinagawa-ku, Tokyo, Japan.

STILNOVO SPA Via F. Borromini 12, 20020 Lainate, Milan, Italy. *Outlets* Belgium: Indoor BV, 137 Chaussée de Charleroi, Brussels. France: Stilnovo France sarl, 123 Rue de Reuilly, 75012 Paris. USA: Thunder & Light Inc., 230 5th Avenue, Suite 400, New York, NY 10001. West Germany: Georg Hartl, Contractfunction, Siedlungsweg 10, 8894 Hollenbach.

STRÄSSLE SÖHNE AG 9533 Kirchberg, Switzerland. *Outlets* Denmark: Don Batchelor Aps, Strandvejen 163

A, 2900 Hellerup. France: Philippe Morel Lab., Aria, 31 Rue E. Dubois, 01000 Bourg. Italy: Costi C S, Via Trebbia 22, 20135 Milan. Japan: Asahi Grant KK, 11F Maison Mita No. 1103, 2-8-20 Mita, Minato-ku, Tokyo. The Netherlands: Andrea Kok Agenturen, Bilderdijkkade 5, 1052 RS Amsterdam. UK: Roger Procter Assoc. Ltd, Euro House, Lower Lane, Wellesbourne, Warwickshire CV35 9RB. USA: Monel Contract Furniture Inc., PO Box 291, Oakland Gardens, NY 11364. West Germany: WK-Verband Ges f. Wohngestaltung GmbH, Heilbronnerstrasse 4, 7022 Leinfelden-Echterdingen 2.

SWID POWELL DESIGN 55 E. 57 Street, New York, NY 10022, USA. *Outlets* Europe: Anton Wandinger, Bestform, 19 Gewerbestrasse, D-5905, Frendenberg, West Germany.

T

T & S BRASS AND BRONZE WORKS Route 4, Old Buncombe Road, Travelers Rest, South Carolina 20690, USA.

TARZAN FURNITURE FACTORY Pohjoisesplanaeli 25 A, PO Box 111, 00100 Helsinki, Finland. *Outlets* Italy: Fin Form, Viale Montesanto 4, 20124 Milan. Sweden: Swedese Möbler Ab, Formvagen, 56700 Vaggeryd. UK: Bristol International Business Interiors, Unit 10, Euroway Industrial Park, Swindon SN5 8YW.

TECTA MÖBEL Sohnreystr, 4471 Lauenförde, West Germany. *Outlets* France: Nova Distribution sarl, Cit Tour de Montparnasse, 3 Rue de l'Arrivée, BP 258, 75749 Paris. Italy: Fai srl Internazionaale, Via Garibaldi 6, Casella Postale 129, 20033 Desil, Milan. Japan: Actus GmbH, 2-1-13 Shibuya, Shibuya-ku, Tokyo 150. The Netherlands: Ton J. de Geus, Kogge 03/77, 8242 Lelystad. Sweden: Ergo Form, Göte Samuelsson, Gustav Dalensgaten 11, 41705 Gothenburg. USA: Global Furniture, 40 Prince Street, New York, NY 10021.

TELENOVA INC. 102-B Cooper Court, Los Gatos, California 95030 USA.

TERADA Tekkosho Umeda 8-11-5, Adachi-ku, Tokyo, Japan.

GEBRÜDER THONET GMBH Michael Thonet Strasse 1, 3558 Frankenberg, West Germany. *Outlets* UK: Aram Designs Ltd, 3 Kean Street, London WC2 4AT.

GEBRÜDER THONET VIENNA 11A Untere Weissgerberstrasse, A-1030, Vienna, Austria. *Outlets* Belgium: Ruud Claushuis BV, Rijksweg 70, Naarden, Postbus 293, 1400 AG Bussum. Italy: Poltrona Frau Spa, SS 77-Km 74, 5, 62029 Tolentino (MC). Japan: Actus Corporation, 19-1, 2-Chome, Shinjuku-Shinjuku-ku, Tokyo 160. Norway: Berg Interior, Sagveien 28, 0458 Oslo 4. UK: The Conran Shop Ltd, 77–79 Fulham Road, London SW3 6RE. USA: Gordon International, 200 Lexington Avenue, New York, NY 10016.

THORN EMI MAJOR ELECTRICAL APPLIANCES LTD New Lane, Havant, Hants PO9 2NH, UK.

TIME SPACE ART INC. 2-11-13 Aoyama Success Building, Minami Aoyama, Minato-ku, Tokyo 107, Japan.

TOP TONE CO. LTD Higashi-Yotsugi 3-44, Katsushita, Tokyo, Japan.

TOSHIBA KK 33 Shin-Isogo-cho, Isogo-ku, Yohohama-shi, Japan.

TRIBU 88 Avenue Klèbes, 75116 Paris, France.

3 SUISSES FRANCE SA 12 Rue de la Centenaire, BP 61-59170, Croix, France.

V

VALENTI SRL Via a Volta 2/4, 20090 Cusago, Milan, Italy.
Outlets Denmark: Don Batchelor Aps, Strandvejen 163/A, 2900 Hellerup. France: Protis, 77-101 Avenue du Vieux Chemin de St Denis, 92230, Gennevilliers. Japan: Atic Arflex Trading Inc., 2-9-8 Higashi, Shibuya-ku, Tokyo 150. The Netherlands: AMDA BV, Oosterhoutlaan 37, 1181/AL Amstelveen. UK: Forma Lighting, Unit 4, Mitcham Industrial Estate, 85 Streatham Road, Mitcham, Surrey CR4 2AP. USA: Contract Marketing International, 104 Greene Street, New York, NY 10012. West Germany: Agenhtur Christian Gumpoltsberger Fuer Valenti, Knorrstrasse 39, 8000 München 40.

VEREINIGTE WERKSTÄTTEN Ridlerstrasse 31, 8000 München 2, West Germany.
Outlets UK: Aram Designs Ltd, 3 Kean Street, London WC2 4AT.

VETRERIA NASON & MORETTI Murano, Italy.

WARNER FABRICS 7–11 Noel Street, London W1V 4AL, UK.
Outlets France: Patrick Frey, Ste Pierre Frey-Patifet, 47 Rue des Petits-Champs, 75001 Paris. Italy: Danilo Granata, Viale Corsica 79, 20133 Milan. Japan: N Mori, National Trading Inc, Interior Department, 5-2 Minami-Azabu 4-chome, Minato-ku, Tokyo 106. The Netherlands: Ger van den Bos, Van Diemenlaan 18, 2024 BP Haarlem. Sweden: Harry Lorentzon, Broderna Lorentzon, Petrejusvagen 9, 121 45 Johanneshov, Stockholm. USA: Greeff Fabrics Inc., 150 Midland Avenue, Post Chester, New York, NY 10573. West Germany: K. Dorflinger, Dorflinger & Nichow GmbH, Furstunwall 25, 4 Düsseldorf 1.

W

WILKINSON SWORD LTD Sword House, Totteridge Road, High Wycombe, Bucks HP13 6EJ, UK.

WINDMILL FURNITURE Turnham Green Terrace Mews, Chiswick, London W4 1QU, UK.

FRANZ WITTMANN KG A-3492, Etsdorf am Kamp, Austria.
Outlets France: First Time, 17 Rue Mazarine, Paris 75006. The Netherlands: Fellini, Willemsparkweg 10, 1011 NL Amsterdam. UK: MW United, 19 Dacre Street, London SW1. USA: Stendig Inc., 410 E. 62 Street, New York, NY 10021.

RICK WRIGLEY FURNITURE 80 Race Street, Holyoke, Massachusetts 01040, USA.

Z

ZANOTTA SPA Via Vittorio Veneto 57, 20054 Nova Milanese (Mi), Italy.
Outlets Austria: Prodomo, Flachglasse 35/37, 1060 Vienna. Belgium: Zaira Mis, Boulevard Saint Michel 35, 1040 Brussels. Finland: Funktio, Fredrikinkatu 39, 00120 Helsinki. France: Rose Michel, 45 Avenue G. Clemenceau, 95160 Montmorency L'Ermitage. Japan: Inter Decor, 5-Chome Minato-ku, Tokyo 106-7-11 Roppongi. The Netherlands: Modular Systems, B Toussaintstraat 24, 1054 AR Amsterdam. Sweden: Inside, Hamngatan 37, 11147 Stockholm. Switzerland: Peter Kaufmann, Bergstrasse 3, 8400 Winterthur. UK: Plus Kicker Ltd, 1–2 Cosser Street, London SE1 7BU. USA: International Contract Furnishings, New York, NY 10021.

ZANUSSI ELETTRODOMESTICI SPA Via Giardini Cattaneo 3, 33170 Pordenone, Italy.
Outlets France: IAZ International France SA, 52/56 Rue Emile Zola, 93107 Montreuil Cedex. The Netherlands: IAZ International Nederland BV, Postbus 120, 2400 AC Alphen aan den Rijn. UK: IAZ International (UK) Ltd, Zanussi House, 82 Caversham Road, Reading RG4 8DA. USA: Zanussi Corporation of America, Suite 10267, One World Trade Center, New York, NY 10048. West Germany: IAZ Elektro Vertrieb Deutschland GmbH, Rennbahnstrasse 72/74, 6000 Frankfurt, Main.

ZEUS SRL 8 Via Vigevano, 20144 Milan, Italy.

MAX ZIMMERMANN AG MÖBELFABRIK, Ch-5314 Kleindottingen, Switzerland.
Outlets UK: William Plunkett Furniture Ltd, GB Sinclair, Wiltshire SN2 2PS.

FURTHER READING

BOOKS

Italy: The New Domestic Landscape, New York, 1973. The catalogue of **EMILIO AMBASZ'S** famous exhibition in New York in 1972.

M. CHANDLER, *Ceramics in the Modern World,* London, 1968.

ANDREA BRANZI, *The Hot House: Italian New Wave Design,* London, 1984.
An account of the latest radical developments in the Italian scene in the 1970s and 1980s.

BARBIE CAMPBELL-COLE AND TIM BENTON, *Tubular Steel Furniture,* London, 1979.

Terence Conran's New House Book, London and New York, 1985.

EMMA DENT COAD, FELICE HODGES, PENNY SPARKE AND ANNE STONE, *Design Source Book,* London, 1986.

JAY DOBLIN, *One Hundred Great Product Designs,* New York, 1970.

ARTHUR DREXLER, *Charles Eames: Furniture from the Design Collection,* New York, 1973.

MARC VELLAY AND KENNETH FRAMPTON, *Pierre Chareau,* Paris, 1984 and London, 1986.
The illustrated work of the great pre-war Parisian decorator and an account of his masterpiece, the Maison de Verre.

PHILIPPE GARNER, *Twentieth-Century Furniture,* Oxford, 1980.

GIULIANA GRAMIGNA, *1950–1980 Repertory: Pictures and Ideas Regarding the History of Italian Furniture,* Milan, 1985.

FRANCES HANNAH, *Ceramics, Twentieth Century Design,* London, 1986.

KATHRYN B. HEISINGER, ed., *Design since 1945,* Philadelphia and London, 1983.

BEVIS HILLIER, *The Style of the Century 1900–1980,* New York and London, 1983.
An account of the design and fashion styles of the 20th-century.

CHARLES JENCKS, The Symbolic House, London, 1985.

SYLVIA KATZ, *Classic Plastics from Bakelite to High-Tech,* London, 1984.

EDWARD LUCIE SMITH, *Furniture, A Concise History,* London, 1979.

FIONA McCARTHY, *A History of British Design 1830–1970,* London, 1983.

CLEMENT MEADMORE, *The Modern Chair, Classics in Production,* New York, 1979.

BARBARA RADICE, *Memphis,* London, New York and Milan, 1985.

SUZY SLESIN AND STAFFORD CLIFF, *French Style,* London and New York, 1984.

SUZY SLESIN AND STAFFORD CLIFF, *English Style,* London and New York, 1985.

SUZY SLESIN AND STAFFORD CLIFF, *Caribbean Style,* London and New York, 1986.

SUZY SLESIN AND JOAN KRON, *High Tech,* London and New York, 1978.

PENNY SPARKE, *Furniture,* London, 1986.
A concise account of 20th-century design developments.

DEYAN SUDJIC, *Cult Objects,* London, 1985.

DEYAN SUDJIC, *The Lighting Book,* London and New York, 1985.

CHRISTOPHER WILK, *Thonet: 150 Years of Furniture,* New York, 1980.

CHRISTOPHER WILK, *Marcel Breuer: Furniture and Interiors,* New York, 1981.

Architect Designed Furniture, London (Architectural Press), 1978.

MAGAZINES

AUSTRALIA
Belle (monthly)
Vogue Living (10 times a year)

DENMARK
Hus og Hjem (monthly)
Mobilia (monthly)
Tools (monthly)

FINLAND
Ornamo (monthly)
Form & Function (monthly)

FRANCE
Cent Idées (monthly)
Crée (monthly)
Décoration (monthly)
La Maison de Marie-Claire (monthly)

GERMANY
Ambiente (bi-monthly)
Architektur und Wohnen (monthly)
Das Haus (monthly)
Häuser (monthly)
Schöner-Wohnen (monthly)

ITALY
Abitare (10 times a year) International edition has English text
Ambiente (monthly)
Casa Vogue (11 times a year)
Domus (monthly)
Gran Bazaar (monthly)
Interni (monthly)
Lotus International (quarterly)
Modo (monthly)

JAPAN
Axis (bi-monthly)
Fusion Design (monthly)
Idea (annual)
Styling (monthly)

THE NETHERLANDS
Avenue (monthly)

NEW ZEALAND
New Zealand Home Journal (monthly)

NORWAY
Huset Vart (3 times a year)
Hus og Hjem (quarterly)
Husmorbladet (11 times a year)

SPAIN
Diseño (monthly)

SWEDEN
Form (8 times a year)
Kontur (monthly)

UK
Architects' Journal (weekly)
Architectural Review (monthly)
Blueprint (monthly)
Design (monthly)
Designers' Journal (monthly)
Homes & Gardens (monthly)
House & Garden (monthly)
The World of Interiors (monthly)

USA
Architectural Digest (6 times a year)
Architectural Record (monthly)
House & Garden (monthly)
ID Magazine (bi-monthly)
Interiors (monthly)
Progressive Architecture (monthly)